Morality and Justice in Islamic Economics and Finance

STUDIES IN ISLAMIC FINANCE, ACCOUNTING AND GOVERNANCE

Series Editor: Mervyn K. Lewis, *Professor of Banking and Finance, South Australia and Fellow, Academy of the Social Sciences, Australia*

There is a considerable and growing interest both in Muslim countries and in the West surrounding Islamic finance and the Islamic position on accounting and governance. This important new series is designed to enhance understanding of these disciplines and shape the development of thinking about the theory and practice of Islamic finance, accounting and governance.

Edited by one of the leading writers in the field, the series aims to bring together both Muslim and non-Muslim authors and to present a distinctive East–West perspective on these topics. Rigorous and authoritative, it will provide a focal point for new studies that seek to analyse, interpret and resolve issues in finance, accounting and governance with reference to the methodology of Islam.

Titles in the series include:

Islamic Banking and Finance in the European Union
A Challenge
Edited by M. Fahim Khan and Mario Porzio

Islamic Capitalism and Finance
Origins, Evolution and the Future
Murat Çizakça

What is Wrong with Islamic Finance?
Analysing the Present State and Future Agenda
Muhammad Akram Khan

Islamic Finance in Europe
Towards a Plural Financial System
Edited by Valentino Cattelan

Morality and Justice in Islamic Economics and Finance
Muhammad Umer Chapra

Morality and Justice in Islamic Economics and Finance

Muhammad Umer Chapra

Islamic Development Bank, Saudi Arabia

STUDIES IN ISLAMIC FINANCE, ACCOUNTING AND GOVERNANCE

Edward Elgar

Cheltenham, UK • Northampton, MA, USA

Published by
Edward Elgar Publishing Limited
The Lypiatts
15 Lansdown Road
Cheltenham
Glos GL50 2JA
UK

Edward Elgar Publishing, Inc.
William Pratt House
9 Dewey Court
Northampton
Massachusetts 01060
USA

A catalogue record for this book
is available from the British Library

Library of Congress Control Number: 2014938811

This book is available electronically in the ElgarOnline.com Economics Subject Collection, E-ISBN 978 1 78347 572 8

ISBN 978 1 78347 571 1

Typeset by Columns Design XML Ltd, Reading
Printed and bound in Great Britain by T.J. International Ltd, Padstow

Contents

Preface

Mankind is faced with a number of serious problems which demand an effective solution. The prevalence of injustice and the frequency of financial crises are two of the most serious of these problems. Even though a great deal of effort has been made around the world to reduce injustice, particularly by the welfare states, and also to minimize the frequency and severity of financial crises, both the injustice and the financial crises continue to prevail everywhere in different forms and varying degrees. This causes misery to a large number of people, and particularly the underprivileged. They continue to suffer from economic and financial instability, unemployment, poverty, and lack of adequate need fulfilment.

There are certainly a number of reasons for the financial crises as well as the injustice. It is not the purpose of this book to get into a discussion on all of these. However, two of the most important of these reasons are the excessive expansion of credit and its inequitable allocation. While a great deal of effort has been, and continues to be, made to increase the strength, efficiency and stability of the financial system, not enough attention seems to have been given to the need to make it more equitable. Since the financial institutions mobilize a vast pool of resources from all sectors of the society, the dream of creating a 'just' society may continue to remain unrealized unless the credit extended by them on the basis of these resources serves the interests of all sectors of the society in an equitable manner.

This raises the question of what can be done to not only minimize the frequency and severity of the crises but also make the financial system more equitable. This book is a humble attempt to answer this question. It consists of an 'Introduction' along with a selection of eight of my papers, most of them published in reputed international journals. Four of these papers are on Islamic economics and the other four on Islamic finance. Together they may be able to create a better impact than what they could do individually.

Banks are profit-making institutions. Their own capital is, however, relatively very small. Their primary reliance is on the resources mobilized by them from a vast spectrum of depositors. There are, however, a number of ways in which the banks can utilize these resources to earn profit. How these resources are utilized by them is bound to have a significant impact on the realization of the society's cherished goals, including not only minimization of the frequency and severity of financial crises and realization of a higher rate of growth in output as well as employment, but also ensuring greater justice in society. While making a reasonable amount of profit is bound to be one of their prime objectives, realization of their society's cherished goals needs also to carry a substantial weight in their decision making. Even though a number of the ways in which they utilize these resources may be more or less equally profitable, only some of them may be able to contribute more effectively to the realization of their society's cherished goals.

Therefore, the question is, which of these ways should receive priority. A socially more acceptable preference may be to give priority in the use of the banks' resources to those ways that can help promote not only financial stability and a reasonably high rate of economic development but also greater justice in society. Unless the promotion of justice also carries a significant weight in the utilization of the banks' resources, it may not be possible to make a more meaningful contribution towards the goal of removing hunger, poverty, unemployment and disease. Even though this goal has always existed, it has gained crucial importance after a rise in social tensions that became reflected in the 'Occupy Wall Street Movement' which took place in New York on 17 September 2011. This has intensified the realization that ensuring justice is indispensbale for promoting peace and social harmony in this world. The actualization of justice needs therefore to be considered a matter of utmost concern for all human institutions, and the financial system cannot be an exception.

The financial system does not, however, appear to be attuned to the realization of this goal. It has a built-in tendency towards promoting economic inequality by mobilizing resources from a vast spectrum of society and making them available primarily to a relatively much smaller spectrum. This may also be acceptabe if the credit is granted for purposes that help benefit a large spectrum. This does not, however, seem to be the case. The resources that the financial system mobilizes get used for any purpose, including gambling and speculation in the stock, commodity and foreign exchange markets, production of weapons of mass destruction, luxury goods and status symbols used primarily by the rich, and even pornographic material, when resources needed for the production of some of the goods and services needed by millions of people for a more comfortable and productive life are not available adequately.

While there may be no objection to the effort of banks to earn a reasonable amount of profit, this needs to be done within the framework of promoting justice and helping their society realize its humanitarian goals. The logic behind this expectation is that, since the banks mobilize their vast pool of resources from a large spectrum of the population, it is fair to expect that they would utilize these resources in a way that also helps serve the interests of a large spectrum of the society. This does not necessarily mean that the resources mobilized by banks should be made available to a large number of people. All it means is that these resources should be utilized by them effectively in such a way that the benefit extends to a large number of people by helping promote the kind of economic development that leads to general well-being through a number of ways, including expansion of employment and self-employment opportunities as well as the supply of need-fulfilling and investment goods and services.

This does not, however, seem to be taking place. The resources that the financial system mobilizes become generally available to a relatively small spectrum of high net worth individuals and firms as well as governments without giving due consideration to the use of these resources for fulfilling the people's needs, promoting employment and self-employment opportunities, and solving the society's economic problems. The primary consideration seems to be to make money without giving any significant consideration to the fulfilment of the genuine needs of their society. The consequence is that adequate resources are not available for expanding job opportunities as well as the supply of housing, education, vocational training, and other need-fulfilling and investment goods and services.

This accentuates the need for a meaningful reform of the financial system in a way that would enable the society to solve its problems and realize its humanitarian goals. For greater clarity one may take the example of a banker who is confronted with the demand for credit from two equally creditworthy parties, one from a golf partner who wishes to purchase a luxury yacht and the other from businessmen who wish to import textbooks and uniforms for school children or medical supplies for hospitals. Which of these should receive priority if the resources are limited: his golf partner or the schools and hospitals?

The vision of the Islamic financial system needs to be to transform all human activity, including banking, into a 'blessing' (*rahmah*) for mankind as envisaged by the Qur'an in verse 21:107. This repudiates the idea that 'Islamization' of the financial system can be accomplished by merely introducing some cosmetic changes in the conventional financial system through the employment of 'mark-up' instead of 'interest' without making any worthwhile contribution towards the resolution of the society's serious problems and helping realize some of its crucial goals.

The primary purpose of this book is, therefore, to help fulfil this need without turning banks into charitable institutions. It consists of an introduction plus eight papers, most of which were published in reputed international journals. Even though it is not necessary to get permission for the republication of the author's own papers in his own book, I tried and was able to obtain the permission for most of them. In this respect I am grateful to Professor Robert Whaples, Professor Suzy Howell, Professor Morris Altman, Professor Kosugi Yasushi, and Professor Kabir Hassan for allowing me to include in this book my papers previously published by them. I also wish to thank Mr Iqbal Khan for helping me get permission from Dr S. Nazim Ali for a paper which was published previously by the Islamic Finance Project, Harvard Law School.

I am also grateful to Dr Ahmad Muhammad Ali, President of the Islamic Development Bank (IDB), Dr Abdul Aziz alHinai and Dr Ahmet Tiktik, both Vice Presidents of the IDB, and Professor Azmi Omar, Director General of the Islamic Research and Training Institute, IDB, for the encouragement and support they have all provided unstintingly for the writing and publication of these papers. Without such support, it may have been difficult to write a number of the papers which have been included in this book. I am also grateful to my wife, Khairunnisa, for the help and encouragement she has always provided by taking over a number of household chores which were a part of my domestic responsibilities. Last but not the least, I owe a great deal to Shaikh Mohammad Rashid for the efficient secretarial assistance he has provided over a long period to enable me to not only fulfil my official responsibilities but also to complete this book.

Introduction

We wish to favour those who have been oppressed, so as to make them leaders and successors and establish them firmly in the world.

(al-Qur'an, 28:5–6)

We have sent Our Messengers with Clear Signs as well as the Book and the Balance so that people may establish justice. (al-Qur'an, 57:25)

Those who believe and do not impair their belief with injustice, for them there is peace and they are the guided ones. (al-Qur'an, 6:82)

THE VISION OF ISLAM

The primary vision of Islam in this world, as clearly enunciated by the Qur'an, is to be a 'blessing for mankind'[1] (21:107). A number of Qur'anic verses, three of which have been quoted above, elaborate further the different aspects of this same vision. They emphasize the imperative of not only establishing justice and removing oppression but also uplifting the condition of the downtrodden to enable them to lead a more productive life that could help them become firmly established in this world as leaders and their successors. This is necessary not only to ensure social harmony and long-lasting peace in this world but also to vindicate three of the other most fundamental principles of the Islamic worldview.

One of these three principles is that all human beings, irrespective of their race, wealth, position, sex, age or nationality, are members of a single human family (*ummah wahidah*) as a result of their being created by the One and Only God and being offsprings of the same parents, Adam and Eve (al-Qur'an, 2:213 and 10:19). They are, thus, brothers and sisters with respect to each other and must, therefore, treat everyone fairly and caringly without any discrimination. The second principle is that they are also *khalifahs* or vicegerents of God on earth (al-Qur'an, 2:30). While being the *khalifahs* of the Creator of this universe is undoubtedly a great honour, it is also an immense responsibility. It makes it obligatory for them to try their best to fulfil their primary mission of being a 'blessing' for not only themselves but also everyone and

1

everything else, including animals, birds, insects and the whole environment. Third, the resources that they have at their disposal do not really belong to them; they are rather a trust in their hands from God, their Creator (al-Qur'an, 57:7), for the purpose of being developed and utilized 'efficiently' and 'equitably' for the well-being of all members of the human family and, in particular, those who have been oppressed, as enjoined in the Qur'anic verse quoted above (28:5–6). The financial system cannot be an exception. It must also be a blessing for all by utilizing the resources at its disposal in a way that would help realize the well-being of all and not just a selected few (now being generally referred to as the top one per cent).

The Failure of Muslims to Realize this Vision

Muslim countries do not, however, reflect this vision of Islam at present. There is poverty and unemployment along with a great deal of exploitation and immense inequalities of income and wealth. Even the basic needs of all people do not get fulfilled.[2] A number of Islamic values are being generally violated, particularly by the political elite and the rich and powerful. The well-being of most people, and particularly of the poor and vulnerable, is accordingly not being ensured. Muslims have, thus, failed to become a blessing for even themselves, leave alone the vision of becoming a blessing for also the rest of mankind as envisaged by the Qur'an. What could be the reason for this disappointing performance?

There are a number of moral, socio-economic, political and historical factors that may be able to help explain the prevailing state of affairs.[3] The giving of attention to primarily economic variables may not, therefore, be sufficient. It is necessary to pursue a policy of comprehensive development – development that incorporates all the relevant aspects of moral, educational, socio-economic and political life and does not concentrate primarily on a rise in the aggregate level of output.[4] It should also take into account the different constituents of development as well as the distribution of its benefits. One of the primary goals should be to ensure the availability of adequate employment and self-employment opportunities, particularly for the youth, because youth unemployment shatters their dream for the future and can be a source of great social turmoil and political instability. Without ensuring such comprehensive development, it may not be possible to translate into reality the crucial Islamic goal of overall human well-being (*falah*) to be attained through material as well as spiritual uplift, socio-economic justice, spread of moral and material education, technological advance, good governance, and family and social solidarity.

As a result of centuries of decline, lack of proper education, political illegitimacy, misuse of resources, foreign occupation, and the pursuit of inappropriate policies, the vision has not been realized. It has, consequently, not been possible to attain the need fulfilment of all as well as the kind of family and social solidarity that is enshrined in the teachings of Islam. Moral decline along with crime and social unrest have also been generally on the rise.

Persistently high rates of poverty, unemployment, and glaring disparities in the living standards of the rich and the poor are not only a stigma on the face of humanity but also one of the surest ways of aggravating social discontent and unrest, which are already prevalent not just in most Muslim countries but also in a number of other countries, including some of the relatively rich economies. One of the manifestations of this social discontent is the 'Occupy Wall Street Movement', which took place in New York on 17 September 2011 as a protest against poverty, high rates of unemployment, family disintegration, and social and economic inequality. The simultaneous persistence of these problems in a number of countries around the world clearly reflects the gravity of the prevailing situation. Unless there is comprehensive moral, social, educational, economic and political reform and the condition of the needy and the unemployed improves appreciably, the Movement, which has so far been peaceful, carries the risk of degenerating into violence.

THE CRUCIAL IMPORTANCE OF JUSTICE

The 'Occupy' Movement is, thus, a clear reflection of the social and economic injustice prevailing in a number of countries around the world, including most of the Muslim countries, when the Qur'an has emphatically and unequivocally stressed the crucial importance of justice in society. Accordingly, the primary mission of all the messengers of God was to establish justice in this world (al-Qur'an, 57:25). The absence of justice is considered by the Qur'an to be one of the primary causes of decline and disintegration (20:111). The Qur'an has accordingly warned that it is not possible for a society to maintain social peace and harmony if the faith of its people gets tainted by injustice. This and several other Qur'anic verses have, therefore, clearly and emphatically laid down the absolute and unconditional moral imperative that justice has to be the hallmark of a genuinely Muslim society and that it is not possible for a Muslim society to reflect faithfully the ethos of Islam if justice does not prevail in all its different aspects of life.[5]

This message of the Qur'an has also become reflected in the Prophet's *Sunnah* (peace and blessings of God be upon him). He equated the absence of justice with 'absolute darkness' in the Hereafter.[6] The darkness in the Hereafter will be nothing but a reflection of the darkness that we have perpetuated in this world through injustice, which does not only make the life of the affected individuals miserable but also accentuates social conflict, tension and crime. All of these tend to undermine brotherhood and solidarity, which are inalienable constituents of the ethos of Islam (al-Qur'an, 3:103–105), and ultimately hurt development, perpetuate poverty, and aggravate human problems. Consequently, injustice becomes even more entrenched and the needs of all people do not get satisfied adequately.

This categorical imperative of the Qur'an and *Sunnah* has also become reflected in the writings of nearly all Muslim scholars throughout history. For example, Mawardi (d. 1058) asserted that 'there is nothing that destroys the world and the conscience of the people faster than injustice'.[7] Ibn Taymiyyah (d. 1328) emphasized that 'injustice is absolutely not permissible, irrespective of whether it is to a Muslim or a non-Muslim or even an unjust person'.[8] Ibn Khaldun (d. 1406) weaved a whole philosophy of history around the role of justice in the rise and fall of a civilization and stated unequivocally that it is not possible for a society to achieve and sustain development without justice.[9] This is also reflected in the writings of nearly all modern scholars.

The Role of the Financial System in Promoting Justice

In view of this crucial importance of justice in the Islamic worldview, every effort needs to be made to ensure its prevalence in Muslim societies if they wish to be assured of social peace and harmony and sustainable development. It is, hence, the moral obligation of all sectors of the polity, society and economy of a Muslim society, including the financial system, to contribute towards its actualization.

Banks have a particularly crucial role to play in ensuring justice. They mobilize resources from a large spectrum of the population, and justice demands that these resources should also be employed by them in such a way that the benefit permeates to the whole society. They have, however, not been able generally to live up to this expectation. They have unintentionally accentuated inequalities by mobilizing resources from a large spectrum of the population and making them available generally to a relatively much smaller spectrum of high net-worth individuals. This does not necessarily mean that the banks should make credit available to as large a spectrum of society as that of the depositors. This may not only be very risky but also may not be practical. What is expected of them, however, is to utilize these resources for granting loans and making investments in such a way that a large spectrum of the society is able to benefit from them directly or indirectly through the:

1) Promotion of employment and self-employment opportunities;
2) Promotion of medium and small enterprises as much as possible;
3) Expansion in the production of need-fulfilling and investment goods and services;
4) Reduction as much as possible in the prevailing income and wealth gaps between the rich and the poor; and
5) Minimization of inflationary pressures by ensuring that credit is granted and utilized for productive, and not speculative, purposes.

In contrast with this, the general impression around the world seems to be, as stated above, that the resources mobilized by banks from a large spectrum of society tend to go generally to a relatively much smaller spectrum without due regard for the impact of this on development with justice – development that leads to expansion in job opportunities and need fulfilment along with improvement in the distribution of income. While bank credit has accomplished a great deal that is good and constructive, it has also promoted conspicuous consumption, living beyond means, and exacerbation of inequalities of income and wealth in practically all countries around the world. This is one of the major reasons why, in spite of progressive taxation and the welfare role played by a number of governments, the distribution of income has generally failed to improve significantly in most countries around the world and the needs of all people do not get adequately satisfied.

In the United States, a substantial part of the total credit extended by banks goes to the largest non-financial corporations, which exercise significant political power at both state and federal levels.[10] The Patman Report and the Securities and Exchange Commission Report in the late 1960s and early 1970s had drawn similar conclusions.[11] Although financial institutions generally deny that they exercise significant influence over non-financial corporations to which they supply capital, one would tend to agree with Kotz's observation that 'historical experience indicates that such assurances cannot be taken at face value'.[12] There is so far no indication to lead one to believe that the condition has changed significantly since then.

The position is most probably worse in a number of Muslim and other developing countries because of weak democratic institutions, greater political corruption, lack of a proper vision about the role of banks in the economy, and ineffective regulatory and supervisory framework for banks. For example, in Pakistan, 77.6 per cent of the total bank advances went to less than 1 per cent of total borrowers in 2002 when large depositors provided only 24.8 per cent of total deposits. Consequently, small borrowers received far less than what small depositors had contributed to the banks. It is even worse in nationalized banks where politically well-connected and influential borrowers are sometimes even able to get their loans written off.[13] Such injustice tends to prevail in nearly all countries around the world, more so in countries where the regulatory and supervisory framework for financial institutions is inadequate and the political system promotes cronyism.

Given such inequalities in the allocation of credit, one can only expect inequalities of income to continue to rise rather than decline in the future – an outcome which is grossly in conflict with the socio-economic goals of all societies and particularly those of Islam. While the Basle Committee on Banking Supervision has made valuable recommendations for improving the quality of banking supervision worldwide and, thereby, helping strengthen the financial system, its mandate did not include the making of recommendations for promoting greater justice in the financial system. It is, therefore, imperative that, along with the effort to strengthen the financial system, an effective strategy is also adopted to promote an allocation of credit that is in tune with the universally cherished goal of promoting greater justice.

How Can the Financial System Help Promote Justice?

This raises the question of how to enable the financial system to promote greater justice in society. This does not necessarily require that credit be made available to as large a spectrum of society as that of the depositors. It does, however, require that the resources mobilized by the banks from a large spectrum of society be utilized in such a way that the interest of a large spectrum of the society is served. This would happen if the banks granted credit and pursued their investments in a way that helps further general well-being by promoting the kind of development that leads to an expansion in employment and self-employment opportunities as well as the production of need-fulfilling and investment goods and services.

There seems to be no justification for using the resources provided by a large spectrum of the population in a way that serves primarily the interests of the rich and makes them richer without making any worthwhile contribution towards the goal of expanding employment and self-employment opportunities and promoting development with justice. Credit should under no circumstances be provided for speculation and gambling in the commodity, stock and foreign exchange markets or for hoarding of essential goods to create an artificial shortage and raise prices. If the banks do not live up to this expectation with the resources that they have at their disposal, they cannot become a 'blessing' which the Creator of this universe wishes all human beings to be. Lack of adequate employment and self-employment opportunities can only exacerbate poverty which carries the potential of promoting incapacity, helplessness and, possibly, even crime. The Prophet (pbuh) has, hence, rightly warned that poverty carries the risk of driving a person close to disbelief.[14] Removal of poverty, fulfilment of the basic needs of all individuals, and expansion of employment and self-employment opportunities for all in keeping with their ability and willingness to work should, therefore, be among the primary goals of public policy in all countries. The financial system cannot be an exception.

The financial system should try its best to help realize these goals. This is because the persistence of poverty has the effect of driving a person to begging which is in clear violation of the dignity that is inherent in the status of human beings as the *khalifahs* or vicegerents of God on earth. Begging has, accordingly, been looked down upon in almost all societies and prohibited by Islam except for those who are unable to earn a living because of some disability.[15] An indispensable part of the vision of all societies has, therefore, generally been to enable people to earn an honest living to support themselves and their families.[16] The only exceptions are those who have a disability that prevents them from doing so. For such people every society needs to have a proper social safety net to enable them to fulfil their needs without having to beg. Some welfare-oriented societies have already accomplished this. There is no reason why the Muslim world cannot do this if there is political will, the right policies are pursued for this purpose, and the wealthy realize their Islamic obligation towards those who are in need of their help from the wealth that does not really belong to them but is rather only a trust in their hands from God, its real owner.

A well-known legal maxim of Islamic jurisprudence (*Qawa'id al-fiqhiyyah*) stipulates that 'Something without which an obligation cannot be fulfilled is also obligatory'.[17] Since it is not possible for a person to earn a living without having some skill in demand, the Prophet (pbuh) has enjoined Muslims to acquire skill in some suitable profession so that they can earn a respectable living.[18] Unemployment has, nevertheless, become one of the most serious problems of most Muslim societies just as it has of many other societies around the world. This problem cannot, however, be solved without pursuing the kind of development that leads to an expansion in employment and self-employment opportunities and fulfilment of the people's basic needs. It is, therefore, the collective obligation of both the public and private sectors of a Muslim society to facilitate the training of people in the kind of morally acceptable professions that are in demand and to pursue the kind of development that helps expand the availability of such opportunities. It is only the pursuit of such a policy that would make it possible for anyone who is able and willing to work to find a suitable job to earn an honest living in keeping with his/her ability.

This establishes a crucial role for banks who mobilize a substantial part of the economy's financial resources. They need to utilize these resources in a way that would help promote the kind of development that can help expand employment and self-employment opportunities, fulfil needs and reduce inequalities. This may not be possible unless the banks have a vision of what their responsibility is with respect to the realization of the humanitarian goals of their society.

This may naturally raise in the reader's mind the question of why should the banks be loaded with such a responsibility. Shouldn't their primary objective generally be, like that of other business organizations, to maximize their profit by effectively performing their generally recognized role of intermediation between savers and investors. The pursuit of these higher objectives does not appear to be a widely accepted responsibility of other business organizations and, if imposed on banks, it would tend to create a serious obstacle in the way of satisfying the objectives of their shareholders and other stakeholders. Such an attitude about banks does not appear to be appropriate because they are different from other business organizations. Accordingly, there are a number of reasons to believe that their primary objective should not be to pursue intermediation of *any* kind. They should, rather, pursue intermediation of the kind that would help their society realize some of its crucial goals. Two of these reasons are of particular significance.

One of these is that a preponderant part of their funds does not come from their own shareholders. It comes rather from the deposits provided to them by a large spectrum of society. It is, therefore, fair to expect that, while there is no harm in the banks trying to earn a reasonable amount of profit, they should try to do so in a way that would help serve the interest of a large spectrum of their society. This they can accomplish by helping actualize their society's crucial goals, some of which are:

1)   Promoting a high but sustainable rate of development in conformity with the vision of their society;
2)   Expanding employment and self-employment opportunities;

3) Increasing the supply of need-fulfilling as well as investment goods and services;
4) Reducing the concentration of wealth in a few hands; and
5) Minimizing inflationary pressures.

If the banks use the depositors' resources in a way that hurts the realization of these goals, then they would be violating a trust that has been put in their hands – the trust of utilizing the society's resources for the benefit of the society as a whole. The violation would be even more severe if they also exacerbate inflationary pressures by expanding credit for speculative purposes rather than the growth of the real sector. It is imperative that the banks fulfil this obligation on their own volition as a part of their Islamic as well as corporate responsibility without being subjected to regulatory or supervisory controls. However, if they persist in not doing so, then the central bank would be justified in correcting the situation through persuasion and, if necessary, regulation and supervision.

A second reason for the difference is that by identifying themselves as 'Islamic', the banks have automatically accepted the moral imperative of helping their society realize some of the crucial goals of Islam which generally go under the title of *maqasid (goals of) al-Shari'ah*.[19] This necessitates that they should keep an eye not just on their own profit but also on their Islamic responsibility to extend credit primarily for purposes that would help their society realize some of these goals, particularly the goals of promoting sustainable development with particular emphasis on expanding employment and self-employment opportunities, productive investment and need fulfilment. If, in spite of identifying themselves as 'Islamic', they do not try earnestly to live up to this expectation and indulge in financing speculation and consumption of status symbols, then they would be violating a trust placed in their hands. In societies where the proportion of young people in the population is rising at a relatively high rate and the need for expanding employment and self-employment opportunities is also rising in step with this, the banks cannot remain oblivious to the fulfilment of this crucial need of their society. It is their Islamic as well as corporate responsibility to help their society as much as possible to fulfil this need.

The Real World Scenario

Data are not available to enable one to judge whether the operations of Islamic banks are, or are not, in harmony with this expectation. The general perception, however, seems to be that, even though the deposits of banks come from a large spectrum of the population, the benefit of these deposits does not normally tend to pervade to a reasonably large spectrum of the society even in the case of Islamic banks. It tends to go generally, as in the case of conventional banks, to a much smaller spectrum of relatively high net-worth individuals and businesses without due regard for the dire need of their society to promote development with justice. While it is not possible for the banks to provide credit to as large a spectrum of the population as that of the depositors, it should certainly be possible for them to extend credit in a way that serves the interest of a large spectrum by promoting the kind of development that leads to an expansion in employment and self-employment opportunities as well as an increase in the supply of need-fulfilling and investment goods and services. This shortcoming of banks has had the unintended effect of aggravating the already existing inequalities and social tensions in a number of countries. It is just like diverting, intentionally or unintention-ally, water from numerous small rivers to a few large farms, thus making them thrive at the expense of a large number of small farms which also need this water but are unable to get an equitable share. In addition to this imperative of equitable disbursement of credit, it is also necessary to ensure that credit is extended primarily for productive proposes that would help promote employment and self-employment opportunities and increase the supply of need-fulfilling and investment goods and services. This is what would help the banks make a valuable contribution towards the accelerated development of their society with justice and, thus, becoming a blessing as required by Islam.

The performance of such a role does not seem to constitute a priority in the case of most Islamic banks just as it is in the case of most conventional banks. The general perception seems to be that the Islamic banks do not have any inhibition in providing financing for status symbols just like any other bank. This is in sharp contrast with what is required for the actualization of the *maqasid*. It is the responsibility of Islamic banks to help their society actualize these goals. In addition, the internationally recognized goals of ensuring safety of the depositors' funds and health and stability of the financial system should also be among their primary objectives and should not be neglected under any circumstances.

In addition to a general deficiency in the vision of both conventional as well as Islamic banks regarding the productive use and equitable distri-bution of credit, the allocation of credit in the conventional financial system suffers from another problem. This arises from the absence of risk-sharing which tends to create an incentive on the part of banks to extend credit excessively. Since it is now well-recognized that excessive lending is one of the major causes of financial crises,[20] introduction of risk-sharing has become a clear imperative. Consequently, Islamic finance should be able to make a rich contribution to the international financial system if risk-sharing, which constitutes one of its fundamental principles, is conscienciously implemented by both Islamic and conventional banks.[21]

The effort to inject risk-sharing into the financial system should also have the effect of promoting greater discipline and efficiency into the system. This is because risk-sharing would tend to motivate the banks to be more careful in lending. It would, thereby, serve as a constraint not only on lending in excess of the borrowers' ability to repay, but also on promoting living beyond means and speculation. It would also have the effect of helping motivate investment depositors (who would also be sharing in the risk) to keep a close eye on the affairs of their banks to ensure greater transparency and more effective management. Risk-sharing should, thus, help improve loan quality and ensure a more effective use of bank resources. A built-in constraint in the financial system on excessive and imprudent lending, which is now generally recognized to be one of the major causes of financial crises and which Islamic finance is capable of helping bring about, should prove to be a great boon for the financial system.

The introduction of greater discipline need not, however, automatically lead to the flow of a higher volume of credit to small and medium enterprises (SMEs) which is necessary to inject greater justice into the system. The relatively greater potential of SMEs to expand employment and self-employment opportunities gives them a comparative advantage in every society where the population is large and young and the need for employment and self-employment opportunities is great. Nevertheless, they are generally at a great disadvantage in terms of getting financing from banks. It may not, however, be possible for them to benefit from this advantage of theirs if the necessary infrastructure for training, marketing and financing does not exist. It is, therefore, imperative for the governments to promote the necessary infrastructure so as to make it possible for banks to play a crucial role in providing microfinance to those SMEs which have a worthwhile project as well as the requisite expertise and reputation for creditworthiness.

This leads to the question of why the commercial banks are reluctant to extend credit to SMEs. There may be a number of reasons for this phenomenon. Two of these are more important. One is the higher cost of evaluating loan applications from a large number of SMEs and of managing and monitoring the loans once they have been extended. The other reason is the assumed greater risk of default. To enable the banks to give more credit to the SMEs, it is necessary to address both these reasons.

As far as the cost is concerned, there is no doubt that dealing with a large number of small entrepreneurs can be very cumbersome and expensive for banks. It is easier and more economical for them to lend relatively larger amounts to a few high net-worth clients who have adequate cash flow to ensure the repayment of their loans and are also considered to be more trustworthy. Such a practice, however, tends to lead to the unintended adverse consequence of making the rich richer. Even though data are normally not available to confirm this, it is generally understood to be the case almost everywhere around the world.

Among the few exceptions with respect to the availability of data is the State Bank of Pakistan which regularly publishes statistics on the distribution of deposits and advances by size. These statistics, indicate that, as partly reported earlier, small depositors who had deposits of less than one million rupees each and constituted 99.6 per cent of all depositors in 2002, contributed 61.3 per cent of total deposits. However, small borrowers, who borrowed less than one million rupees each and constituted 99.1 per cent of all borrowers, were able to get only 10.5 per cent of the banks' total advances. In sharp contrast with this, big depositors who had deposits of more than 10 million rupees each and constituted only 0.03 per cent of all depositors provided 24.8 per cent of total deposits. However, big borrowers borrowing more than 10 million rupees each and constituting less than 0.9 per cent of total borrowers were able to get 77.6 per cent of total advances. What this indicates is that big borrowers who constituted less than 1 per cent of the total borrowers were able to get more than three quarters of total advances when big depositors contributed only around one quarter of total deposits. Small borrowers, thus, received far less than what small depositors had contributed to the total pool of bank deposits.[22] It is believed to be worse in nationalized banks where, as indicated earlier, a number of politically well-connected big borrowers are even able to get their loans written off.

Allocation of credit of this nature cannot but make the system more unjust by aggravating the prevailing high degree of inequalities in income and wealth. Such injustice seems to be prevalent in almost all countries around the world, in varying degrees. This is the result of a built-in bias in the financial system in favour of inequalities. It mobilizes savings from a large spectrum of society and makes them available to a relatively much smaller spectrum. Only a determined effort to reform the system can help reduce the extent of this bias. One of the most important tasks that needs attention, therefore, is the creation of an institutional framework that is necessary for reducing the cost of evaluation as well as the losses from loan default.

To reduce the cost, it is necessary for the central bank to make some arrangement for the establishment of a databank of all SMEs, and particularly of those who wish to get financing from banks. If they do not provide accurate data, they will be hurting their own long-run interest. The cost of collecting the data may be recovered from a fee charged to those to whom the data are supplied on a confidential basis. Aggregate data should however, be generally made available.

Only when greater justice is injected into the financial system and, thereby, headway is made toward the realization of the vision that the *maqasid al-Shari'ah* stand for, will it be possible to say that Islamization of the financial system has been really accomplished. If no perceptible progress is made in promoting risk-sharing and greater equity in the distribution of credit, expanding employment and self-employment opportunities, and reducing poverty and inequalities of income, then talking about the merits of Islamic finance may not carry much weight. This makes it necessary to evaluate the performance of Islamic financial institutions at least every five years to ensure that they are moving in the direction of helping realize the *maqasid al-Shari'ah*.

NOTES

1. The word used in this Qur'anic verse is *al-'alamin* which is generally translated as 'mankind'. It, however, actually stands for all of God's creation and includes not only human beings but also animals, birds, insects and the whole environment. The implications of being a blessing for not only mankind but also all animate and inanimate objects as well as the environment need no elaboration. It is a moral obligation of all human beings to do whatever they can to enrich the environment, which is a trust in their hands, instead of polluting it.
2. See, for example, the 'Global Hunger Index' prepared by the International Food Policy Research Institute (IFPRI) (en.wikipedia.org/wiki/global_hunger_index). See also the unemployment rates in Muslim countries available in the *World Factbook*.
3. For a discussion of these factors, see Chapra (2008b).
4. For a basic introduction to the concept of comprehensive development in Islam, see Chapra (2008a).
5. See Chapra (1985), pp. 27–28.
6. *Sahih Muslim* (1955), Vol. 4, p. 1996:56, *Kitab al-Birr wa al-Silah wa al-Adab, Bab Tahrim al-Zulm*, from Jabir ibn 'Abdallah. The Prophet, peace and blessings of God be on him', has used the word *zulumat* in this *hadith*. *Zulumat* is the plural of *zulmah* which means darkness, and when used in its plural form, it signifies several layers of darkness, leading ultimately to 'pitch' or 'absolute' darkness, as is also evident in the Qur'anic verse, 24:40.
7. Al-Mawardi, *Adab al-Dunya wa al-Din* (1955), p. 125.

8. Ibn Taymiyyah, *Majmu' al-Fatawa* (1961), Vol. 18, p. 166. See also his *Minhaj al-Sunnah* (1986), Vol. 5, p. 127.
9. Ibn Khaldun, *Muqaddimah* (n.d.), p. 287.
10. Kotz (1978), p. 143.
11. United States Congress, House Banking and Currency Committee, Subcommittee on Domestic Finance (1968), *Commercial Banks and their Trust Activities: Emerging Influence on the American Economy*, 90th Congress, 2nd Session, p. 5. United States, Securities and Exchange Commission, 1971, *Institutional Investor Study Report*, House Document 62-4 referred to the House Committee on Inter-State and Foreign Commerce, pt. 8, pp. 124–25.
12. Kotz (1978), p. 119.
13. Khwaja and Mian, 2005.
14. Reported by al-Bayhaqi from Anas ibn Malik in his *Shu'ab al-Iman*, Vol. 5, p. 267, No. 6612 (Cited by al-Suyuti (d. 911/1505) in his *al-Jami'al-Saghir* from Anas ibn Malik on the authority of Abu Nu'aym's *al-Hilyah*).
15. The Prophet (pbuh) prohibited begging by saying: 'Do not beg anything from people' (Abū Dawud, 1952, Vol. 1, p. 382, from 'Awf ibn Malik), and that 'The hand that is above is better than the hand that is below' (Al-Bukhārī. Vol. 2, p. 133, from 'Abdullah ibn 'Umar).
    The Prophet (pbuh), also declared undesirable the giving of charity to those who are healthy and able-bodied and are, thus, capable of earning their own livelihood (Abū Dāwūd, 1952, Vol. I, p. 379; Nasā'ī, 1964, Vol. 5, p. 74 and Ibn Mājah, 1952, Vol. Ī. p. 589:1839).
    He, therefore, assigned a place of high esteem to earning one's own living by saying: 'He who seeks the world lawfully to refrain from begging, to cater for his family, and to be kind to his neighbour, will meet God on the Day of Judgment with his face shining like the full moon'.
    (Tabrizi, *Mīshkāt*, 1381AH., Vol. 2, p. 658:5207, from Abū Hurayrah, on the authority of Bayhaqī's *Shu'ab al-Īmān*).
16. The Qur'an instructs Muslims to go out into the world and seek of God's bounties after having attended to their prayers (62:10). The Prophet (pbuh) said that: 'Earning a lawful livelihood is obligatory upon every Muslim' (Suyūtī, *Aī-Jami' al-Saghir*, from Anas ibn Malik. p. 54). He elaborated this point further by saying: 'A man has not earned better income than that which is from his own effort' (*Sunan Ibn Mājah*, 1952, Vol. 2, p. 723:2138, from Miqdam ībn Ma'di Karib). According to the Prophet (pbuh), trust in God does not imply that a Muslim should refrain from making an effort. He should in fact do his utmost, and then trust in God for the best results. This is the implication of his displeasure at a man who left his camel untied thinking that the camel would not stray because God would take care of him. The Prophet admonished him to tie the camel first and then trust in God (see '*Kitāb al-Kasb*' of Muhammad Ibn al-Hasan al-Shaybānī in al-Sarakhsī, *Kitāb al-Mabsūt*, Vol. 30, p. 249.
    Caliph 'Umar emphasized the Islamic injunction to earn one's own livelihood by saying that the sky does not rain gold and silver. God provides livelihood to people through the rendering of service to each other. Therefore no one should stay away from earning his livelihood ('Ali al-Tantawi and Naji al-Tantawi, *Akhbaru 'Umar*, p. 268).
17. 'Izz al-Din 'Abd al-Salam (n.d.), Vol. 1, p. 46; and al-Shatibi (n.d.), Vol. 2, p. 394; see also Mustafa al-Zarqa (1967), pp. 784 and 1088; and Nadvi (2000), Vol. 1, p. 480.
18. The Prophet (pbuh) said: 'God loves a Muslim who has a professional skill' (Narrated by al-Mundhiri, Vol. 2, p. 524, from Ibn 'Umar on the authority of al-Tabarani's *al-Kabir* and *al-Bayhaqi*).

19. For some elaboration of the *maqasid al-Shari'ah*, see Chapra (2008).
20. See for example, Bank for International Settlements (2012), *82nd Annual Report* (1 April 2011–31 March 2012) (Basel, 24 June), p. 26.
21. For an elaboration of this, see Chapra (2009).
22. Calculated from the data available in the State Bank of Pakistan, *State Bank Bulletin*.

REFERENCES

Al-'Abbadi, 'Abd al-Salam Dawud al- (1974, 1975 and 1977), *Al-Milkiyyah fi al-Shari'ah al-Islamiyyah* (Amman, Jordan: Maktabah al-Aqsa, 3 volumes), Vols 1–3.
Al-Qur'an – Translations are my own. I have, however, benefited from the translations of Marmaduke Pickthal and Abdullah Yusuf Ali.
Bank for International Settlements (2012), *82nd Annual Report* (1 April 2011–31 March 2012) (Basel, 24 June), p. 26.
Bayhaqi, Imam Abu Bakr al- (d. 1065) (1990), *Shu'ab al-Iman*, Muhammad al-Sa'id Bisyuni Zaghlul (ed.) (Beirut: Dar al-Kutub al-'Ilmiyyah).
Bukhari, Imam Abu 'Abdallah Muhammad ibn Isma'il al- (d. 869) (1987), *Sahih al- Bukhari*, al-Shaykh Qasim al-Shamma'i al-Rifa'i (ed.) (Beirut: Dar al-Qalam, 1987).
Chapra, M. Umer (2008a), *The Islamic Vision of Development in the Light of Maqasid al-Shari'ah* (Jeddah: IRTI/IDB).
Chapra, M. Umer (2008b), *Muslim Civilization: The Causes of Decline and the Need for Reform* (Leicester, UK: The Islamic Foundation).
Chapra, M. Umer (2009), *The Global Financial Crises: Some Suggestions for Reform of the Global Financial Architecture in the Light of Islamic Finance* (Kyoto: Research Centre for Islamic Area Studies).
Ibn Khaldun, 'Abd al-Rahman (d. 1406) (n.d.), *Muqaddimah* (Cairo: Al-Maktabah al-Tijariyyah al-Kubra).
Ibn Mājah (d. 886) (1952), *Sunan Ibn Majah* (Cairo: 'Isā al-Bābī al-Halabī).
Ibn Taymiyyah (1986), *Minhaj al-Sunnah al-Nabawiyyah*, M. Rashad Salim (ed.) (Riyadh: Imam Muhammad Islamic University).
Ibn Taymiyyah, Imam Ahmad (d. 1328) (1961), *Majmu' al-Fatawa Shaykh al-Islam Ahmad Ibn Taymiyyah*, 1st edn, 'Abd al-Rahman al 'Asimi (ed.) (Riyadh: Matabi' al-Riyadh).
International Food Policy Research Institute (IFPRI), *Global Hunger Index* (en.wikipedia, org/wiki/global_hunger_index).
'Izz al-Din 'Abd al-Salam (d. 1252) (n.d.), *Qawa'id al-Ahkam fi Masalih al-Anam* (Beirut: Dar al-Ma'rifah).
Khwaja, Asim and Atif Mian (2005), 'Do Lenders Favour Politically Connected Firms?: Rent Provision in an Emerging Financial Market', *Quarterly Journal of Economics*.
Kotz, D.M. (1978), *Bank Control of Large Corporations in the U.S.* (Berkeley: University of California Press).
Mawardi Abū 'Ali al- (d. 1058) (1955), *Adab al-Dunya wa al-Din*, Mustafa al-Saqqa (ed.) (Cairo: Mustafa al-Babi al-Halabi).

Mundhiri, 'Abd al-'Azim al- (d. 1258) (1986), *Al-Targhib wa al-Tarhib*, Mustafa M. Al-Amarah (ed.) (Beirut: Dar al Kutub al-'Ilmiyyah).

Muslim, Imam Abu al-Husayn Muslim Ibn al-Hajjaj al-Naysaburiy (1955), *Sahih Muslim*, Muhammad Fu'ad 'Abd al-Baqi (ed.) (Cairo: 'Isa al-Babi al-Halabi).

Nadvi, 'Ali Ahmad al- (2000), *Jamharah al-Qawa'id al-Fiqhiyyah fi al-Mu'amalat al-Maliyyah* (Riyadh: Sharikah al-Rajhi al-Masrafiyyah li al-Istithmar).

Sarakhsi, Shams al-Din al- (d. 1090) (n.d.), *Kitab al-Mabsut* (Beirut: Dar al-Ma'rifah), particularly '*Kitab al-Kasb*' of al-Shaybani in Vol. 30, pp. 245–87.

Shatibi, Abu Ishaq, al- (d. 1388) (n.d.), *al-Muwafaqat fi Usul al-Shari'ah* (Cairo: al-Maktabah al-Tijariyyah al-Kubra).

State Bank of Pakistan, *State Bank Bulletin*, different relevant issues.

Suyuti, Jalal al-Din, al- (d. 1505) (n.d.), *Al-Jami' al-Saghir* (Cairo: 'Abd al-Hamid Ahmad Hanafi) Vol. 2.

Tabrīzī, Walī al-Dīn al- (1966), *Mīshkāt al-Masabih*, M. Nāsir al-Dīn al-Albānī (ed.) (Damascus: al-Maktab al-Islāmī).

Zarqa, Mustafa A., al- (1967), *Al-Fiqh al-Islami fi Thawbihi al-Jadid* (Damascus: Matabi' Alif Ba' al-Adib).

PART I

Islamic economics

1. Is it necessary to have Islamic economics?

> If Islam can be shown to be capable of providing fruitful vision to illuminate the modern conscience, then all mankind and not only Muslims, have a stake in the outcome. (Marshall Hodgson, 1977, Vol. 3, p. 441)

> Apart from the Islamic world, where fundamentalist political tendencies are quite marked, the global political scene is dominated by rhetoric and values that are primarily consumption-oriented and that stress personal self-gratification as the primary purpose of political action.
> (Zbigniew Brzezinsky, 1995, p. 53)

1.1 INTRODUCTION

Conventional economics, which dominates modern economic thinking, has become a well-developed and sophisticated discipline after going through a long and rigorous process of development over more than a century. The development continues uninterrupted, as reflected in the publication of innumerable journals, books, and research reports throughout the world. Individuals, universities, research organizations, and governments are all participating actively in this development. As a result of accelerated development in Western industrial countries over a long period, substantial resources are available to scholars to pursue their research. It goes to the credit of the West that there is a great quest for knowledge; researchers are willing to work rigorously, and creative work gets richly rewarded in terms of both prestige and material benefits.

Islamic economics has, however, had its resurgence only over the last three to four decades. The number of individuals, universities, governments, and research organizations participating in its development is relatively very small. Since most Muslim countries are poor and in the initial stage of development, the resources they have available at their disposal for financing research activities are also relatively meagre. Moreover, some of the governments in Muslim countries consider the resurgence of Islam, with its unmistakable call for political accountability and socio-economic justice, to be a threat to their survival. They are, therefore, reluctant to render any moral or material support for the development of Islamic social sciences.

An unavoidable question, therefore, is whether it is really necessary to have Islamic economics when conventional economics is already there in a highly developed form. This question acquires particular significance because the subject matter of both disciplines is nearly the same: allocation and distribution of scarce resources among their infinite uses. The justification would be there only if the effort to develop Islamic economics is directed toward the realization of a purpose that cannot be realized by the analysis developed by conventional economics. The need would be all the more acute if the set of variables employed for the analysis is broader, and the mechanisms and method to be used for the allocation and distribution of resources are also different.

1.2   THE VISION

Every activity of rational human beings generally has a purpose, and it is usually the purpose that determines its nature, differentiates it from other activities, and also helps evaluate its performance. The first question that one may, therefore, wish to ask is about the purpose behind studying the allocation and distribution of resources. Such a study may not have been necessary if resources were unlimited. However, resources *are* limited and *not* sufficient to satisfy all the claims on them by all individuals and groups in society. We are, therefore, posed with the perplexing question of which uses and whose claims to choose and how to make the choice. A simple answer may perhaps be to use them in a way that would help the society realize its vision. A vision essentially incorporates the dream of a society about what it would like to be in the future. It may consist of a number of goals, which the society aspires to achieve. All of these goals may together serve as a guiding star and indicate the direction in which the society wishes to proceed. This may help channel the society's efforts and energies in the desired direction and thereby minimize waste. The vision may never be fully realized. It may, nevertheless, continue to inspire the society to persist in the struggle for its realization by keeping the faith in the future perennially kindled.

Different societies may have different visions. Nevertheless, there is one dimension that seems to be common among the visions of most societies. This is the goal of realizing human well-being. However, the term well-being, even though used by a number of economists (Oswald et al., 1997) is itself a controversial term and may be defined in a number of ways. It may be defined in a purely material sense, totally ignoring its spiritual content, or in a way that also takes into account the spiritual aspect. Depending on which definition of well-being one adopts, there may arise the need for an entirely different configuration of goods and services to be produced by the society with the scarce resources at its disposal. This may lead to different mechanisms for allocation and distribution.

If well-being were to be defined in a purely material and hedonist sense, then it would be perfectly rational for economics to give prominence to the serving of self-interest and the maximization of wealth, bodily pleasures, and sensual satisfactions. Because pleasures and sensual satisfactions depend primarily on individual tastes and preferences, value judgments may have to be kept out to allow individuals total freedom to decide for themselves what they wish. All goods and services that provide bodily pleasures and sensual satisfactions to individuals in accordance with their own tastes and preferences may become acceptable. The impartial market forces may then be considered sufficient to bring about such an allocation and distribution of resources. Redistribution[1] of the wealth produced may be important, but only to the extent to which it does not interfere with the freedom of the individual to pursue his/her self-interest. The government's role may also have to be kept at a minimum, except to the extent to which it is necessary to enable the individual and the market to perform effectively.

However, if well-being were to be defined in a way that rises above the materialist and hedonist sense and incorporates humanitarian and spiritual goals, then economics may not be able to avoid a discussion of what these goals are and how they may be realized. These goals may include not only economic well-being, but also human brotherhood and socio-economic justice, mental peace and happiness, and family as well as social harmony. One of the tests for the realization of these goals may be the extent to which social equality, need-fulfilment of all, full employment, equitable distribution of income and wealth, and economic stability have been attained without heavy debt-servicing burden, high rates of inflation, undue depletion of nonrenewable resources, or damage to the ecosystem in a way that endangers life on earth. Another test may be the realization of family and social solidarity, which would become reflected in the mutual care of members of the society for each other, particularly the children, the aged, the sick, and the vulnerable, and absence, or at least minimization, of broken families, juvenile delinquency, crime, and social unrest.

Once economics gets into a discussion of human well-being in this comprehensive sense, then the task of economics may become wider and more difficult and complex. It may not be able to confine itself to just economic variables. It may have to take into account all those factors, including moral, psychological, social, political, demographic and historical, that determine well-being in this comprehensive sense. It may also have to answer a number of questions that may not need an answer if its goal were only to help maximize wealth and consumption. One of these questions may be about whether the serving of self-interest would be sufficient as a motivating force to realize comprehensive well-being, or would it also be necessary to have some other motivating force. Could such well-being be realized more effectively if all the agents operating in the market observed certain rules of behaviour and had certain desirable qualities? If so, then it may be necessary to impose certain constraints on individual behaviour. The individual may not then remain totally free to do what he/she pleases in accordance with his/her tastes and preferences. The question that would then arise is about who will determine these constraints, and how would it be ensured that the individual's freedom is not unduly restricted. This is because individual freedom is also essential for human well-being and cannot be compromised except to a certain agreed extent.

In addition, there are a number of institutions in human society that influence individual and social outcomes. The market is only one of them. Some others are family, society, and the state. Family may perhaps be the most important of these because it provides the human input for the market, the society, and the state. It is the primary breeding place and training ground for all individuals. It is here that a substantial part of individual tastes and preferences, personalities, and behaviour patterns get formed. The family's health and solidarity would hence be of crucial importance. If the family disintegrates, would it be possible to provide the future generation with the kind of upbringing that it needs? If the quality of upbringing goes down, then it may not be possible for a society to sustain its development and supremacy for long in the economic, technological, or military fields. Because economics is also concerned with the rise and fall of a society, then would it be realistic on its part to ignore the integrity and stability of the family?

If the market, the family, the society, and the state all have a role to play in human well-being, then the question is how to make them play their roles in a manner that complements and does not hinder the effective performance of their role by others? Although the market may operate efficiently if every individual tries to serve his/her self-interest, would it also be possible for families, the society, and the state to operate effectively and harmoniously if everyone were to behave in the same self-interested manner?

These are not new questions. They have been addressed by social philosophers for centuries. The majority seems to hold the view that the serving of self-interest is only one of the motivating forces in human society, and maximization of wealth and consumption is only one of the goals. The spiritual and humanitarian goals stated above are of equal, if not greater importance. Some of these goals may in fact be in conflict with each other, and a compromise may need to be struck. Would it be possible for a society to arrive at such a compromise if it sets maximization of wealth and consumption as its primary goal, and its members are not willing to sacrifice their self-interest for realizing the society's humanitarian goals?

Sacrifice is of particularly great importance in the case of the family and the society. Experience shows that the more the parents are attached to each other and adopt an attitude of mutual sacrifice and cooperation, the greater harmony and stability is likely to be there in the family. The upbringing of children also requires a substantial degree of mutual cooperation and sacrifice of self-interest on the part of parents. Similarly social harmony may also require members to cooperate with each other and to sacrifice for the common good and to take care of the poor and the vulnerable. Even in the case of the market and the state, sacrifice may not be avoidable. In spite of competition, which helps safeguard social interest, it may be possible for operators in the market to make unjustified gains by cheating and obstructing competition in a manner that may be difficult to detect. Similarly, although democracy, public accountability, and a free press do help in protecting the public interest, it may nevertheless be possible for government officials to use their authority for personal benefit at the expense of the taxpayer.

Therefore, there has to be some motivating force that prevents individuals from wrongdoing even when it is possible for them to get away unscathed. Government coercive power has proved to be an effective motivating force. However, if this were the only force in human society to prevent wrongdoing, the costs of enforcement may tend to be very high. Is it possible to supplement competition, public accountability, and government coercive power by some other motivating force that might induce members of society to abide willingly to agreed values or rules of behaviour and to fulfil their contracts and social obligations faithfully even when this involves a sacrifice of self-interest?

This brings us to the question of why should any person sacrifice his/her self-interest to serve social interest in the market place, the family, the society, or the government. If economics concentrates only on self-interest and has no place for a motivating force other than self-interest, then it may not be able to answer this question. If maximizing wealth and consumption is the only goal in the life of an individual, then there is no need to make any sacrifice for others. Serving self-interest may be the best policy. The family may then suffer; the quality of the future generation may decline, and even the performance of the market and the government may ultimately be adversely affected. The question, therefore, is how to motivate individuals to fulfil their contracts and other commitments honestly and not to undermine competition or to resort to unfair means of earning, even when it is possible for them to get away with it? This is a question that religions have tried to address by providing rules of behaviour in the form of moral obligations of individuals towards other human beings, animals, and the environment and trying to motivate their followers to abide by these rules even when doing so hurts their self-interest in this world. Whether or not they have succeeded in this task is a different matter. However, economics may not be able to ignore religious values and the associated motivating force if its goal is the realization of comprehensive well-being.

A society may have attained the pinnacle of glory in the material sense, but it may not be able to sustain it for long if the moral fibre of individuals and society is weakening, the family is disintegrating, the new generation is unable to get the kind of attention and upbringing that are necessary for an achieving civilization, and social tensions and anomie are rising. The material and the spiritual aspects of well-being are not, therefore, independent of each other. They are closely interrelated. Greater family harmony may help raise better individuals to operate in the market, and better social harmony may create a more conducive environment for effective government and accelerated development. If this is true, then the emphasis on serving self-interest and maximizing wealth and consumption may have to be toned down to some extent to serve social interest and optimize human well-being. Some uses of resources that serve self-interest and fit well into the hedonist framework may have to be reduced to fulfil the needs of all individuals in society and thereby promote family and social harmony.

Available evidence supports the contention that material advance is not by itself sufficient to increase happiness and social harmony. 'Rich countries are not typically happier than poor countries', concludes Richard Easterlin after 30 surveys conducted in 19 developed and developing countries (Easterlin, 1973, 1995; Oswald, 1997). There is something else that is also needed to create happiness and harmony and to remove tensions and anomie. Therefore, if economics concerns itself with well-being in its comprehensive sense, then it may not be able to confine its discussion to just material prosperity.[2]

1.3 THE MECHANISMS

How human well-being is defined is, therefore, an extremely crucial factor in the allocation and distribution of resources. If there is a difference in the concept of well-being, then there will also be a difference in the mechanisms and method for realizing it. There are three important mechanisms that determine the use of resources in any society or economic system. These are filtering, motivation, and socio-economic and political restructuring (Chapra, 1992, pp. 213–33). Just as it is possible to define well-being in a number of ways, it is also possible to have different mechanisms for filtering, motivation, and socio-economic restructuring.

First, all the different claims on limited resources need to be passed through a filter, in a way that realization of spiritual or humanitarian goals is not jeopardized, to create equilibrium between all the claims on these resources and their supply. There may be different ways of filtering. Three of these are central planning, market mechanism, and moral values (Chapra, 1992, pp. 71–112). Experience of socialist countries has shown that central planning is not an effective mechanism for filtering, even in the material sense, and almost all of them have abandoned it by now, except perhaps Cuba. However, market mechanism has performed extremely well. Prices determined through the interaction of supply and demand in perfectly competitive markets help filter out the various uses of resources in a way that equilibrium gets established. But the problem with the use of market mechanism for filtering is that it is possible to have several market equilibria depending on which tastes and preferences of individuals and firms interact with each other in the market place. *Any* and *every* market equilibrium may not lead to the realization of humanitarian goals. It may be desirable to complement the market system by some other mechanism that would help change individual tastes and preferences in a way that would lead to the desired kind of equilibrium. Could moral values help bring about such a change?

Second, if coercion is ruled out, then the desired kind of filtering may have to be brought about by motivating all individuals sufficiently to put in their best performance and to abstain from the use of resources in a way that frustrates the realization of the desired kind of well-being. Motivation acquires a great significance in economics as compared with, say physics, because economics deals with human beings who may or may not always behave in a standard manner that would be conducive to goal realization. The serving of self-interest has proved to be an effective motivating mechanism for increasing efficiency, whereas competition, public accountability, and government intervention have helped safeguard social interest. Would it be possible to safeguard social interest even more effectively if both market mechanism and government intervention are complemented by a sense of moral obligation?

Third, the physical, social, and political environments also influence human behaviour and the use of scarce resources. It may hence be necessary to supplement the filter mechanism and the motivating system by creating an enabling environment of economic, social, and political values and institutions that influence individuals positively, in a manner that would be conducive to the realization of well-being in its comprehensive sense. This would bring into focus the need for socio-economic and political reform.

For example, if the need-fulfilment of all is accepted as a goal, and the operation of market forces does not automatically lead to this, then some arrangement may need to be made to realize this goal. If budgetary constraints prevent the state from playing an important role, then is it possible for the family and the society to share the burden? However, if the values or the structure of the families and the society have changed over time, making them unwilling or unable to share the burden, then is it possible for economics to not discuss the kind of socio-economic change that is necessary to realize its humanitarian goals. Its refusal to do so may be tantamount to giving blessings to the prevailing inequities. These might accentuate social unrest and tensions, which may lead ultimately to a decline of the society even in the material sense. Similarly, even if a society has values, but individuals are able to get away with dishonesty, bribery, and other unfair means of earning, there being no effective system for detecting and punishing the culprits, then such practices may become locked-in through the long-run operation of path dependence and self-reinforcing mechanisms. Everyone may then condemn the practice, but may not be able to eliminate it single-handedly by him or herself being honest and fair. Is it possible to eliminate the undesired practices by just giving sermons and not undertaking comprehensive reform through socio-economic and political restructuring'? If such restructuring is needed, could it be brought about without the state also playing a supportive role? Would it be possible for economics to abstain from discussing the kind of change that is needed and the role of the state in it?

If the mechanisms chosen by economics are not in conformity with the desired concept of well-being, or if the desired restructuring is not, or cannot be, brought about, then that kind of well-being may fail to be realized. Within this perspective, anything that prevents the kind of filtering, motivation, and restructuring that the desired well-being requires may be termed as distortion, and any use of resources that does not directly or indirectly contribute to, or that is in conflict with, goal realization may be considered *unproductive, inessential,* or *wasteful.* The role that the state plays in the economy may also be determined by the kind of filtering, motivation, and restructuring that are necessary for realizing its vision.

1.4 ROLE OF THE WORLDVIEW

The concept of well-being selected by economics as well as the filtering, motivation, and restructuring mechanisms adopted by it are determined essentially by its worldview. Some of the questions that the worldview tries to answer are about how the universe has come into existence, the meaning and purpose of human life, the ultimate ownership and objective of the limited resources at the disposal of human beings, and the rights and responsibilities of individuals and families towards each other and their physical and social environment.

The answers to these questions have a far-reaching influence on human thought and behaviour and lead to different theoretical frameworks and policy prescriptions. For example, if the universe is believed to have come into existence by itself, and human beings are not accountable to anyone, then they would be free to live as they please. Their purpose in life would be to serve their self-interest through the realization of maximum wealth and consumption. The measure of their well-being would, in this case, be the extent to which they attain bodily pleasures and sensual satisfactions. Survival of the fittest may perhaps be the most logical behaviour pattern. Value judgments may be unwarranted, and all the three mechanisms of filtering, motivation, and restructuring may be developed by human beings alone through reliance on their own reason and experience.

However, if all human beings have been created by the Supreme Being and the resources they have at their disposal are a trust from Him, then they would automatically become related to each other by a natural bond of brotherhood and also be accountable to Him. They would then not be absolutely free to do what they please, but would rather be expected to use the scarce resources and behave with each other and their environment in a way that would help realize the well-being of *all* individuals, irrespective of whether they are rich or poor, white or black, male or female, and children or adults. They would also be expected to ensure not only the realization of the material goals but also spiritual and humanitarian goals, particularly social harmony and absence of anomie.

Revelation and reason would both in this case play an important role in filtering, motivation, and restructuring, and value judgments would not be out-of-bounds.

1.5 THE METHOD

The method of economics is also determined by its worldview. Linguistically, the term method refers to the rules and procedures of a discipline followed in a certain logical order to achieve a desired end (Blaug, 1980, p. xi; Caws, 1967, p. 339). Essentially, what the method does is to provide criteria for the acceptance or rejection of certain propositions as a part of the discipline (Blaug, 1980, p. 264; Machlup, 1978, p. 54). The steps taken and the criteria for acceptance or rejection thus depend, as Caws (1967, p. 339) has rightly indicated, on the end sought.

If survival of the fittest is an acceptable behaviour pattern, and if individuals are free to do what they wish in accordance with their preferences and their wealth, then the allocation and distribution brought about by market forces could not be questioned. There would be no point in talking about humanitarian goals. Economics would accept the status quo, pass no judgment on it, and make no policy recommendations to change it. Its method would then be just to describe (make positive statements about) how resources are actually allocated and distributed by the operation of market forces and to analyze, theoretically as well as empirically, the relationship among the different variables involved in such allocation and distribution, with a view to help make predictions about what may happen in the future. Economics would then be strictly a positive science with no normative role to play.

If, however, the purpose of economics is also to help realize the humanitarian goals, then the method may not be just to describe, analyze, and predict, but also to compare the actual results with the desired goals, to analyze the reasons for the gap between the two, and to show how the gap may be removed without unduly sacrificing individual freedom. Value judgments may not then be out-of-bounds. Because the purpose of revelation is to help in making such value judgments, it may also be welcome, and economics may then be based on both revelation and reason and experience. There may then be no justification for creating a watertight distinction between its positive and normative functions because both may be closely integrated and together constitute an indispensable part of its raison d'être.

1.6 THE RELEVANCE OF ISLAMIC ECONOMICS

The vision, the mechanisms, and the method of economics are all, therefore, the logical outcome of its worldview. Even though none of the prevailing major worldviews is either totally materialist and hedonist nor totally humanitarian and spiritual, there are, nevertheless, significant differences among them in terms of the emphasis they put on the material or the spiritual goals. The greater the difference in the emphasis, the greater may be the difference in the economic disciplines of these societies. Feyerabend (1993) has frankly recognized this in the introduction to the Chinese edition of his thought-provoking book *Against Method*, by stating that 'First world science is only one science among many; by claiming to be more it ceases to be an instrument of research and turns into a (political) pressure group' (p. 3, parentheses are in the original). Even if the worldviews are the same, as is the case with institutional and conventional economics (Blaug, 1985, pp. 708–11), which are believed by a number of economists to be complementary, the Nobel Laureate, Professor Douglass North, clearly stated: 'Introducing institutional analysis into static neoclassical theory entails modifying the existing body of theory. But devising a model of economic change requires the construction of an entire theoretical framework, because no such model exists' (North, 1990, p. 112).

However, if there is a substantial difference even in the worldviews and the visions, there is no reason why there cannot be greater differences in the disciplines. One discipline may just try to explain what exists, refuse to make value judgments, and not concern itself with socio-political change for realizing a certain vision of life. Another discipline may not find *what is* to be acceptable and aim at helping realize the desired social vision. It may not then be able to avoid a discussion of how, and through what process, the vision may be realized. This need not make the disciplines mutually exclusive. The rational and amicable discussion of different worldviews and disciplines may in fact promote greater depth and breadth in the analysis of both disciplines through cross-pollination, thus making the world richer and better off. Feyerabend (1993) is hence right in asserting that 'proliferation of theories is beneficial for science while conformity impairs its critical power. Uniformity also impairs the free development of the individual' (p. 5).

1.7 THE ISLAMIC WORLDVIEW

This brings us to the very pertinent question of whether the worldview of Islamic economics is significantly different from that of conventional economics. Although there is a great deal that is common among the worldviews of most major religions of the world, particularly those of Islam, Christianity, and Judaism, it may not be possible to say the same about the worldviews of Islamic and conventional economics. The worldviews of both disciplines are radically different. The Islamic worldview is not secularist, value-neutral, materialist, or social-Darwinist. It is rather based on a number of concepts that strike at the root of these doctrines. It gives primary importance to moral values, human brotherhood, and socio-economic justice and does not rely primarily on either the state or the market for realizing its vision. It relies rather on the integrated roles of values and institutions, market, families, society, and the state, to ensure the realization of its vision of ensuring the well-being of all. It puts great emphasis on social change through a reform of the individual and his/her society, without which the market and the state could both perpetuate inequities.

The fundamental Islamic belief is that this universe and everything in it, including human beings, has been created by the One and the Only God. All human beings are His vicegerents and brothers unto each other. There is no superiority of one over the other because of race, sex, nationality, wealth, or power. Their sojourn in this world is temporary. Their ultimate destination is the Hereafter where they *will* be accountable before God. Their well-being in the Hereafter depends on whether or not they live in this world, and fulfil their obligations towards others, in a way that helps ensure the well-being of all individuals in society.[3]

One of the things that seriously affects the well-being of all individuals in society is the way the scarce resources, which are a trust from God, are used. God, the Creator and Owner of these resources, has provided certain values, rules of behaviour, or institutions, within the framework of which human beings are expected to use these resources and to interact with each other. These values have been given not just to any one specific group of human beings, but rather to all people at different times in history through a chain of His messengers (who were all human beings), including Abraham; Moses: Jesus; and, the last of them, Muhammad, peace and blessings of God be on them all.[4] Thus according to Islam, there is a continuity and similarity in the value systems of all revealed religions to the extent to which the message has not been lost or distorted over the ages.

The prophets did not, however, bring just the values. They also struggled to reform their societies. Socio-economic and political reform is, therefore, the major thrust of the Islamic message. To accept *what is* and not to struggle for the realization of the vision or *what ought to be* is a vote in favour of prevailing inequities and doing nothing to remove them. Such an attitude cannot be justifiable within the Islamic worldview. The mission of human beings is not just to abide themselves by the Islamic values, but also to struggle for the reform of their societies in accordance with these. This is what is meant by righteous living.

Righteous living would, it is believed, help promote a balance between individual and social interest and help actualize the *maqasid al- Shari'ah* (the goals of the *Shari'ah*), or what may be referred to as the vision of Islam, two of the most important constituents of which are socio-economic justice and the well-being of all life created by God.[5] Injustice cannot but thwart the realization of true well-being, accentuate tensions and social unrest, discourage individuals from putting in their best, and thus retard development. However, whereas conventional economics assumes the prevalence of self-interested behaviour on the part of individuals, Islam does not assume the prevalence of ideal behaviour. It believes that, although some people may normally act in an ideal manner, the behaviour of most people may tend to be anywhere between the two extremes of selfishness and altruism and hence a constant effort (*jihad*) needs to be made on the part of both individuals and society for moral uplift.

Islam, however, rules out the use of force for moral uplift: 'There shall be no compulsion in religion' (al-Qur'an, 2:256), and 'Say that the Truth has come from your Lord: Whoever wishes may either believe in it or reject it' (al-Qur'an, 18:29).[6] It rather lays stress on proper upbringing, creating conviction through logical reasoning and friendly dialogue (al-Qur'an, 16:125), and creating an enabling environment for motivating individuals to do what is right and to abstain from doing what is wrong. This is, however, not sufficient. It is also necessary to provide both material and spiritual incentives and deterrents to motivate individuals to do their best for their own good as well as that of others and to prevent them from causing harm to others. Smoothly functioning competitive markets, where people interact with each other in their self-interest, are necessary for ensuring maximum efficiency. However, although competition does help safeguard social interest to a certain extent, total reliance cannot be placed on it because some people may use unfair means to enrich themselves. Hence governments have tried to pass and enforce regulations. But regulations may not be possible without having a perception of what is the right thing to do. Therefore, once we regulate, we do not remain value-neutral. Moreover, it may not be realistic to depend primarily on regulations because regulations may be circumvented and need to be effectively enforced. The cost of enforcing them may be lower if there is some effective mechanism for self-enforcement.

This self-enforcement is believed to come from two sources. One of these is the innate goodness of the human being himself or herself. Within the framework of Islamic beliefs, people are good by nature because God has created them in His own image (al-Qur'an, 30:30). The individual does not necessarily always act in his self-interest. He/she also acts in the interest of others and even makes sacrifices for them under a feeling of moral obligation. However, because the individual is also free and his/her behaviour is not determined, he/she may or may not preserve his/her innate goodness and may act in ways that are against his/her nature. This may hurt him/her and his/her society. Therefore, it is necessary to provide incentives and deterrents as well as an enabling environment. The problem with a number of this-worldly incentives and deterrents is that they may be insufficient and may not even be justly implemented.

Therefore, the second source of self-enforcement is belief in the reward and punishment in the Hereafter. If I abstain from doing anything wrong and also sacrifice my material self-interest for the sake of others, I will improve my well-being in the Hereafter. The concept of Hereafter thus gives a long-term perspective to self-interest by extending it beyond a person's lifespan in this world. It is not possible for competition and government intervention to *always* motivate a person to do what is morally right and to abstain from what is morally wrong, to cooperate with others and to make sacrifices for them. Governments can try to ensure competition and to pass laws to safeguard social interest. However, there are so many clandestine ways of restraining competition and of cheating and exploiting others without being caught that it may be difficult for governments to succeed unless there is an inner urge on the part of operators in the market themselves to do what is right, to fulfil their contracts and other commitments faithfully, and not to try to undermine competition or resort to unfair means of earning. In the last analysis, therefore, it may not be possible to safeguard social interest effectively without the help of moral values and without creating an effective motivating force and a proper environment for their enforcement. This may reduce the burden on the government of safeguarding social interest.

1.8 THE HISTORICAL LINK

Islamic economics had been developing gradually as an interdisciplinary subject in keeping with the Islamic worldview in the writings of Qur'an commentators, jurists, historians, and social, political, and moral philosophers. A large number of scholars, including Abu Yusuf (d. 798), al-Mas'udi (d. 957), al-Mawardi (d. 1058), Ibn Hazm (d. 1064), al-Sarakhsi (d. 1090), al-Tusi (d. 1093), al-Ghazali (d. 1111), al-Dimashqi (d. after 1175), Ibn Rushd (d. 1198), Ibn Taymiyyah (d. 1328), Ibn al-Ukhuwwah (d. 1329), Ibn al-Qayyim (d. 1350), al-Shatibi (d. 1388), Ibn Khaldun (d. 1406), al-Maqrizi (d. 1442), al-Dawwani (d. 1501), and Shah Waliyullah (d. 1762), made valuable contributions over the centuries.[7] These scholars were not, however, specialists in economics. Strict compartmentalization of disciplines had not developed by then. They were masters of a number of different intellectual disciplines, and their contributions are, therefore, spread over a vast literature, some of which has been lost because of the vicissitudes of time and a wave of invasions particularly by the Mongols (Rosenthal, 1947, p. 19; Sarton, 1927, Vol. 1, p. 662). It was perhaps because of this multidisciplinary nature of their contributions that human well-being never got conceived as an isolated phenomenon dependent primarily on economic variables. It was seen as the end-product of a number of economic as well as moral, psychological, social, demographic, and political factors in such an integrated manner that it was not possible to realize overall human well-being without an optimum contribution from all. Justice occupied a pivotal place in this whole framework. This was to be expected because of its crucial importance within the Islamic worldview.

These diverse contributions over the centuries seem to have reached their consummation in Ibn Khaldun's (n.d.) *Muqaddimah*, or *Introduction to Histon*, where he tried to analyze the closely interrelated roles of moral, psychological, political, economic, social, demographic, and historical factors over a period of three generations, or 120 years, in the rise and fall of a dynasty (*dawlah*) or civilization (*umran*). His analysis was thus not static and was not based on only economic variables. It was, rather, dynamic and multidisciplinary. The need for such an analysis was felt by him because he lived at a time (1332–1406) when the Muslim civilization was already in a process of decline and, as a conscientious Muslim, he was keen to see a reversal of the tide. However, this is not all that he did. The *Muqaddimah* also contains a considerable discussion of economic principles, a significant part of which is undoubtedly Ibn Khaldun's original contribution to economics.[8]

His contributions did not, unfortunately, get fertilized and developed further in the Muslim world. As he rightly theorized himself, sciences progress only when a society is itself progressing (Ibn Khaldun, n.d., p. 434). This theory has become clearly upheld by Muslim history. Sciences progressed rapidly in the Muslim world from the middle of the 8th century to the middle of the 12th century. The development continued at a decelerated pace for two more centuries (Sarton, 1927–1948; Sezgin, 1983 and ff.). Thereafter, there appeared a brilliant star only once in a while on an otherwise unexciting firmament. Economics was no exception. It also continued to be in a state of limbo in the Muslim world. No major contributions were made after Ibn Khaldun, except by a few isolated luminaries such as al-Maqrizi (d. 1442), al-Dawwani (d. 1501), and Shah Waliyullah (d. 1762).

Consequently, whereas conventional economics became a separate scientific discipline in the West in the 1890s after the publication in 1890 of Alfred Marshall's great treatise, *Principles of Economics* (Schumpeter, 1954, p. 21)[9] and has continued to develop since then, Islamic economics remained primarily an integral part of the unified social and moral philosophy of Islam until the Second World War. The independence of most Muslim countries after the War and the need to develop their economies in a way that would help realize the Islamic vision has given boost to the reemergence of Islamic economics. This need not give anyone the impression that the attempt is to bypass the good and valuable analytical work done by conventional economics and its offshoots. It would be difficult not to agree with Blaug (1980) when he said that 'any methodological prescription that amounts to wiping clean the entire slate of received economics and to starting all over again from scratch may be dismissed out of hand as self-defeating' (p. 121).

1.9 ACHIEVEMENTS, SHORTCOMINGS AND FUTURE PROSPECTS

Islamic economics has so far, however, been able to scratch only the surface of what Ibn Khaldun's multidisciplinary dynamics entails. Greater emphasis has been laid so far on explaining what the ideal Islamic economic system is, how it differs from socialism and capitalism, and why the operation of markets within the framework of the Islamic worldview would help minimize some of the glaring inequities of the market system and exert a positive impact on the realization of overall human well-being without *excessive* reliance on the state. Most of the discussion is, however, of a normative nature – how all economic agents (individuals and households, firms, altruistic organizations, markets and governments) are expected to behave in the light of Islamic norms. This has been accompanied by some sporadic historical data to show that the system has actually been in existence for at least short periods at different times in Muslim history and that this has produced positive results. This was natural and in fact necessary. Economics is so closely related to the worldview and the economic system of a society that without clarity about these, Islamic economics may have groped in the dark for the direction in which to proceed.[10]

The other area where substantial, although still far from adequate, literature has become available is Islamic finance. An effort has been made to show why an economy that relies less on credit and more on equity may be superior in its overall performance to the one that relies substantially on credit, particularly on short-term credit (Mills and Presley, 1999, pp. 58–72 and 114–20; Chapra, 1985, pp. 107–45; 1992, pp. 327–34). Some progress has also been made in macroeconomics. There has been a considerable discussion of the Islamic vision (Ahmad and Awan, 1992; Khan, 1994). There is, however, no theoretical macroeconomic model that would show how the Islamic values and institutions, and different sectors of the economy, society and polity would interact to help realize the vision. An appropriate macroeconomic policy package has hence not developed. The field where very little progress has been made is microeconomics. It has not been possible to establish the relationship among the macroeconomic goals and the behaviour of different economic agents and the kind of socio-economic and political reform that the realization of goals may require. Yalcintas (1986) is perhaps right in stating that 'Construction of microeconomic theory under the Islamic constraints might be the most challenging task before Islamic economics' (p. 38).

Although there is undoubtedly some merit in showing how the injection of a moral dimension into economics might help realize the Islamic vision without excessive dependence on the state, such a discussion does not take us very far. Due to centuries of decline, disintegration, and lack of proper education, Islamic values are not reflected either in individual or social behaviour or in the prevailing legal, social, political, and economic institutions of Muslim countries. There is a great deal of deviation from Islamic norms. A number of morally wrong practices, such as dishonesty, corruption, extravagance, wastefulness, and lack of punctuality and conscientiousness have become securely locked-in through the long-run operation of path dependence and self-reinforcing mechanisms. The deviation is taking a heavy toll of justice, development, and general well-being (see Chapra, 1992, pp. 251–338). The task of

Islamic economics does not, therefore, get fully accomplished if it does not show the causes of this deviation. Other societies have translated their values into formal institutions in spite of an external secularist and value-neutral stance (Organisation for Economic Co-operation and Development, 1996). They have formulated a legal framework and a proper code of conduct for government officials and put in place mechanisms for transparency, rule of law, public accountability, and protection of whistle-blowers. They have also created sufficient checks and balances and adopted measures that would make it difficult for violators to get away unscathed. Muslim countries have generally lagged behind here. The question is why. It may not be possible to answer this question without also injecting psychological, social, political, and historical dimensions into the analysis. One of the major reasons for the Muslim malaise may be the failure of the political system. There is hardly any Muslim country where there is a truly democratic government, accountable to the people, where the press is really free, where the courts are independent of political interference, and where the law of the land gets applied fairly and impartially to all, irrespective of their wealth and power. This is in clear violation of the Islamic norms related to the polity. The result is that senior government functionaries are able to get away with corruption, inequities, and incompetence. This frustrates the effective and impartial operation of incentives and deterrents and creates a favourable climate for the general violation of Islamic norms. The country's resources do not, therefore, get used efficiently and equitably for the well-being of the people. In addition, there is a glaring omission in Islamic economics of a scientific analysis of some of the crucial problems of Muslim countries, including budgetary and balance of payments deficits, high debt-servicing burden, low levels of saving, investment and real growth, high rates of inflation and unemployment, extreme inequalities of income and wealth, and miserable socio-economic condition of the poor.

There could be no escape from what Ibn Khaldun (1950) did for his society – adopting a multidisciplinary approach to find out the causes of the various problems and suggesting, in the light of such analysis, a comprehensive, well-integrated, and practical reform program. Within the framework of his multidisciplinary dynamic model, concentrating only on moral or economic variables may not be able to take the Muslim world very far on the path of development with justice.

Islamic economics also needs to collect reliable data on a number of important economic variables. Without knowing the actual position and the reasons for it, it may not be possible to prepare a well-conceived program for social, economic, and political change. Data create transparency and reveal the true picture, which some governments do not welcome. Hence one of the essential prerequisites for reform is the collection and publication of necessary data and their scientific analysis. Missing in particular are data on distribution of income and wealth, extent of need-fulfilment, and nature and quality of life, particularly of the downtrodden people. Without such data, it is not possible to know the degree of equity prevailing in the allocation and distribution of resources, which is the most crucial criterion for judging the Islamization of a Muslim economy. There are also inadequate data about government revenues and expenditures, consumption, saving and investment behaviour of individuals and different sectors of the population, employment and unemployment, bonded, female and child labour, wages and salaries, working conditions, work habits, and productivity, along with a rational explanation for the deviation from Islamic norms. Once this is done, it may be possible for Islamic economics to do a more meaningful job of analyzing the impact that the introduction of Islamic values and institutions may have on aggregate consumption, saving and investment. economic growth and stability, and distribution of income.

The practical wisdom of Islamic economics has thus been unable to come to grips with the task of explaining the rise and fall of Muslim economies in the past, the lag between Islamic norms and the actual behaviour of economic agents, and the causes of problems faced by Muslim countries. It has been unable to suggest a balanced package of policy proposals in the light of Islamic teachings to enable Muslim countries to perform the difficult task of reducing their imbalances and simultaneously actualizing the Islamic vision. Moreover, its theoretical core has also thus far been unable to come out of the straitjacket of conventional economics, which takes into account primarily the economic variables that are measurable and generally avoids a discussion of the complex historical interplay of moral, psychological, economic, social and political factors. Islamic economics has thus 'failed to escape the centripetal pull of Western economic thought, and has in many regards been caught in the intellectual web of the very system it set out to replace' (Nasr, 1991, p. 388). It is thus unable to explain the difference in the performance of various societies with respect to overall human well-being.

The potential is, however, great but the expectations for the near future should not be pitched at a very high level. It may not be possible to raise Muslim societies, at least in the near future, to the high spiritual level that Islam demands and that Muslim economists assume in their analysis. Moreover, the performance of all the functions that are expected from

Islamic economics may not be immediately feasible because of the lack of resources and political support, the non-availability of data, and the difficulty of measuring a number of the socio-economic and political variables that need to be incorporated into the models. It is possible that even after a great effort, the achievements may not be significantly great. The discipline will mature over time after passing through an evolutionary process. It has, fortunately, the advantage of benefiting from the tools of analysis developed by conventional, social, humanistic, and institutional economics as well as other social sciences.

ACKNOWLEDGEMENT

I gratefully thank Mr Mobin Ahmad for the secretarial assistance provided by him in the preparation of this chapter.

NOTES

1. It may be desirable to be clear about the difference between the terms distribution and redistribution. Distribution refers to the allocation of resources that takes place automatically through the operation of market forces. However, when a society uses extramarket or other nonmarket processes to change that distribution in accordance with the concept of justice embodied in its worldview, it is referred to as redistribution.
2. The literature on the determinants of human well-being has been growing rapidly. For a survey of this literature, see David Myers (1993).
3. For greater detail on the fundamentals of the Islamic worldview, see Chapra (1992), pp. 201–12.
4. The Qur'an does not make any mention of the prophets sent by God to people other than those in the Middle East. Their names were not familiar to them, and the Qur'an is not intended to be an encyclopedia. However, it states clearly that 'And indeed We have sent Our Messengers to every community in every period' (al-Qur'an, 16:36). 'And We sent Messengers before you; some of them We have mentioned to you, while some others We have not mentioned' (al-Qur'an, 40:78).
5. For a brief discussion of the vision of Islam or the *maqasid al-Shari'ah*, see Chapra (1992), pp. 7–9. There has been a substantial discussion of the *maqasid al-Shari'ah* in the *fiqh* literature, some of the most prominent exponents being al-Matridi (d. 945), al-Shashi (d. 975), al-Baqillani (d. 1012), al-Juwayni (d. 1085), al-Ghazali (d. 1111), Fakhr al-Din al-Razi (d. 1209), al-Amidi (d. 1234), 'Izz al-Din 'Abd al-Salam (d. 1262), Ibn Taymiyyah (d. 1327), and al-Shatibi (d. 1388). For a modern discussion of these, see Masud (1977); al-Raysuni (1992), pp. 25–55; and Nyazee (1994), pp. 189–268.
6. The Qur'an repeats the same message in a number of other places. For example, 'Are you going to compel people to believe' (al-Qur'an, 10:99) and 'You are not there to force them to believe. Exhort through the Qur'an whoever takes heed of the Warning' (al-Qur'an, 50:45).

7. For a brief account of some of these contributions, see De Shmogyi (1965), Islahi (1996), Mirakhor (1987), Siddiqi (1992), and Spengler (1964).
8. See also *Muqaddimah's* translation under Rosenthal (1967) and selections from it under Issawi (1950). For details of Ibn Khaldun's multidisciplinary dynamic model, see Chapter 5 of my forthcoming book, *The Future of Economics: An Islamic Perspective* (Leicester, UK: The Islamic Foundation).
9. According to Blaug (1985, p. 3), economics became an academic discipline in the 1880s.
10. According to Zarqa (1986), Islamic economics is 'the "economic system", on the one hand, and "the economic analysis thereof", on the other' (p. 52).

REFERENCES

Ahmad, A., and Awan, K.R. (eds) (1992), *Lectures on Islamic Economics* (Jiddah: IDB).

Blaug, M. (1980), *The Methodology of Economics or How Economists Explain* (Cambridge: Cambridge University Press).

Blaug, M. (1985), *Economic Theory in Retrospect*, 4th edn (Cambridge: Cambridge University Press).

Brzezinsky, Z. (1995), *Out of Control: Global Turmoil on the Eve of the 21st Century* (New York: Touchstone Books).

Caws, P. (1967), Scientific method. In P. Edwards (ed.), *The Encyclopedia of Philosophy* (London: Macmillan), pp. 339–43.

Chapra, M.U. (1985), *Towards Just Monetary System* (Leicester, UK: The Islamic Foundation).

Chapra, M.U. (1992), *Islam and the Economic Challenge* (Leicester, UK: The Islamic Foundation).

Chapra, M.U. (1996), *What is Islamic Economics?* (Jeddah: IRTI).

De Shmogyi, J.N. (1965), Economic theory in classical Arabic literature. *Studies in Islam* (January), 1–6.

Easterlin, R. (1973), Does money buy happiness? *The Public Interest* (Winter).

Easterlin, R. (1995), Will raising the incomes of all increase the happiness of all? *Journal of Economic Behavior and Organization*, 27, 35–48.

Feyerabend, P. (1993), *Against Method*, 3rd edn (London: Verso).

Hodgson, M.G.S. (1977), *The Venture of Islam: Conscience and History in a World Civilization* (Chicago, IL: University of Chicago Press).

Ibn Khaldun (n.d.), 'Abd al-Rahman. *Muqaddimah* (Cairo: AI-Maktabah al-Tijariyyah al-Kubra).

Islahi, A.A. (1996), *History of Economic Thought in Islam* (Aligarh, India: Department of Economics, Aligarh Muslim University).

Islamic Research and Training Institute, Islamic Development Bank (1986), *Problems of Research in Islamic Economics* (Jeddah: Islamic Research and Training Institute).

Issawi, C. (1950), *An Arab Philosophy of History. Selections from: the Prolegomena of Ibn Khaldun of Tunis (1332–1406)* (London: John Murray).

Khan, M.F. (1994), *Essays in Islamic Economics* (Leicester, UK: The Islamic Foundation).

Machlup, F. (1978), *Methodology of Economics and Other Social Sciences* (New York: Academic Press).

Masud, M.K. (1977), *Islamic Legal Philosophy: A Study of Abu Ishaq al-Shatibi's Life and Thought* (Islamabad: Islamic Research Institute).

Mills, P.S. and Presley, J.R. (1999), *Islamic Finance: Theory and Practice* (London: Macmillan Press).

Mirakhor, A. (1987), The Muslim scholars and the history of economics: A need for consideration. *American Journal of Islamic Social Sciences* (December), 245–76.

Myers, D.G. (1993), *The Pursuit of Happiness. Who is Happy and Why?* (New York: Avon).

Nasr, S.V.R. (1991), Islamisation of knowledge: a critical overview. *Islamic Studies* (Autumn), 30, 3, 387–400.

North, Douglass C. (1990), *Institutions, Institutional Change, and Economic Performance* (Cambridge: Cambridge University Press).

Nyazee, I.A.K. (1994), *Theories of Islamic Law. The Methodology of Ijtihad* (Islamabad: IIIT).

OECD (1996), *Ethics in the Public Service. Current Issues and Practice* (Paris: OECD, Public Management Occasional Papers, No. 14).

Oswald, A.J. (1997), Happiness and economic performance. *Economic Journal* (November), 815–31.

Oswald, A.J., Frank, R.H. and Ng, Y.-K. (1997), Economics and happiness. *Economic Journal* (November), 1812–58.

Raysuni, A. (1992), *al-Nazariyyah al-Maqasid 'Inda al-!mam al-Shatibi*, 2nd edn (Riyadh: Al-Dar al-Alamiyyah lil Kitab al-Islami).

Rosenthal, F. (1947), The technique and approach of Muslim scholarship. *Analecta Orientelia* (Rome: Pontificam Institutum Biblicum), 24.

Rosenthal, F. (1958), *Ibn Khaldun. The Muqaddimah, An Introduction to History*, 1st edn (2nd edn 1967; 3 volumes) (London: Routledge and Kegan Paul).

Sarton, G. *Introduction to the History of Science.* (3 volumes issued between 1927 and 1948, the 2nd and 3rd in two parts each) (Washington: Carnegie Institute).

Schumpeter, J.A. (1954), *History of Economic Analysis*, Elizabeth B. Schumpeter (ed.) (New York: Oxford University Press).

Sezgin, F. (1983), *Tarikh al-Turath al-'Arabi* [History of Arab Legacy] (First volume, followed by other volumes in later years) (Mahmud Fahmi Hijazi, Trans.) (Riyadh: Imam Muhammad ibn Saud Islamic University).

Siddiqi, M.N. (1992), History of Islamic economic thought. In Ahmad and Awan (1992), pp. 69–90.

Spengler, J. (1964), Economic thought of Islam: Ibn Khaldun. *Comparative Studies in Society and History*, 6, 268–306.

Yalcintas, N. (1986), Problems of research in Islamic economics: General background. In Islamic Research and Training Institute (1986), pp. 23–41.

Zarqa, M.A. (1986), Problems of research in the theory of Islamic economics: Suggested solutions. In Islamic Research and Training Institute (1986), pp. 52–63.

2. Islamic economics: what it is and how it developed

Islamic economics has been having a revival over the last few decades. However, it is still in a preliminary stage of development. In contrast with this, conventional economics has become a well-developed and sophisticated discipline after going through a long and rigorous process of development over more than a century. This raises a number of questions, some of which are: Is it necessary to have a new discipline in economics? If so, what is Islamic economics, how does it differ from conventional economics needed, and has it made any worthwhile contributions over the centuries? This chapter tries to briefly answer these questions in three parts.

2.1 IS A NEW DISCIPLINE IN ECONOMICS NEEDED?

It is universally recognized that resources are scarce compared with the claims on them. However, it is also simultaneously recognized by practically all civilizations that the well-being of all human beings needs to be ensured. Given the scarcity of resources, the well-being of all may remain an unrealized dream if the scarce resources are not utilized efficiently and equitably. For this purpose, every society needs to develop an effective strategy, which is consciously or unconsciously conditioned by its worldview. If the worldview is flawed, the strategy may not be able to help the society actualize the well-being of all. The prevailing worldviews may be classified for the sake of ease into two board theoretical constructs: (1) secular and materialist, and (2) spiritual and humanitarian.

2.1.1 The Role of the Worldview

The secular and materialist worldviews attach maximum importance to the material aspect of human well-being and tend generally to ignore the importance of the spiritual aspect. They often argue that maximum

material well-being can be best realized if individuals are given unhindered freedom to pursue their self-interest and to maximize their want
satisfaction in keeping with their own tastes and preferences.[1] In their
extreme form they do not recognize any role for Divine guidance in
human life and place full trust in the ability of human beings to chalk out
a proper strategy with the help of their reason. In such a worldview there
is little role for values or government intervention in the efficient and
equitable allocation and distribution of resources. When asked about how
social interest would be served when everyone has unlimited freedom to
pursue his/her self-interest, the reply is that market forces will themselves
ensure this because competition will keep self-interest under check.

In contrast with this, religious worldviews give attention to both the
material as well as the spiritual aspects of human well-being. They do not
necessarily reject the role of reason in human development. They,
however, recognize the limitations of reason and wish to complement it
by revelation. They do not also reject the need for individual freedom or
the role that the serving of self-interest can play in human development.
They, however, emphasize that both freedom and the pursuit of self-
interest need to be toned down by moral values and good governance to
ensure that everyone's well-being is realized and that social harmony and
family integrity are not hurt in the process of everyone serving his/her
self-interest.

2.1.2   Material and Spiritual Needs

Even though *none* of the major worldviews prevailing around the world
is totally materialist and hedonist, there are, nevertheless, significant
differences among them in terms of the emphasis they place on material
or spiritual goals and the role of moral values and government intervention in ordering human affairs. While material goals concentrate primarily on goods and services that contribute to physical comfort and
well-being, spiritual goals include nearness to God, peace of mind, inner
happiness, honesty, justice, mutual care and cooperation, family and
social harmony, and the absence of crime and anomie. These may not be
quantifiable, but are, nevertheless, crucial for realizing human well-being.
Resources being limited, excessive emphasis on the material ingredients
of well-being may lead to a neglect of spiritual ingredients. The greater
the difference in emphasis, the greater may be the difference in the
economic disciplines of these societies. Feyerabend (1993) has frankly
recognized this in the introduction to the Chinese edition of his thought
provoking book, *Against Method*, by stating that 'First world science is
only one science among many; by claiming to be more it ceases to be an

instrument of research and turns into a (political) pressure group' (p. 3, parentheses are in the original).

2.1.3   The Enlightenment Worldview and Conventional Economics

There is a great deal that is common between the worldviews of most major religions, particularly those of Judaism, Christianity and Islam. This is because, according to Islam, there is a continuity and similarity in the value systems of all Revealed religions to the extent to which the Message has not been lost or distorted over the ages. The Qur'an clearly states that: 'Nothing has been said to you [Muhammad] that was not said to the Messengers before you' (al-Qur'an, 41:43). If conventional economics had continued to develop in the image of the Judo–Christian worldview, as it did before the Enlightenment Movement of the seventeenth and eighteenth centuries, there may not have been any significant difference between conventional and Islamic economics. However, after the Enlightenment Movement, all intellectual disciplines in Europe became influenced by its secular, value-neutral, materialist and social-Darwinist worldview, even though this did not succeed fully. All economists did not necessarily become materialist or social-Darwinist in their individual lives and many of them continued to be attached to their religious worldviews. Koopmans (1969) has rightly observed that 'scratch an economist and you will find a moralist underneath'. Therefore, while theoretically conventional economics adopted the secular and value neutral orientation of the Enlightenment worldview and failed to recognize the role of value judgments and good governance in the efficient and equitable allocation and distribution of resources, in practice this did not take place fully. The pre-Enlightenment tradition never disappeared completely (see Baeck, 1994, p. 11).

There is no doubt that, in spite of its secular and materialist worldview, the market system led to a long period of prosperity in the Western market-oriented economies. However, this unprecedented prosperity did not lead to the elimination of poverty or the fulfilment of everyone's needs in conformity with the Judo–Christian value system even in the wealthiest countries. Inequalities of income and wealth have continued to persist and there has also been a substantial degree of economic instability and unemployment which have added to the miseries of the poor. This indicates that both efficiency and equity have remained elusive in spite of rapid development and phenomenal rise in wealth.

Consequently there has been persistent criticism of economics by a number of well-meaning scholars, including Thomas Carlyle (*Past and Present*, 1843), John Ruskin (*Unto this Last*, 1862) and Charles Dickens

(*Hard Times*, 1854–55) in England, and Henry George (*Progress and Poverty*, 1879) in America. They ridiculed the dominant doctrine of laissez-faire with its emphasis on self-interest. Thomas Carlyle called economics a 'dismal science' and rejected the idea that free and un-controlled private interests will work in harmony and further the public welfare (see Jay and Jay, 1986). Henry George condemned the resulting contrast between wealth and poverty and wrote: 'So long as all the increased wealth which modern progress brings goes but to build great fortunes, to increase luxury and make sharper the contrast between the House of Have and the House of Want, progress is not real and cannot be permanent' (George, 1955, p. 10).

In addition to failing to fulfil the basic needs of a large number of people and increasing inequalities of income and wealth, modern economic development has been associated with the disintegration of the family and rise in the disintegration of the family, crime and anomie, and a decline in peace of mind failure to bring peace of mind and inner happiness. (Easterlin, 2001, 1995 and 1974; Oswald, 1997; Blanchflower and Oswald, 2000; Diener and Oishi, 2000; and Kenny, 1999). The laissez-faire approach, for example, lost ground, particularly after the Great Depression of the 1930s as a result of the Keynesian revolution and the socialist onslaught. However, most scholars have concluded that government intervention alone cannot by itself remove all socio-economic ills. It is also necessary to motivate individuals to do what is right and abstain from doing what is wrong. This is where the moral uplift of society can be helpful. Without it, more and more difficult and costly regulations are needed. Nobel Laureate, Amartya Sen has, there-fore, rightly argued that 'the distancing of economics from ethics has impoverished welfare economics and also weakened the basis of a good deal of descriptive and predictive economics' and that economics 'can be made more productive by paying greater and more explicit attention to ethical considerations that shaped human behaviour and judgment' (Sen, 1987, pp. 78 and 79). Hausman and McPherson also conclude in their survey article in the *Journal of Economic Literature* on 'Economics and Contemporary Moral Philosophy' that 'An economy that is engaged actively and self-critically with the moral aspects of its subject matter cannot help but be more interesting, more illuminating and, ultimately, more useful than the one that tries not to be' (Hausman and McPherson, 1993, p. 723).

2.2 WHAT IS ISLAMIC ECONOMICS AND HOW DOES IT DIFFER FROM CONVENTIONAL ECONOMICS?

While conventional economics is now in the process of returning to its pre-Enlightenment roots, Islamic economics never got entangled in a secular and materialist worldview. It is based on a religious worldview which strikes at the roots of secularism and value neutrality. To ensure the true well-being of all individuals, irrespective of their sex, age, race, religion or wealth, Islamic economics does not seek to abolish private property, as was done by Communism, nor does it prevent individuals from serving their self-interest. It recognizes the role of the market in the efficient allocation of resources, but does not find competition to be sufficient to safeguard social interest. It tries to promote human brotherhood, socio-economic justice and the well-being of all through an integrated role of moral values, market mechanism, families, society, and 'good governance'. This is because of the great emphasis in Islam on human brotherhood and socio-economic justice.

2.2.1 The Integrated Role of the Market, Families, Society and Government

The market is not the only institution where people interact in human society. They also interact in the family, the society and the government and their interaction in all these institutions is closely interrelated. There is no doubt that the serving of self-interest does help raise efficiency in the market place. However, if self-interest is overemphasized and there are no moral restraints on the individual, other institutions may not work effectively – families may disintegrate, the society may be uncaring, and the government may be corrupt, partisan, and self-centred. Mutual sacrifice is necessary for keeping the families glued together. Since the human being is the most important input of not only the market, but also of the family, the society and the government, and the family is the source of this input, nothing may work if the families disintegrate and are unable to provide loving care to children. This is likely to happen if both the husband and wife try to serve just their own self-interest and are not attuned to the making of sacrifices that the proper care and upbringing of children demands. Lack of willingness to make such sacrifice can lead to a decline in the quality of the human input of all other institutions, including the market, the society and the government. It may also lead to a fall in fertility rates below the replacement level, making it difficult for the society not only to sustain its development but also its social security system.

2.2.2 The Role of Moral Values

While conventional economics generally considers the behaviour and tastes and references of individuals as given, Islamic economics does not do so. It places great emphasis on individual and social reform through moral uplift. This is the purpose for which all God's messengers, including Abraham, Moses, Jesus, and Muhammad, came to this world. Moral uplift aims at the change in human behaviour, tastes and preferences and, thereby, it complements the price mechanism in promoting general well-being. Before even entering the market place and being exposed to the price filter, the consumers are expected to pass their claims through the moral filter. This will help filter out conspicuous consumption and all wasteful and unnecessary claims on resources. The price mechanism can then take over and reduce the claims on resources even further to lead to the market equilibrium. The two filters can together make it possible to have optimum economy in the use of resources, which is necessary to satisfy the material as well as spiritual needs of all human beings, to reduce the concentration of wealth in a few hands, and to raise savings, which are needed to promote greater investment and employment. Without complementing the market system with morally based value judgments, we may end up perpetuating inequities in spite of our good intentions through what Solo calls inaction, non-choice and drifting (Solo, 1981, p. 38).

From the above discussion, one may easily notice the similarities and differences between the two disciplines. While the subject matter of both is the allocation and distribution of resources and both emphasize the fulfilment of material needs, there is an equal emphasis in Islamic economics on the fulfilment of spiritual needs. While both recognize the important role of market mechanism in the allocation and distribution of resources, Islamic economics argues that the market may not by itself be able to fulfil even the material needs of all human beings. This is because it can promote excessive use of scarce resources by the rich at the expense of the poor if there is undue emphasis on the serving of self-interest. Sacrifice is involved in fulfilling our obligations towards others and excessive emphasis on the serving of self-interest does not have the potential of motivating people to make the needed sacrifice. This, however, raises the crucial question of why would a rational person sacrifice his self-interest for the sake of others?

2.2.3 The Importance of the Hereafter

This is where the concepts of the innate goodness of human beings and of the Hereafter come in – concepts which conventional economics ignores but on which Islam and other major religions place a great deal of emphasis. Because of their innate goodness, human beings do not necessarily always try to serve their self-interest. They are also altruistic and are willing to make sacrifices for the well-being of others. In addition, the concept of the Hereafter does not confine self-interest to just this world. It rather extends it beyond this world to life after death. We may be able to serve our self-interest in this world by being selfish, dishonest, uncaring, and negligent of our obligations towards our families, other human beings, animals, and the environment. However, we cannot serve our self-interest in the Hereafter except by fulfilling all these obligations.

Thus the serving of self-interest receives a long-run perspective in Islam and other religions by taking into account both this world as well as the next. This serves to provide a motivating mechanism for sacrifice for the well-being of others that conventional economics fails to provide. The innate goodness of human beings along with the long-run perspective given to self-interest has the potential of inducing a person to be not only efficient but also equitable and caring. Consequently, the three crucial concepts of conventional economics – rational economic man, positivism, and laissez-faire – were not able to gain intellectual blessing in their conventional economics sense from any of the outstanding scholars who represent the mainstream of Islamic thought.

2.2.4 Rational Economic Man

While there is hardly anyone opposed to the need for rationality in human behaviour, there are differences of opinion in defining rationality (Sen, 1987, pp. 11–14). However, once rationality has been defined in terms of overall individual as well as social well-being, then rational behaviour could only be that which helps us realize this goal. Conventional economics did not define rationality in this way. It equates rationality with the serving of self-interest through the maximization of wealth and want satisfaction. The drive of self-interest was considered to be the 'moral equivalent of the force of gravity in nature' (Myers, 1983, p. 4). Within this framework society came to be conceptualized as mere collection of individuals united through ties of self-interest.

The concept of 'rational economic man' in this social-Darwinist, utilitarian, and material sense of serving self-interest could not find a foothold in Islamic economics. 'Rationality' in Islamic economics does not get confined to the serving of one's self-interest in this world alone; it also gets extended to the Hereafter through the faithful compliance with moral values that help rein self-interest to promote social interest. Al-Mawardi (d. 1058) considered it necessary, like all other Muslim scholars, to rein individual tastes and preferences through moral values (al-Mawardi, 1955, pp. 118–120). Ibn Khaldun (d. 1406) emphasized that moral orientation helps remove mutual rivalry and envy, strengthens social solidarity, and creates an inclination towards righteousness (Ibn Khaldun, n.d., p. 158).

2.2.5 Positivism

Similarly, positivism in the conventional economics sense of being 'entirely neutral between ends' (Robbins, 1935, p. 240) or 'independent of any particular ethical position or normative judgment' (Friedman, 1953) did not find a place in Muslim intellectual thinking. Since all resources at the disposal of human beings are a trust from God, and human beings are accountable before Him, then there is no other option but to use them in keeping with the terms of trust. These terms are defined by beliefs and moral values. Human brotherhood, one of the central objectives of Islam, would be a meaningless jargon if it were not reinforced by justice in the allocation and distribution of resources.

2.2.6 Pareto Optimum

Without justice, it would be difficult to realize even development. Muslim scholars have emphasized this throughout history. Development Economics has also started emphasizing its importance, more so in the last few decades.[2] Abu Yusuf (d. 798) argued that: 'Rendering justice to those wronged and eradicating injustice, raises tax revenue, accelerates development of the country, and brings blessings in addition to reward in the Hereafter' (Abu Yusuf, 1933–34, p. 111: see also pp. 3–17). Al-Mawardi argued that comprehensive justice 'inculcates mutual love and affection, obedience to the law, development of the country, expansion of wealth, growth of progeny, and security of the sovereign' (al-Mawardi, 1955, p. 27). Ibn Taymiyyah (d. 1328) emphasized that 'justice towards everything and everyone is an imperative for everyone, and injustice is prohibited to everything and everyone. Injustice is absolutely not permissible irrespective of whether it is to a Muslim or a non-Muslim or even to an unjust person' (Ibn Taymiyyah, 1961–63, Vol. 18, p. 166).

Justice and the well-being of all may be difficult to realize without a sacrifice on the part of the well-to-do. The concept of Pareto optimum does not, therefore, fit into the paradigm of Islamic economics. This is because Pareto optimum does not recognize any solution as optimum if it requires a sacrifice on the part of a few (rich) for raising the well-being of the many (poor). (It is the concept of Pareto optimum which prompted John Rawls to state that one must never act solely to increase general happiness, if in doing so one makes any person unhappy [Rawls, 1958].) Such a position is in clear conflict with moral values, the raison d'être of which is the well-being of all. Hence this concept did not arise in Islamic economics. In fact Islam makes it a religious obligation of Muslims to make a sacrifice for the poor and the needy, by paying *Zakat* at the rate of 2.5 per cent of their net worth. This is in addition to the taxes that they pay to the governments as in other countries.

2.2.7 The Role of State

Moral values may not be effective if they are not observed by all. They need to be enforced. It is the duty of the state to restrain all socially harmful behaviour[3] including injustice, fraud, cheating, transgression against other people's person, honour and property, and the non-fulfilment of contracts and other obligations through proper upbringing, incentives and deterrents, appropriate regulations, and an effective and impartial judiciary. The Qur'an can only provide norms. It cannot by itself enforce them. The state has to ensure this. That is why Prophet Muhammad said: 'God restrains through the sovereign more than what He restrains through the Qur'an' (cited by al-Mawardi, 1955, p. 121). This emphasis on the role of the state has been reflected in the writings of all leading Muslim scholars throughout history.[4] Al-Mawardi emphasized that an effective government (*Sultan Qahir*) is indispensable for preventing injustice and wrongdoing (al-Mawardi, 1960, p. 5). Say's Law could not, therefore become a meaningful proposition in Islamic economics.

How far is the state expected to go in the fulfilment of its role? What is it that the state is expected to do? This has been spelt out by a number of scholars in the literature on what has come to be termed as 'Mirrors for Princes'.[5] None of them visualized regimentation or the owning and operating of a substantial part of the economy by the state. Several classical Muslim scholars, including al-Dimashqi (d. after 1175) and Ibn Khaldun, clearly expressed their disapproval of the state becoming directly involved in the economy (al-Dimashqi, 1977, pp. 12 and 61; Ibn Khaldun, pp. 281–83). According to Ibn Khaldun, the state should not acquire the character of a monolithic or despotic state resorting to a high degree of regimentation (p. 188). It should not feel that, because it has authority, it can do anything it likes (p. 306). It should be welfare-oriented, moderate in its spending, respect the property rights of the people, and avoid onerous taxation (p. 296). This implies that what these scholars visualized as the role of government is what has now been generally referred to as 'good governance'.

2.3   SOME OF THE CONTRIBUTIONS MADE BY ISLAMIC ECONOMICS

The above discussion should not lead one to an impression that the two disciplines are entirely different. One of the reasons for this is that the subject matter of both disciplines is the same, allocation and distribution of scarce resources. Another reason is that all conventional economists have never been value neutral. They have made value judgments in conformity with their beliefs. As indicated earlier, even the paradigm of conventional economics has been changing – the role of good governance has now become well recognized and the injection of a moral dimension has also become emphasized by a number of prominent economists. Moreover, Islamic economists have benefited a great deal from the tools of analysis developed by neoclassical, Keynesian, social, humanistic and institutional economics as well as other social sciences, and will continue to do so in the future.

2.3.1   The Fallacy of the 'Great Gap' Theory

A number of economic concepts developed in Islamic economics long before they did in conventional economics. These cover a number of areas including an interdisciplinary approach; property rights; division of labour and specialization; the importance of saving and investment for development; the role that both demand and supply play in the determination of prices and the factors that influence demand and supply; role of money, exchange, and market mechanism; characteristics of money, counterfeiting, currency debasement, and Gresham's Law; the development of cheques, letters of credit and banking; labour supply and population; the role of the state, justice, peace, and stability in development; and principles of taxation. It is not possible to provide a comprehensive coverage of all the contributions Muslim scholars made to economics. Only some of their contributions will be highlighted below to remove the concept of the 'Great Gap' of 'over 500 years' that exists in the history of conventional economic thought as a result of the false assumption by Joseph Schumpeter in his book, *History of Economic Analysis* (1954), that the intervening period between the Greeks and the Scholastics was sterile and unproductive.[6] This concept has become well embedded in the conventional economics literature as may be seen from the reference to this even by the Nobel Laureate, Douglass North, in his December 1993 Nobel lecture (North, 1994, p. 365). Consequently, as Todd Lowry has rightly observed, 'the character and sophistication of Arabian writings has been ignored' (see his 'Foreword' in Ghazanfar, 2003, p. xi).

The reality, however, is that the Muslim civilization which benefited greatly from the Chinese, Indian, Sassanian and Byzantine civilizations, itself made rich contributions to intellectual activity, including socio-economic thought, during the 'Great Gap' period, and thereby played a part in kindling the flame of the European Enlightment Movement. Even the Scholastics themselves had been greatly influenced by the contributions made by Muslim scholars. The names of Ibn Sina (Avicenna, d. 1037), Ibn Rushd (Averroes, d. 1198) and Maimonides (d. 1204) (a Jewish philosopher, scientist, and physician who flourished in Muslim Spain), appear on almost every page of the 13th century summa (treatises written by scholastic philosophers) (Pifer, 1978, p. 356).

2.3.2 Multidisciplinary Approach for Development

One of the most important contributions of Islamic economics, in addition to the above paradigm discussion, was the adoption of a multidisciplinary dynamic approach. Muslim scholars did not focus their attention primarily on economic variables. They considered overall human well-being to be the end product of interaction over a long period of time between a number of economic as well as moral, social, political, demographic and historical factors in such a way that none of them is able to make an optimum contribution without the support of the others. Justice occupied a pivotal place in this whole framework because of its crucial importance in the Islamic worldview There was an acute realization that justice is indispensable for development and that, in the absence of justice, there will be decline and disintegration.

The contributions made by different scholars over the centuries seem to have reached their consummation in Ibn Khaldun's *Maquddimah*, which literally means 'introduction', and constitutes the first volume of a seven-volume history.[7] Ibn Khaldun lived at a time (1332–1406) when the Muslim civilization was in the process of decline. He wished to see a reversal of this tide, and, as a social scientist, he was well aware that such a reversal could not be envisaged without first drawing lessons (*'ibar*) from history to determine the factors that had led the Muslim civilization to bloom out of humble beginnings and to decline thereafter. He was, therefore, not interested in knowing just what happened. He wanted to know the how and why of what happened. He wanted to introduce a cause and effect relationship into the discussion of historical phenomena. The *Muqaddimah* is the result of this desire. It tries to derive the principles that govern the rise and fall of a ruling dynasty, state (*dawlah*) or civilization (*umran*).

Since the centre of Ibn Khaldun's analysis is the human being, he sees the rise and fall of dynasties or civilizations to be closely dependent on the well-being or misery of the people. The well-being of the people is in turn not dependent just on economic variables, as conventional economics has emphasized until recently, but also on the closely interrelated role of moral, psychological, social, economic, political, demographic and historical factors. One of these factors acts as the trigger mechanism. The others may, or may not, react in the same way. If the others do not react in the same direction, then the decay in one sector may not spread to the others and either the decaying sector may be reformed or the decline of the civilization may be much slower. If, however, the other sectors react in the same direction as the trigger mechanism, the decay will gain momentum through an interrelated chain reaction such that it becomes difficult over time to identify the cause from the effect. He, thus, seems to have had a clear vision of how all the different factors operate in an interrelated and dynamic manner over a long period to promote the development or decline of a society.

He did not, thus, adopt the neoclassical economists' simplification of confining himself to primarily short-term static analysis of only the markets by assuming unrealistically that all other factors remain constant. Even in the short-run, everything may be in a state of flux through a chain reaction to the various changes constantly taking place in human society, even though these may be so small as to be imperceptible. Therefore, even though economists may adopt the *ceteris paribus* assumption for ease of analysis, Ibn Khaldun's multidisciplinary dynamics can be more helpful in formulating socio-economic policies that help improve the overall performance of a society. Neoclassical economics is unable to do this because, as North has rightly asked, 'How can one prescribe policies when one does not understand how economies develop?' He, therefore, considers neoclassical economics to be 'an inappropriate tool to analyze and prescribe policies that will induce development' (North, 1994, p. 549).

However, this is not all that Islamic economics has done. Muslim scholars, including Abu Yusuf (d. 798), al-Mawardi (d. 1058), Ibn Hazm (d. 1064) al-Sarakhsi (d. 1090), al-Tusi (d. 1093), al-Ghazali (d. 1111), al-Dimashqi (d. after 1175), Ibn Rushd (d. 1187), Ibn Taymiyyah (d. 1328), Ibn al-Ukhuwwah (d. 1329), Ibn al-Qayyim (d. 1350), al-Shatibi (d. 1388), Ibn Khaldun (d. 1406), al-Maqrizi (d. 1442), al-Dawwani (d. 1501), and Shah Waliyullah (d. 1762), made a number of valuable contributions to economic theory. Their insight into some economic concepts was so deep that a number of the theories propounded by them could undoubtedly be considered the forerunners of some more sophisticated modern formulations of these theories.[8]

2.3.3 Division of Labour, Specialization, Trade, Exchange and Money and Banking

A number of scholars emphasized the necessity of division of labour for economic development long before this happened in conventional economics. For example, al-Sarakhsi (d. 1090) said: 'the farmer needs the work of the weaver to get clothing for himself, and the weaver needs the work of the farmer to get his food and the cotton from which the cloth is made … , and thus everyone of them helps the other by his work' (al-Sarakhsi, 1978, Vol. 30, p. 264). Al-Dimashqi, writing about a century later, elaborates further by saying: 'No individual can, because of the shortness of his lifespan, burden himself with all industries. If he does, he may not be able to master the skills of all of them from the first to the last. Industries are all interdependent. Construction needs the carpenter and the carpenter needs the ironsmith and the ironsmith needs the miner, and all these industries need premises. People are, therefore, necessitated by force of circumstances to be clustered in cities to help each other in fulfilling their mutual needs' (al-Dimashqi, 1977, pp. 20–21).

Ibn Khaldun ruled out the feasibility or desirability of self-sufficiency, and emphasized the need for division of labour and specialization by indicating that: 'It is well-known and well-established that individual human beings are not by themselves capable of satisfying all their individual economic needs. They must all cooperate for this purpose. The needs that can be satisfied by a group of them through mutual cooperation are many times greater than what individuals are capable of satisfying by themselves' (Ibn Khaldun, p. 360). In this respect he was perhaps the forerunner of the theory of comparative advantage, the credit for which is generally given in conventional economics to David Ricardo who formulated it in 1817.

The discussion of division of labour and specialization, in turn, led to an emphasis on trade and exchange, the existence of well-regulated and properly functioning markets through their effective regulation and supervision (*hisbah*), and money as a stable and reliable measure and medium of exchange and store of value. However, because of bimetallism (gold and silver coins circulating together) which then prevailed, and the different supply and demand conditions that the two metals faced, the rate of exchange between the two full-bodied coins fluctuated. This was further complicated by debasement of currencies by governments in the later centuries to tide over their fiscal problems. This had, according to Ibn Taymiyyah (d. 1328) (1961–63, Vol. 29, p. 649), and later on al-Maqrizi (d. 1442) and al-Asadi (d. 1450), the effect of bad coins driving good coins out of circulation (al-Misri, 1981, pp. 54 and 66), a phenomenon which was recognized and referred to in the West in the 16th century as Gresham's Law. Since debasement of currencies is in sheer violation of the Islamic emphasis on honesty and integrity in all measures of value, fraudulent practices in the issue of coins in the 14th century and afterwards elicited a great deal of literature on monetary theory and policy. The Muslims, according to Baeck, should, therefore, be considered forerunners and critical incubators of the debasement literature of the 14th and 15th centuries (Baeck, 1994, p. 114).

To finance their expanding domestic and international trade, the Muslim world also developed a financial system, which was able to mobilize the 'entire reservoir of monetary resources of the mediaeval Islamic world' for financing agriculture, crafts, manufacturing and long-distance trade (Udovitch, 1970, pp. 180 and 261). Financiers were known as *sarrafs*. By the time of Abbasid Caliph al-Muqtadir (908–932), they had started performing most of the basic functions of modern banks (Fischel, 1992). They had their markets, something akin to the Wall Street in New York and the Lombard Street in London, and fulfilled all the banking needs of commerce, agriculture and industry (Duri, 1986, p. 898). This promoted the use of checks (*sakk*) and letters of credit (*hawala*). The English word 'check' comes from the Arabic term *sakk*.

2.3.4   Demand and Supply

A number of Muslim scholars seem to have clearly understood the role of both demand and supply in the determination of prices. For example, Ibn Taymiyyah (d. 1328) wrote: 'The rise or fall of prices may not necessarily be due to injustice by some people. They may also be due to the shortage of output or the import of commodities in demand. If the demand for a commodity increases and the supply of what is demanded declines, the price rises. If, however, the demand falls and the supply increases, the price falls' (Ibn Taymiyyah, 1961–63, Vol. 8, p. 523).

Even before Ibn Taymiyyah, al-Jahiz (d. 869) wrote nearly five centuries earlier that: 'Anything available in the market is cheap because of its availability [supply] and dear by its lack of availability if there is need [demand] for it' (al-Jahiz, 1983, p. 13), and that 'anything the supply of which increases, becomes cheap except intelligence, which becomes dearer when it increases' (p. 13).

Ibn Khaldun went even further by emphasizing that both an increase in demand or a fall in supply leads to a rise in prices, while a decline in demand or a rise in supply contributes to a fall in prices (Ibn Khaldun, pp. 393 and 396). He believed that while continuation of 'excessively low' prices hurts the craftsmen and traders and drives them out of the market, the continuation of 'excessively high' prices hurts the consumers. 'Moderate' prices in between the two extremes were, therefore, desirable, because they would not only allow the traders a socially acceptable level of return but also lead to the clearance of the markets by promoting sales and thereby generating a given turnover and prosperity (p. 398). Nevertheless, low prices were desirable for necessities because they provide relief to the poor who constitute the majority of the population (p. 398). If one were to use modem terminology, one could say that Ibn Khaldun found a stable price level with a relatively low cost of living to be preferable, from the point of view of both growth and equity in comparison with bouts of inflation and deflation. The former hurts equity while the latter reduces incentive and efficiency. Low prices for necessities should not, however, be attained through the fixing of prices by the state; this destroys the incentive for production (pp. 279–83).

The factors which determined demand were, according to Ibn Khaldun, income, price level, the size of the population, government spending, the habits and customs of the people, and the general development and prosperity of the society (pp. 398–404). The factors which determined supply were: demand (pp. 400 and 403), order and stability (pp. 306–308), the relative rate of profit (pp. 395 and 398), the extent of human effort (p. 38), the size of the labour force as well as their knowledge and skill (pp. 363 and 399–400), peace and security (pp. 394–95 and 396), and the technical background and development of the whole society (pp. 399–403). All these constituted important elements of his theory of production. If the price falls and leads to a loss, capital is eroded, the incentive to supply declines, leading to a recession. Trade and crafts also consequently suffer (p. 398).

This is highly significant because the role of both demand and supply in the determination of value was not well understood in the West until

the late 19th and the early 20th centuries. Pre-classical English economists like William Petty (1623–87), Richard Cantillon (1680–1734),
James Steuart (1712–80), and even Adam Smith (1723–90), the founder
of the Classical School, generally stressed only the role of the cost of
production, and particularly of labour, in the determination of value. The
first use in English writings of the notions of both demand and supply
was perhaps in 1767 (Thweatt, 1983). Nevertheless, it was not until the
second decade of the 19th century that the role of both demand and
supply in the determination of market prices began to be fully appreci-
ated (Groenewegen, 1973). While Ibn Khaldun had been way ahead of
conventional economists, he probably did not have any idea of demand
and supply schedules, elasticities of demand and supply and most
important of all, equilibrium price, which plays a crucial role in modern
economic discussions.

2.3.5 Public Finance

Taxation
Long before Adam Smith (d. 1790), who is famous, among other things,
for his canons of taxation (equality, certainty, convenience of payment,
and economy in collection) (see Adam Smith, 1937, pp. 777–79), the
development of these canons can be traced in the writings of pre-Islamic
as well as Muslim scholars, particularly the need for the tax system to be
just and not oppressive. Caliphs Umar (d. 644), Ali (d. 661) and Umar
ibn Abd al-Aziz (d. 720), stressed that taxes should be collected with
justice and leniency and should not be beyond the ability of the people to
bear. Tax collectors should not under any circumstances deprive the
people of the necessities of life (Abu Yusuf, 1933–34, pp. 14, 16 and 86).
Abu Yusuf, adviser to Caliph Harun al-Rashid (786–809), argued that a
just tax system would lead not only to an increase in revenues but also to
the development of the country (Abu Yusuf, 1933–34, p. 111; see also
pp. 14, 16, 60, 85, 105–19 and 125). Al-Mawardi also argued that the tax
system should do justice to both the taxpayer and the treasury – 'taking
more was iniquitous with respect to the rights of the people, while
taking less was unfair with respect to the right of the public treasury'
(al-Mawardi, 1960, p. 209; see also pp. 142–56 and 215).[9]

Ibn Khaldun stressed the principles of taxation very forcefully in the
Muqaddimah. He quoted from a letter written by Tahir ibn al-Husayn,
Caliph al-Ma'mun's general, advising his son, 'Abdullah ibn Tahir,
Governor of al-Raqqah (Syria): 'So distribute [taxes] among all people
making them general, not exempting anyone because of his nobility or
wealth and not exempting even your own officials or courtiers or

followers. And do not levy on anyone a tax which is beyond his capacity to pay' (p. 308).[10] In this particular passage, he stressed the principles of equity and neutrality, while in other places he also stressed the principles of convenience and productivity. The effect of taxation on incentives and productivity was so clearly visualized by Ibn Khaldun that he seems to have grasped the concept of optimum taxation. He anticipated the gist of the Laffer Curve, nearly 600 years before Professor Arthur Laffer, in two full chapters of the *Muqaddimah*.[11]

At the end of the first chapter, he concluded that 'the most important factor making for business prosperity is to lighten as much as possible the burden of taxation on businessmen, in order to encourage enterprise by ensuring greater profits [after taxes]' (Ibn Khaldun, p. 280). This he explained by stating that 'when taxes and imposts are light, the people have the incentive to be more active. Business therefore expands, bringing greater satisfaction to the people because of low taxes ... , and tax revenues also rise, being the sum total of all assessments' (p. 279). He went on to say that as time passes the needs of the state increase and rates of taxation rise to increase the yield. If this rise is gradual people become accustomed to it, but ultimately there is an adverse impact on incentives.

Business activity is discouraged and declines, and so does the yield of taxation (pp. 280–81). A prosperous economy at the beginning of the dynasty, thus, yields higher tax revenue from lower tax rates while a depressed economy at the end of the dynasty, yields smaller tax revenue from higher rates (p. 279). He explained the reasons for this by stating: 'Know that acting unjustly with respect to people's wealth, reduces their will to earn and acquire wealth ... and if the will to earn goes, they stop working. The greater the oppression, the greater the effect on their effort to earn ... and, if people abstain from earning and stop working, the markets will stagnate and the condition of people will worsen' (pp. 286–87); tax revenues will also decline (p. 362). He, therefore, advocated justice in taxation (p. 308).

Public expenditure

For Ibn Khaldun the state was also an important factor of production. By its spending it promotes production and by its taxation it discourages production (Ibn Khaldun, pp. 279–81). Since the government constitutes the greatest market for goods and services, and is a major source of all development (pp. 286 and 403), a decrease in its spending leads to not only a slackening of business activity and a decline in profits but also a decline in tax revenue (p. 286). The more the government spends, the better it may be for the economy (p. 286).[12] Higher spending enables the government to do the things that are needed to support the population and to ensure law and order and political stability (pp. 306 and 308). Without order and political stability, the producers have no incentive to produce. He stated that 'the only reason [for the accelerated development of cities] is that the government is near them and pours its money into them, like the water [of a river] that makes green everything around it, and irrigates the soil adjacent to it, while in the distance everything remains dry' (p. 369).

Ibn Khaldun also analyzed the effect of government expenditure on the economy and is, in this respect, a forerunner of Keynes. He stated:

> A decrease in government spending leads to a decline in tax revenues. The reason for this is that the state represents the greatest market for the world and the source of civilization. If the ruler hoards tax revenues, or if these are lost, and he does not spend them as they should be, the amount available with his courtiers and supporters would decrease, as would also the amount that reaches through them to their employees and dependents [the multiplier effect]. Their total spending would, therefore, decline. Since they constitute a significant part of the population and their spending constitutes a substantial part of the market, business will slacken and the profits of businessmen will decline, leading also to a decline in tax revenues … . Wealth tends to circulate between the people and the ruler, from him to them and from them to him. Therefore, if the ruler withholds it from spending, the people would become deprived of it. (p. 286)

2.3.6 Economic Mismanagement and Famine

Ibn Khaldun established the causal link between bad government and high grain prices by indicating that in the later stage of the dynasty, when public administration becomes corrupt and inefficient, and resorts to coercion and oppressive taxation, incentive is adversely affected and the farmers refrain from cultivating the land. Grain production and reserves fail to keep pace with the rising population. The absence of reserves causes supply shortages in the event of a famine and leads to price escalation (Ibn Khaldun, pp. 301–302).

Al-Maqrizi (d. 1442) who, as *muhtasib* (market supervisor), had intimate knowledge of the economic conditions during his times, and applied Ibn Khaldun's analysis in his book (1956) to determine the reasons for the economic crisis of Egypt during the period 1403–1406. He identified that the political administration had become very weak and corrupt during the Circassian period. Public officials were appointed on the basis of bribery rather than ability.[13] To recover the bribes, officials resorted to oppressive taxation. The incentive to work and produce was adversely affected and output declined. The crisis was further intensified by debasement of the currency through the excessive issue of copper *fulus*, or fiat money, to cover state budgetary deficits. All these factors joined hands with the famine to lead to a high degree of inflation, misery of the poor, and impoverishment of the country.

Hence al-Maqrizi laid bare the socio-political determinants of the prevailing 'system crisis' by taking into account a number of variables like corruption, bad government policies, and weak administration. All of these together played a role in worsening the impact of the famine, which could otherwise have been handled effectively without a significant adverse impact on the population. This is clearly a forerunner of Sen's entitlement theory, which holds the economic mismanagement of illegitimate governments to be responsible for the poor people's misery during famines and other natural disasters (Sen, 1981). What al-Maqrizi wrote of the Circassian Mamluks was also true of the later Ottoman period (see Meyer, 1989).

2.3.7 Stages of Development

Ibn Khaldun stated the stages of development through which every society passes, moving from the primitive bedouin stage to the rise of villages, towns and urban centres with an effective government, development of agriculture, industry and sciences, and the impact of values and environment on this development (*Muqaddimah*, pp. 35, 41–44, 87–95, 120–48, 172–76). Waliyullah[14] (d. 1762) also analyzed the development of society later on through four different stages from primitive existence to a well-developed community with *khilafah* (morally based welfare state), which tries to ensure the spiritual as well as material well-being of the people. Like Ibn Khaldun, he considered political authority to be indispensable for human well-being. To be able to serve as a source of well-being for all and not of burden and decay, it must have the characteristics of the *khilafah*. He applied this analysis in various writings to the conditions prevailing during his lifetime. He found that the luxurious lifestyle of the rulers, along with their exhausting military campaigns, the increasing corruption and inefficiency of the civil service, and huge stipends to a vast retinue of unproductive courtiers, led them to the imposition of oppressive taxes on farmers, traders and craftsmen, who constituted the main productive section of the population. These people had, therefore, lost interest in their occupations, output had slowed down, state financial resources had declined, and the country had become impoverished (Waliyullah, 1992, Vol. I, pp. 119–52). Thus, in step with Ibn Khaldun and other Muslim scholars, al-Maqrizi and Waliyullah combined moral, political, social and economic factors to explain the economic phenomena of their times and the rise and fall of their societies.

2.3.8   Muslim Intellectual Decline

Unfortunately, the rich theoretical contribution made by Muslim scholars up until Ibn Khaldun did not get fertilized and irrigated by later scholars to lead to the development of Islamic economics, except by a few isolated scholars like al-Maqrizi, al-Dawwani (d. 1501), and Waliyullah. Their contributions were, however, only in specific areas and did not lead to a further development of Ibn Khaldun's model of socio-economic and political dynamics. Islamic economics did not, therefore, develop as a separate intellectual discipline in conformity with the Islamic paradigm along the theoretical foundations and method laid down by Ibn Khaldun and his predecessors. It continued to remain an integral part of the social and moral philosophy of Islam.

One may ask here why the rich intellectual contributions made by Muslim scholars did not continue after Ibn Khaldun. The reason may be that, as indicated earlier, Ibn Khaldun lived at a time when the political and socio-economic decline of the Muslim world was already under-way.[15] He was perhaps 'the sole point of light in his quarter of the firmament' (Toynbee, 1935, Vol. 3, p. 321). According to Ibn Khaldun himself, sciences progress only when a society is itself progressing (Ibn Khaldun, p. 434). This theory is clearly upheld by Muslim history. Sciences progressed rapidly in the Muslim world for four centuries from the middle of the 8th century to the middle of the 12th century and continued to do so at a substantially decelerated pace for at least two more centuries, tapering off gradually thereafter. (Sarton, 1927, Vol. 1 and Book 1 of Vol. 2). Once in a while there did appear a brilliant star on an otherwise unexciting firmament. Economics was no exception. It also continued to be in a state of limbo in the Muslim world. No worthwhile contributions were made after Ibn Khaldun.

The trigger mechanism for this decline was, according to Ibn Khaldun, the failure of political authority to provide good governance. Political illegitimacy, which started after the end of *khilafah* in 661 gradually led to increased corruption and the use of state resources for private benefit at the neglect of education and other ration-building functions of the state. This gradually triggered the decline of all other sectors of the society and economy.[16]

The rapidly rising Western civilization took over the torch of knowledge from the declining Muslim world and has kept it burning with even greater brightness. All sciences, including the social sciences, have made phenomenal progress. Conventional economics became a separate academic discipline after the publication of Alfred Marshall's great treatise, *Principles of Economics*, in 1890 (Schumpeter, 1954, p. 21),[17] and has continued to develop since then at a remarkable speed. With such a great achievement to its credit, there is no psychological need to allow the 'Great Gap' thesis to persist. It will help promote better understanding of the Muslim civilization in the West if textbooks start giving credit to Muslim scholars. They were 'the torchbearers of ancient learning during the medieval period' and 'it was from them that the Renaissance was sparkcd and the Enlightenment kindled' (Todd Lowry in his 'Foreword' in Ghazanfar, 2003, p. xi). Watt has been frank enough to admit that, 'the influence of Islam on Western Christendom is greater than is usually realized' and that, 'an important task for Western Europeans, as we move into the era of the one world, is … to acknowledge fully our debt to the Arab and Islamic world' (Watt, 1972, p. 84).

Conventional economics, however, took a wrong turn after the Enlightenment Movement by stripping itself of the moral basis of society emphasized by Aristotelian and Judo–Christian philosophies. This deprived it of the role that moral values and good governance can play in helping the society raise both efficiency and equity in the allocation and distribution of scarce resources needed for promoting the well-being of all. However, this has been changing. The role of good governance has already been recognized and that of moral values is gradually penetrating the economics orthodoxy. Islamic economics is also reviving now after the independence of Muslim countries from foreign domination. It is likely that the two disciplines will converge and become one after a period of time. This will be in keeping with the teachings of the Qur'an, which clearly states that mankind was created as one but became divided as a result of their differences and transgression against each other (10:19, 2:213 and 3:19). This reunification (globalization, as it is now called), if reinforced by justice and mutual care, should help promote peaceful coexistence and enable mankind to realize the well-being of all, a goal the realization of which we are all anxiously looking forward to.

NOTES

1. This is the liberal version of the secular and materialist worldviews. There is also the totalitarian version which does not have faith in the individuals' ability to manage private property in a way that would ensure social well-being. Hence its prescription is to curb individual freedom and to transfer all means of production and decision-making to a totalitarian state. Since this form of the secular and materialist

worldview failed to realize human well-being and has been overthrown practically everywhere, it is not discussed in this chapter.

2. The literature on economic development is full of assertions that improvement in income distribution is in direct conflict with economic growth. For a summary of these views, see Cline (1973), Chapter 2. This has, however, charged and there is hardly any development economist now who argues that injustice can help promote development.

3. North has used the term 'nasty' for all such behaviour. See the chapter 'Ideology and Free Rider', in North (1981).

4. Some of these scholars include: Abu Yusuf (d. 798), al-Mawardi (d. 1058), Abu Ya'la (d. 1065), Nazam al-Mulk (d. 1092), al-Ghazali (d. 1111), Ibn Taymiyyah (d. 1328), Ibn Khaldun (d. 406), Shah Waliyullah (d. 1762), Jamaluddin al-Afghani (d. 1897), Muhammad 'Abduh (d. 1905), Muhammad Iqbal (d. 1938), Hasan al-Banna (d. 1949), Sayyid Mawdudi (d. 1979), and Baqir al-Sadr (d. 1980).

5. Some of these authors include: al-Katib (d. 749), Ibn al-Muqaffa (d. 756) al-Nu'man (d. 974), al-Mawardi (d. 1058), Kai Ka'us (d. 1082), Nizam al-Mulk (d. 1092), al-Ghazali (d. 1111), and al-Turtushi (d. 1127). (For details, see Essid, 1995, pp. 19–41).

6. For the fallacy of the 'Great Gap' thesis, see Mirakhor (1987); and Ghazanfar (2003), particularly the 'Foreword' by Todd Lowry and the 'Introduction' by Ghazanfar, called Kitab al-'Ibar or the Book of Lessons [of History].

7. The full name of the book (given in the References) may be freely translated as 'The Book of Lessons and the Record of Cause and Effect in the History of Arabs, Persians and Berbers and their Powerful Contemporaries'. Several different editions of the Muqaddimah are now available in Arabic. The one I have used is that published in Cairo by al-Maktabah al-Tijarriyah al-Kubra without any indication of the year of publication. It has the advantage of showing all vowel marks, which makes the reading relatively easier. The Muqaddimah was translated into English in three volumes by Franz Rosenthal. Its first edition was published in 1958 and the second edition in 1967. Selections from the Muqaddimah by Charles Issawi were published in 1950 under the title, *An Arab Philosophy of History: Selections from the Prolegomena of Ibn Khaldun of Tunis (1332–1406)*. A considerable volume of literature is now available on Ibn Khaldun. Some of this is: Spengler (1964); Boulakia (1971); Mirakhor (1987) and Chapra (2000).

8. For some of these contributions, see Spengler (1964); DeSmogyi (1965); Mirakhor (1987); Siddiqi (1992); Essid (1995); Islahi (1996); Chapra (2000); and Ghazanfar (2003).

9. For a more detailed discussion of taxation by various Muslim scholars, see the section on 'Literature on Mirrors for Princes' in Essid (1995), pp. 19–41.

10. This letter is a significant development over the letter of Abu Yusuf to Caliph Harun al-Rashid (1933–34, pp. 3–17). It is more comprehensive and covers a larger number of topics.

11. These are: 'On tax revenues and the reason for their being low and high' (pp. 279–80) and 'Injustice ruins development' (pp. 286–410).

12. Bear in mind the fact that this was stated at the time when commodity money, which it is not possible for the government to 'create', was used, and fiduciary money had not become the rule of the day.

13. This was during the Slave (Mamluk) Dynasty in Egypt, which is divided into two periods. The first period was that of the Bahri (or Turkish) Mamluks (1250–1382), who have generally received praise in the chronicles of their contemporaries. The second period was that of the Burji Mamluks (Cirassians, 1382–1517). This period was beset by a series of severe economic crises. (For details see Allouche, 1994).

14. Shah Waliyullah al-Dihlawi, popularly known as Waliyullah, was born in 1703, four years before the death of the Mughal Emperor, Aurangzeb (1658–1707). Aurangzeb's

rule, spanning a period of 49 years, was followed by a great deal of political instability – 10 different changes in rulers during Waliyullah's lifespan of 59 years – leading ultimately to the weakening and decline of the Mughal Empire.

15. For a brief account of the general decline and disintegration of the Muslim world during the 14th century, see Muhsin Mahdi (1964), pp. 17–26.
16. For a discussion of the causes of Muslim decline, see Chapra (2000), pp. 173–252.
17. According to Blaug (1985, p. 3), economics became an academic discipline in the 1880s.

REFERENCES

Abu Yusuf, Ya 'qub ibn Ibrahim (d. 798) (1933–1934), *Kitab al-Kharaj*, 2nd edn (Cairo: al-Matab'ah al-Salafiyyah). This book has been translated into English by A. Ben Shemesh (1969), *Taxation in Islam* (Leiden: E.J. Brill, Vol. 3).

Allouche, Adel (1994), *Mamluk Economics: A Study and Translation of Al-Maqrizi's* Ighathah (Salt Lake City: University of Utah Press).

Baeck, Louis (1994), *The Mediterranean Tradition in Economic Thought* (London: Routledge).

Blanchflower, David, and Oswald, Andrew (2000), Well-being over time in Britain and US. NBER Working Paper 7487.

Blaug, Mark (1985), *Economic Theory in Retrospect* (Cambridge: Cambridge University Press).

Boulakia, Jean David C. (1971), Ibn Khaldun: A fourteenth century economist, *Journal of Political Economy*, 1105–18.

Brittan, Samuel (1995), *Capitalism with a Human Face* (Aldershot, UK and Brookfield, VT, USA: Edward Elgar Publishing).

Chapra, M. Umer (2000), *The Future of Economics: An Islamic Perspective* (Leicester, UK: The Islamic Foundation).

Cline, William R. (1973), *Potential Effects of Income Redistribution on Economic Growth* (New York: Praeger).

DeSmogyi, Joseph N. (1965), Economic theory in classical Arabic literature, in *Studies in Islam* (Delhi), pp. 1–6.

Diener E., and Oishi, Shigehiro (2000), Money and happiness: Income and subjective well-being, in E. Diener and E. Suh (eds), *Culture and Subjective Well-being* (Cambridge, MA: The MIT Press).

Dimashqi, Abu al-Fadl Ja'far ibn 'Ali al- (d. 1175) (1977), *Al-Isharah ila Mahasin al-Tijarah*, Al-Bushra al-Shurbaji (ed.) (Cairo: Maktabah al-Kulliyat al-Azhar).

Duri, A.A. (1986), Baghdad, *The Encyclopedia of Islam* (Leiden: Brill), pp. 894–9.

Easterlin, Richard (1974), Does economic growth improve the human lot?: Some empirical evidence, in Paul David and Melwin Reder (eds), *Nations and Households in Economic Growth: Essays in Honour of Moses Abramowitz* (New York: Academic Press).

Easterlin, Richard (1995), Will raising the income of all increase the happiness of all?, *Journal of Economic Behaviour and Organization*, 27:1, 35–48.

Easterlin, Richard (2001), Income and happiness: Towards a unified theory, *Economic Journal*, 111: 473.

Essid, M. Yassine (1995), *A Critique of the Origins of Islamic Economic Thought* (Leiden: Brill).

Feyerabend, Paul (1993), *Against Method*, 3rd edn (London: Verso).

Fischel, W.J. (1992), Djahbadh, in the *Encyclopedia of Islam*, Vol. 2, pp. 382–3.

Friedman, Milton (1953) *Essays in Positive Economics* (Chicago: The University of Chicago Press).

George, Henry (1955), *Progress and Poverty* (New York: Robert Schalkenback Foundation).

Ghazanfar, S.M. (2003), *Medieval Islamic Economic Thought: Filling the Great Gap in European Economics* (London and New York: Routledge Curzon).

Groenewegen, P.D. (1973), A note on the origin of the phrase, supply and demand, *Economic Journal*, June, pp. 505–9.

Hausman, Daniel and McPherson, Michael (1993), Taking ethics seriously: economics and contemporary moral philosophy, *Journal of Economic Literature*, June, pp. 671–731.

Ibn Khaldun (n.d.), *Muqaddimah* (Cairo: Al-Maktabah al-Tijariyyah al-Kubra). See also its translation under Rosenthal (1967), and selections from it under Issawi (1950).

Ibn Taymiyyah (d. 728/1328) (1961–63), *Majmu' Fatawa Shaykh al-Islam Ahmad Ibn Taymiyyah*, 1st edn, 'Abd al-Rahman al-'Asimi (ed.) (Riyadh: Matabi' al-Riyad).

Islahi, A. Azim (1996), *History of Economic Thought in Islam* (Aligharh, India: Department of Economics, Aligharh Muslim University).

Issawi, Charles (1950), *An Arab Philosophy of History: Selections from the Prolegomena of Ibn Khaldun of Tunis (1332–1406)* (London: John Murray).

Jahiz, Amr ibn Bahr al- (d. 869) (1983), *Kitab al-Tabassur bi al-Tijarah* (Beirut: Dar al-Kitab al-Jadid).

Jay, Elizabeth, and Jay, Richard (1986), *Critics of Capitalism: Victorian Reactions to Political Economy* (Cambridge: Cambridge University Press).

Kenny, Charles (1999), Does growth cause happiness, or does happiness cause growth?, *Kyklos*, 52:1, 3–26.

Koopmans, T.C. (1969), Inter-temporal distribution and 'optimal' aggregate economic growth, in Fellner et al., *Ten Economic Studies in the Tradition of Irving Fisher* (John Wiley and Sons).

Mahdi, Mohsin (1964), *Ibn Khaldun's Philosophy of History* (Chicago: University of Chicago Press).

Maqrizi, Taqi al-Din Ahmad ibn Ali al- (d. 1442) (1956), *Ighathah al-Ummah bi Kashf al-Ghummah* (Hims, Syria: Dar ibn al-Wahid). See its English translation by Allouche (1994).

Mawardi, Abu al-Hasan 'Ali al- (d. 1058) (1955), *Adab al-Dunya wa al-Din*, Mustafa al Saqqa (ed.) (Cairo: Mustafa al-Babi al Halabi).

Mawardi, Abdu al-Hasan (1960), *Al-Ahkam al-Sultaniyyah wa al-Wilayat al-Diniyyah* (Cairo: Mustafa al-Babi al-Halabi). The English translation of this book by Wafa Wahba has been published under the title *The Ordinances of Government* (Reading: Garnet, 1996).

Meyer, M.S. (1989), Economic thought in the Ottoman Empire in the 14th – early 19th centuries, *Archiv Orientali*, 4:57, 305–18.

Mirakhor, Abbas (1987), The Muslim scholars and the history of economics. A need for consideration, *The American Journal of Islamic Social Sciences*, December, 245–76.

Misri Rafiq Yunus al- (1981), *Al-Islam wa al-Nuqud* (Jeddah, King Abdulaziz University).

Myers, Milton L. (1983), The soul of modern economic man: Ideas of self-interest, *Thomas Hobbes to Adam Smith* (Chicago: University of Chicago Press).

North, Douglass C. (1981), *Structure and Change in Economic History* (New York: W.W. North).

North, Douglass C. (1994), Economic performance through time, *The American Economic Review*, June, 359–68.

Oswald, A.J. (1997), Happiness and economic performance, *Economic Journal*, 107:445, 1815–31.

Pifer, Josef (1978), Scholasticism, in *Encyclopedia Britannica*, Vol. 16, pp. 352–7.

Rawls, John (1958), Justice is fairness, *Philosophical Review*, 67, 164–94.

Robbins, Lionel (1935), *An Essay on the Nature and Significance of Economic Science*, 2nd edn (London: Macmillan).

Rosenthal, Franz (1967), *Ibn Khaldun: the Muqaddimah, An Introduction to History* (London: Routledge and Kegan Paul, 3 volumes).

Sarakhsi, Shams al-Din al- (d. 1090) (1978), *Kitab al-Mabsut*, 3rd edn (Beirut: Dar al- Ma'rifah), particularly '*Kitab al-Kasb*' of al-Shaybani in Vol. 30, pp. 245–97.

Sarton, George, *Introduction to the History of Science* (Washington, DC: Carnegie Institute, 3 volumes issued between 1927 and 1948, each of the 2nd and 3rd volumes has two parts).

Schumpeter, Joseph A. (1954), *History of Economic Analysis*, Elizabeth B. Schumpeter (ed.) (New York: Oxford University Press).

Sen, Amartya (1981), *Poverty and Famines: An Essay on Entitlement and Deprivation* (Oxford: Clarendon Press).

Sen, Amartya (1987), *On Ethics and Economics* (Oxford: Basil Blackwell).

Siddiqi, M. Nejatullah (1992), History of Islamic economic thought, in Ausaf Ahmad and K.R. Awan, *Lectures on Islamic Economics* (Jeddah: IDB/IRTI), pp. 69–90.

Smith, Adam (d. 1790) (1937), *An Inquiry into the Nature and Causes of the Wealth of Nations* (1776) (New York: The Modern Library).

Solo, Robert A. (1981), Values and judgments in the discourse of the sciences, in Robert A. Solo and Charles A. Anderson (1981), *Value Judgment and Income Distribution* (New York: Praeger), pp. 9–40.

Spengler, Joseph (1964), Economic thought in Islam: Ibn Khaldun, *Comparative Studies in Society and History*, pp. 268–306.

Thweatt, W.O. (1983), Origins of the terminology, supply and demand, *Scottish Journal of Political Economy*, November, pp. 287–94.

Toynbee, Arnold J. (1935), *A Study of History*, 2nd edn (London: Oxford University Press).

Udovitch, Abraham L. (1970), *Partnership and Profit in Medieval Islam* (Princeton; NJ: Princeton University Press).

Waliyullah, Shah (d. 1762) (1992), *Hujjatullah al-Balighah*, 2nd edn, M.Sharif Sukkar (ed.) (Beirut: Dar Ihya al- Ulum), 2 volumes. An English translation of this book by Marcia K. Hermansen was published in 1966 by E.J. Brill, Leiden.

Watt, W. Montgomery (1972), *The Influence of Islam on Medieval Europe* (Edinburgh: Edinburgh University Press).

3. Ethics and economics: the Islamic imperative*

3.1 INTRODUCTION

All human beings living on this planet wish to ensure their well-being. This is but natural and in conformity with human nature. Accordingly, there seems to be hardly any difference of opinion among all societies around the world that the ultimate purpose of development has to be the promotion of human well-being. There is, however, considerable difference of opinion in the understanding of what constitutes real well-being. Although some people tend to emphasize primarily the material contents of well-being, the general tendency seems to be that the realization of true well-being requires the satisfaction of both the material as well as non-material and spiritual needs of the human personality. While a rise in income and wealth can help satisfy the basic material needs of the human personality,[1] it may not necessarily be able to satisfy by itself all the non-material and spiritual needs. This leads us to another related question of what these non-material and spiritual needs are that a rise in income and wealth may not necessarily be able to satisfy. This is where ethics and economics interact with each other meaningfully. While ethics specifics the goals and values as well as the non-material needs the satisfaction of which is necessary to ensure the true well-being of all, economics helps analyze the ways through which these goals may be realized within the framework of available resources and agreed values.

One of the most important non-material or spiritual needs is mental peace and happiness. While the satisfaction of this need does demand 'adequate' income and wealth, it also requires the fulfilment of some other human aspirations. Most of these aspirations are generally embedded in a society's ethical system which is generally a reflection of its religious paradigm. Among the most important of these other aspirations are justice and social harmony which demand that all individuals be considered as socially equal and treated with dignity and respect, that their basic needs be satisfied, and that the fruits of development be shared equitably by all irrespective of their race, colour, age, sex, religion or nationality. Some of the other equally important and generally recognized

67

requirements for sustained well-being are the noble traits of character which enable people to live together caringly and peacefully and co-operate with each other effectively for the well-being of all. It is generally recognized that the inculcation of these traits is facilitated by moral uplift and an inner urge on the part of individuals to sacrifice at least some of their self-interest for the well-being of others. Without these traits it may be difficult to ensure family and social harmony, security of life and property, individual freedom, proper upbringing of children, hard and efficient work, and minimization of crime, tensions and anomie. It is also necessary to curb wasteful spending for the purpose of promoting saving, investment and charitable giving, all three of which are indispensable for promoting not only development and employment but also the well-being of the poor and disabled.

Historical experience indicates that the material and non-material needs are both interdependent and reinforce each other. If any one of these two is neglected, the other may also tend to suffer ultimately. For example, if a person is not treated with respect and dignity in his workplace, his feelings may be hurt and he may not be able psycho-logically to render his best. Similarly if he is selfish and quarrelsome, he may not be able to get along well with his wife as well as colleagues. Accordingly, the spirit of cooperation, mutual care, and family and social solidarity that are needed at home as well as in the workplace will suffer and, thereby, adversely affect efficiency and well-being. It may not, therefore, be possible to sustain the long-run health and development of a society without ensuring the fulfilment of both the material and non-material needs. This confronts us with the perplexing question of how the spiritual and non-material needs may be satisfied if a rise in income and wealth is not by itself capable of satisfying them.

3.2 NEED FOR A PROPER WORLDVIEW

Spiritual and non-material needs may be difficult to satisfy if the society does not have a proper worldview. The worldview tries to answer some crucial questions about how the universe and human beings came into existence, the meaning and purpose of human life, the ultimate ownership and objective of the limited resources at the disposal of human beings, and the relationship of human beings to each other as well as their environment. For example, if the worldview assumes that the universe has come into existence by itself, then the implication would be that human beings are not accountable before a Supreme Being and are free to live as they please. Their purpose in life may then be to seek maximum pleasure, irrespective of how it affects others or the environment. The serving of self-interest and survival of the fittest may then seem to be the most logical norms of behaviour. If, instead, it is believed that human beings are pawns on the chessboard of history and their life is determined by external forces over which they have no control, then, they cannot be held responsible for what goes on around them and need have no qualms about the prevailing inequities.

However, if the worldview is founded on the belief that human beings and what they possess have been created by the Supreme Being and are accountable before Him individually as well as collectively for the well-being of all, then they may not be justified in considering themselves as either absolutely free to behave as they please or helpless pawns on the chessboard of history, unconcerned about how their behaviour affects the well-being of others and the direction in which history is moving. They would rather tend to have the conviction that they have a mission to perform – the mission of being, in the words of the Qur'an, a 'blessing for mankind' (21:107) by ensuring the well-being of all rather than that of just a few (the top 1 per cent). They would also have the conviction that by striving for the happiness of others they will also be able to ensure their own happiness. This would also make them realize that the resources they have at their disposal, as well as the environment, are a trust and that it is their obligation to work hard and conscienciously for using these resources efficiently as well as equitably for the purpose of fulfilling their mission successfully.

3.3 RELIGIOUS WORLDVIEWS

The differences in the worldviews would not have been significant if the religious worldview had remained in its pristine purity and continued to dominate human societies. This is because, according to the Qur'an, God has sent His Messengers, who were all human beings, to all societies around the world at different times in history.[2] The gist of these messages was to provide a proper worldview along with certain essential norms of behaviour (moral values) the faithful observance of which could lead to the well-being of all. They also provided a motivating mechanism to ensure the observance of these norms by as many people as possible. A new Messenger came when the message of the previous Messenger was either lost, distorted, or became unheeded. Accordingly, all revealed religions have their origin in the teachings of one or the other of these Messengers. This is the primary reason why there is a continuity and great deal of similarity in the worldviews and value systems of all revealed religions to the extent to which the original message has not been lost or distorted. They all emphasize belief in God and the Hereafter, and provide certain essential norms of behaviour for harmonizing individual, socio-economic and political relations.

The basic worldview of all revealed religions in their pristine form is, therefore, more or less the same even though there are differences in details as a result of changes in circumstances over space and time. The Qur'an clearly states that: 'Nothing has been said to you [Muhammad], which was not said to the Messengers before you' (al-Qur'an, 41:43). This is what adds a dimension of tolerance to the Islamic faith. The Qur'an says: 'Do not argue with the People of the Book except in the best manner unless it be those of them who have been unjust. Tell them: We believe in what has been revealed to us and what was revealed to you. Our God and your God is One and we submit ourselves to Him' (29:46–47). The Qur'an also instructs Muslims not to revile the gods to whom the followers of other religions pray because this will make them react adversely and revile, in turn, the One and only God out of ignorance and spite. This is because the beliefs and practices of all people seem attractive to them (6:108).

3.4 THE ENLIGHTENMENT MOVEMENT AND ITS IMPACT

The Enlightenment Movement of the 17th and 18th centuries has, however, directly or indirectly influenced almost all societies around the world in different degrees by its secular and materialist worldview. Although initially it had the laudable objective of freeing Europe from the dictatorship of the Church, it gradually slid to the extreme and ended up declaring all the revealed truths of religion as 'simply figments of imagination, non-existent, indeed at the bottom priestly inventions designed to keep men ignorant of the ways of Reason and Nature'.[3] It thus succeeded in realizing one of its major objectives which was to deny any role for revelation in the management of human affairs. It placed undue emphasis on the ability and power of reason alone to distinguish right from wrong and to manage all aspects of human life in a manner that would help ensure the well-being of all. This dented the sanctity that religion assigns to moral values for the realization of humanitarian goals. Values, therefore, became relative and got shifted unwittingly to the private domain of individuals to be determined by their self-interest on the basis of the unsubstantiated assumption that if everyone served his/her self-interest social interest would be served automatically. However, moral values are not concerned with the reform of only the private life of individuals. Their objective is to reform all sectors of human life, including the individual, social, economic, political, military, and international and, therefore, affect everyone's well-being directly or indirectly by linking all these sectors together in a purposeful manner. Their sphere of influence does not, therefore, get confined to only the personal preferences of individuals. The sanctity that religion provides to these values or social norms, helps greatly in their general acceptance and observance. Any other way of formulating values may not be able to have the sanctity that religion provides to these values. The loss of sanctity paved the way for the introduction of philosophies of social Darwinism, materialism, determinism and existentialism. This deprived society of the harmony and consistency with which the moral dimension combines all aspects of human life into an integrated whole and, thereby, helps in ensuring comprehensive well-being.

Social Darwinism injected the principle of survival of the fittest in place of human brotherhood and altruism into the spectrum of human relationships. This inadvertently provided tacit justification for the concept of 'might is right' in the ordering of human relations and for holding the poor and downtrodden as totally responsible for their own poverty and misery. Materialism made wealth maximization, bodily gratification and sensual pleasures the objective of human endeavour. This served to provide the foundation for today's consumer culture which has continually raised consumption to the position of a status symbol and led to the multiplication of human wants beyond the ability of available resources to satisfy. The result has been an excessive resort to unfair means of earning or to over indulgence in debt, which has now become one of the major causes of financial crises. Determinism implied that human beings had little control over their own behaviour. Their behaviour was, instead, assumed to be determined by mechanical and automatic responses to external stimuli as in animals (Watson and Skinner), or by unconscious mental states beyond the individual's conscious control (Freud) or by social and economic conflict (Engel and Marx). Determinism, thus, did not merely negate the distinctiveness and complexity of the human self, it also led, in step with social Darwinism, to the repudiation of moral responsibility for individual behaviour. This unrealistic stance of determinism tilted the pendulum towards the other extreme of existentialism, which declared human beings to be absolutely free.[4] There can be no justification for having agreed values and for imposing restrictions on individual freedom to create harmony between individual and social interests not automatically brought about by market forces. Such a concept of absolute freedom could not but lead to the concept of value neutrality, sensual pleasures, and laissez-faire.

If these ideas had penetrated fully into the human psyche, they would have greatly increased the misery of human societies. Fortunately, there were several protests against the Enlightenment worldview by a number of scholars like Sismondi (1773–1842), Carlyle (1795–1881), Ruskin (1819–1900), Hobson (1858–1940), Tawney (1880–1962), Schumacher (1891–1971), Myrdal (1898–1987), and Boulding (1910–93) during the entire history of conventional economics.[5] The Enlightenment Movement could not, therefore, succeed in totally eroding the humanitarian values of the Christian, Muslim and other worldviews even though it did succeed in undermining the authority of the Church. Some scholars even emphasized the need for a new paradigm.[6]

Secularism succeeded, however, in driving a wedge between the moral and the material and, thereby, segregating these into two separate unrelated compartments. This had two very adverse effects on human society. First, it removed the religious and moral education from schools. In the beginning this did not have a significant damaging effect because the families and the churches continued to provide the needed moral education. However, now that the families are rapidly disintegrating and the attendance at churches has also declined substantially, moral education fails to be imparted. The moral quality of the new generation is, therefore, gradually declining, particularly when the TV and the Internet are constantly promoting consumerism along with an overdose of pornography and violence. Secondly, it has also severed the close link between reason and revelation, which are both essentially interdependent and absolutely necessary for reinforcing each other in contributing to human well-being. Without guidance from revelation, primary reliance on reason may lead to more and more ways of deceiving and exploiting people and creating weapons of mass destruction. Similarly, without an important role for reason, not only would the intellectual and technological progress of mankind slowdown, but the religious worldview may also lose its focus with the real world and, thereby, become unable to meet successfully the challenges faced by it in a continually changing intellectual and material environment. This would tend to make them both (reason as well as revelation) less effective in helping realize the humanitarian goals of society. The severing of the link between reason and revelation has already given rise in economics to an excessive emphasis on the serving of self-interest and maximization of wealth and want satisfaction as well as a number of other concepts like the Pareto optimum which have tended to neglect the role of sacrifice in human societies for the well-being of all and particularly the children, the disabled, the sick and the poor.[7]

3.5 INDIVIDUAL REFORM, SOCIAL SOLIDARITY AND GENERAL WELL-BEING

The undeniable fact, however, is that, if human beings are the end as well as the means of development, then their reform and well-being need to be given the utmost importance. It is the religious worldview which, if properly understood and implemented, carries the potential of enabling the reform of the human self and promoting an equitable use of resources to ensure the well-being of all through the fulfilment of all the spiritual as well as material needs of the human personality. This is because the religious worldview is capable of injecting a meaning and purpose into life and providing the right direction to all human effort with the objective of transforming the individuals into better human beings and changing their behaviour, lifestyle, tastes, preferences, and attitude towards themselves as well as their Creator, other human beings, resources at their disposal, and the environment. Such a constructive and humantarian change in individuals and their behaviour can help promote social solidarity and a more efficient and equitable use of resources which is needed for the well-being of all. This is something which conventional economics has avoided discussing under the veil of value neutrality.

Toynbee and the Durants have, therefore, rightly concluded after their extensive study of history, that moral uplift and social solidarity are not possible without the moral sanction that religions provide. Toynbee asserts that 'religions tend to quicken rather than destroy the sense of social obligation in their votaries' and that 'the brotherhood of man presupposes the fatherhood of God – a truth which involves the converse proposition that, if the divine father of the human family is left out of the reckoning, there is no possibility of forging any alternative bond of purely human texture which will avail by itself to hold mankind together'.[8] Will and Ariel Durant have also observed forcefully in their valuable book, *The Lessons of History*, that 'there is no significant example in history, before our time, of the society successfully maintaining moral life without the aid of religion'.[9] This is all in conformity with what the Qur'an stated fourteen centuries ago that 'Whoever turns away from My (God's) Message will have a distressful life' (20:124).

3.6 RULES OF BEHAVIOUR AND MOTIVATING SYSTEM

This raises the question of why are moral uplift and social solidarity not possible without the aid of faith. This is because two of the foremost requisites for moral uplift as well as social solidarity are: first, the existence of values or rules of behaviour which command such a wide and unconditional acceptance that they become categorical imperatives; and secondly, the consciencious observance of these rules by everyone with a sense of moral obligation. This leads us to another question of how to arrive at rules which are unconditionally accepted and observed by everyone. Is it possible to arrive at such rules by means of 'social contract' as suggested by some modern philosophers and political scientists? The answer may be yes only if all participants in the discussion are socially, economically and intellectually equal so that everyone has an equal weight in the formulation of the desired rules. Since such equality is not only non-existent but also almost impossible to create in the real world, the rich and powerful will tend to dominate the decision-making process and lead to the formulation of rules that serve their own vested interest. This would tend to frustrate the universal acceptance and observance of these rules as well as the realization of general well-being.

It is, therefore, necessary that an omniscient and benevolent outsider be assigned this task – an outsider who is impartial, who knows the strengths and weaknesses of all human beings, who treats them all as equals, who cares for the well-being of all without any discrimination, and who is capable of analyzing not only the short-term but also the long-term effects of the rules given by him. Who could be more qualified to perform this task than the Creator of this universe and human beings Himself? The Creator has done this job. He has sent His Messengers who were all human beings and came to this world at different times in history to guide others. There is no reason to assume that the Merciful and Beneficent Creator would create human beings and leave them without any guidance to grope in the dark. Bernard Williams is, therefore, right in observing that 'social morality is not an invention of philosophers'.[10]

However, even when we have the values that command relatively wide and unconditional acceptance, there arises the question of how to ensure the observance of these values by everyone. Since these values try to create a balance between self-interest and social interest, living up to these values requires a certain degree of sacrifice of self-interest on the part of all individuals. Secularism, which preaches individualism and places excessive emphasis on the serving of self-interest, has no mechanism to motivate individuals to make this sacrifice. It assumes that the serving of self-interest will almost always automatically lead to the serving of social interest. Although this does happen some of the times it need not and does not happen all the time.

This raises the question of how does faith try to motivate an individual to live up to these values and to fulfil all his/her social, economic and political obligations that normally involve some sacrifice of self-interest. Faith tries to accomplish this by giving self-interest a long-term perspective – stretching it beyond the span of this world, which is finite, to the Hereafter, which is eternal. An individual's self-interest may be served in this world by being selfish and not fulfilling his obligations towards others. His interest in the Hereafter cannot, however, be served except by fulfilling all these obligations. The more he fulfils these, the better will his well-being be in the Hereafter. Since this world is finite and the Hereafter is eternal, no rational person would tend to hurt his eternal self-interest for the sake of his transient this-worldly self-interest.

It is this long-term perspective of self-interest, along with the individual's innate good nature, accountability before the Supreme Being, and the reward and punishment in the Hereafter, which has the potential of motivating individuals and groups to faithfully fulfil their family and social obligations even when this may appear to hurt their short-term this-worldly self-interest. It may be possible for a person to adopt different stratagems to escape punishment for his wrongdoing in this world. He cannot, however, do this to escape punishment in the Hereafter. God is All-Knowing and Just and cannot be cheated or misguided. This long-term dimension of self-interest in the Hereafter has been generally ignored by conventional economics after being cast in its secularist Enlightenment worldview. It has, therefore, no mechanism to motivate individuals to sacrifice for the well-being of others.

In fact, the dimension of sacrifice seems to be generally missing from conventional economics as a result of excessive emphasis on the serving of self-interest. The result is the concept of Pareto optimum which has given its blessing to the line of thinking that only that position is optimum which makes someone better off without making anyone worse off. This rules out the role of sacrifice in human societies for the purpose of making others better off. Thus while charitable giving involves a material sacrifice on the part of the giver, it does not only give him an inner satisfaction but also has the potential of playing an important role in improving overall human well-being. Sacrifice, however, receives hardly any mention in economics textbooks. Such an omission is not in harmony with the innate goodness of human nature and the generally accepted transcendental values of nearly all societies. It has, therefore, received a great deal of opposition and, accordingly, Francis Fukuyama, who in his earlier book, *The End of History* (1992), declared liberalism to be the final culmination of human achievement,[11] turned about-face in his later book, *The End of Order* (1997), and declared that 'without the transcendental sanctions posed by religion … modern societies would come apart at the seams'.[12]

3.7 FAILURE TO REALIZE THE WELL-BEING OF ALL

The other objective of the Enlightenment Movement was to rid mankind of state despotism. While this objective was laudable in itself, it went to the extreme of giving rise to the concept of laissez-faire which stood for government non-intervention in the operation of the market and of rejecting the role that 'good governance' can play in the realization of general human well-being. This raised the question of how order and harmony would be created in the economy and how social interest would be protected in a laissez-faire environment where everyone was totally free to do whatever he/she wishes to serve his/her self-interest. It was argued that competition would help prevent excesses on the part of both individuals and firms and thus create 'harmony' between self-interest and social interest. There was, therefore, no need for imposing any moral or institutional constraints on the behaviour of individuals or firms and the operation of market forces. It was perhaps not realized that moral values given by religion provide not only a code of conduct for individuals, families, society, and the government to ensure the well-being of all but also a sanctity to these values, something that no secular social contract may be able to provide. The sanctity helps motivate most people, if not everyone, to accept and observe these values faithfully. Without this sanctity, the code of behaviour may require a coercive power to ensure the faithful acceptance and observance of these rules, making it difficult to reform individual and social behaviour in a democratic way to ensure the well-being of all.

The great merit of the age-old free enterprise system is that it promotes private ownership of property and recognizes the profit motive, thus enabling individuals to benefit from their hard work, creativity and entrepreneurship. It is also democratic – by their purchases of goods and services in the market place, individuals cast their votes in favour of the production of those goods and services that they desire. However, the contention that this would automatically promote by itself the well-being of all was based on flawed logic. The system was therefore unable to promote the well-being of all.

The flaws in the logic are not difficult to visualize. First, since the voting strength of the rich and the poor is grossly unequal, the rich have the potential to swing the outcome of market forces in their favour. This can act against the interest of the poor and underprivileged. Second, since the restraining influence of the moral filter was also undermined, materialism took its place, Materialism, however, promoted the consumer culture which persuaded individuals through advertising and the culture of 'keeping up with the Joneses' to purchase a maximum amount of goods and services. Wants thus tended to become maximized as compared with needs. The only constraint was individual income. However, even this constraint became weakened by the conventional financial system where banks tend to act as loan pushers and try constantly to promote living beyond means by both the private and public sectors. The proportional reserve system has played an important role in enabling them to do so. Claims on resources, have, therefore, multiplied and generated not only inflationary pressures but also financial crises by an excessive rise in debt and debt-serving burden beyond the ability of the borrowers or the governments to repay.

Third, the excessive rise in claims has indirectly hurt the need fulfilment of the poor. This is because the rich are able to buy whatever they wish. Since luxury and conspicuous consumption goods and services constitute a substantial part of their spending, a large proportion of the scarce resources gets diverted to the production of these goods and services, leaving inadequate resources for the production of goods and services that are needed to satisfy the basic needs of the poor. All the essential needs of the poor do not, thus, get satisfied and their well-being suffers. This has hurt the well-being of not only the present generation but also that of future generations and given rise to discontent, social tensions, crime and anomie. The natural result is a number of protests like the 'Tea Party' and 'Occupy Wall Street'.

3.8   THE WELFARE STATE

The welfare state has no doubt been a healthy and welcome development around the world. It gained momentum after the Great Depression and particularly after the Second World War. Its immediate objective was to mitigate some of the most conspicuous excesses of capitalism and to serve as an acceptable alternative to communism. Hence it attracted nearly all sections of the population. However, since it was as secularist in its outlook as capitalism, it did not believe in the injection of a moral dimension into the management of the economy. Initially, it relied primarily on four basic policy instruments. These were: (1) nationalization of certain key industries; (2) a strong labour movement; (3) regulation; and (4) the crucial role of the government in providing welfare services, promoting growth, and ensuring full employment. However, the movement for the nationalization of major industries lost momentum because of the general disenchantment with the performance of nationalized industries. The trade union movement, which was considered to be a panacea for raising the incomes of labourers, improving their working conditions, and providing them with a sense of economic security also lost momentum as a result of the excesses of labour unions and relatively high rates of unemployment. While a certain degree of regulation is indispensable to ensure competition, maintain order in the economy, and safeguard the rights of others, excessive regulation can prove to be a great burden. Therefore, even though regulation initially received a great deal of support, questions began to be raised against its long-term feasibility, and business interests joined hands with conservative governments to push for deregulation, which gained momentum in many industrial countries.

The increased welfare role of the government hence became the primary tool of the welfare state. However, since the welfare state did not have any mechanism other than taxation to filter out excessive claims on resources and since the raising of taxes is generally not welcome by the public, it has become plagued by the threat of rising monetary creation and public debt. While the deficits of individual countries lead to inflationary pressures and balance of payment deficits for those specific countries, the high and continuous budgetary deficits of a reserve currency country like the US have become a problem not only for the US but also for the whole world. They provide high-powered reserves to banks around the world and, thereby, enable them to expand credit excessively.

This is a phenomenon from which the world is suffering at present. As long as there is confidence in the dollar there may not be any significant problem. However, if the confidence gets shaken as it did in the late 1960s there will be difficulties for the US as well as other countries. The world will then be under pressure to look for a substitute which can serve not only as a medium of exchange but also as a stable store of value. The development of such a medium could also help put a brake on the spendthrift spending of the US public and private sectors and the consequent flow of excessive high-powered reserves to the international financial system.

The welfare state has, no doubt, done a valuable job of reducing inequities. This has proved to be a great blessing for all and particularly for the poor and the vulnerable. It has, however, led to an exponential growth in public spending and taxation. However, in spite of high rates of taxation, there are excessive levels of budgetary deficits. Moreover, in spite of high rates of government spending, rates of growth in many industrial countries have not been high enough to help realize the cherished goal of full employment and the well-being of all. Consequently, even though the welfare states have made a valuable contribution, the dream of an egalitarian society remains far from realization in spite of substantial economic development over the years. What is needed, therefore, is to inject morality and justice into the financial system to help reduce the excessive spending of the rich on status symbols and speculation to offset the increased spending of the welfare states. This can help create the kind of an egalitarian society that is needed to promote growth with justice, without accentuating speculation and inflationary pressures.

3.9 A RISE IN SOCIAL PROBLEMS

The tragedy of the secularist philosophy of capitalism was not merely that the unhindered pursuit of self-interest by individuals did not, and could not, serve the interest of all, but that it also led to a number of insoluble social problems. The race for the maximization of wealth and want satisfaction and of keeping up with the Joneses has shoved most of the other requisites for human well-being into the background, including family integrity, proper upbringing of children, and social solidarity. There is a decline in the individuals' ability and willingness to make credible long-term commitments to their spouses, children, parents and extended families. It is not possible to keep husband and wife together in a mutually loving and caring relationship if both of them are not willing to sacrifice some of their self-interest for the well-being of each other as well as their children. Therefore, Lundberg and Pollak have rightly concluded that 'long-term marriage combined with child-bearing is no longer a near-universal adult experience'.[13] Consequently, most of the industrial countries have experienced a substantial increase in divorce rates along with a rise in cohabitation rates.[14] This has substantially undermined the family institution, which has historically served as the foundation of human society and civilization. Divorce tends to adversely affect the well-being of most, if not all, people who get divorced. According to the finding of Stevenson and Wolfers, 'On average, divorced people are worse off – and married people are better off – financially, physically, and emotionally'.[15] It tends to have a more serious effect on men who have to pay the alimony. They get impoverished.[16] The disintegration of the family cannot but ultimately lead to reduced overall well-being, particularly if it expands excessively and leads to social breakdown.

High divorce rates also lead to a neglect of the proper upbringing of children and exert a bad influence on their moral, psychological and intellectual development.[17] McLanahan and Sandefur find that, on average, children reared with both biological parents do substantially better than those reared in other family structures.[18] This is because children brought up in broken families are unable to get the love and care of both parents. Daly and Wilson have concluded from their research that children were anywhere from ten to over a hundred times more likely to suffer abuse at the hands of substitute rather than natural parents.[19] Consequently, they develop psychological problems which adversely affect their moral and intellectual development and lead to juvenile delinquency. The quality of the future generation consequently declines. Any society where the quality of the future generation goes down significantly may not be able to maintain its moral, intellectual, technological and military supremacy in the long-run.

In addition to the rise in family disintegration, there is also a decline in the willingness to get married. The marriage rate is currently at its lowest point in recorded history. Many families form without any intention of begetting children.[20] This, combined with excessive resort to birth control, has steeply reduced the birth rate in Europe so much so that *The Times* went to the extent of foreboding that 'Europeans are a vanishing species'.[21] Germany's birthrate is now below what is needed to replace the present population.[22] If the present German birthrate is sustained and immigration is zero, Germany's population is predicted to fall from 82 million to 38.5 million at the century's end, a drop of 53 per cent.[23] Consequently, the proportion of young people will tend to decline and that of old people to increase. In addition to creating problems for the pension funds of the countries where this phenomenon takes place, there will also be difficulty in maintaining their economic activity at a desired level[24] without increased dependence on labour imported from other countries.

In short, what secularism has done is to undermine the collective sanction that religion provides to social values to ensure their general acceptance and observance as rules of behaviour for the proper ordering of socio-economic and political life. This has led to a weakening of the crucial role that the moral filter plays in maintaining a healthy balance between self-interest and social interest in all aspects of human society. Consequently, maximization of wealth and want satisfaction has become the primary purpose of human endeavour. This has promoted a substantial rise in meaningless purchases, particularly of status symbols, and led to a resort to over indulgence in debt beyond the ability of the people to repay along with a rise in overtime work to earn more and more to repay the debt, leaving little time for leisure and family. All these developments have together contributed to a rise in the different symptoms of anomie, indicating, thereby, a lack of inner happiness in the life of individuals. Moral philosophers throughout history as well as a number of modern scholars have, therefore, rightly questioned the identification of well-being with a rise in income and wealth.[25] They have emphasized that while the material contents of well-being are important, the non-material and spiritual contents cannot be ignored if true well-being needs to be ensured.

This has been further vindicated by empirical research which has shown the importance of both the material as well as spiritual ingredients of well-being. This is because, even though real income has dramatically risen in several countries around the world since the Second World War, the self-reported subjective well-being of their populations has not only failed to increase, it has in fact declined.[26] The reason is that happiness is positively associated with higher income only up to the level where all basic biological needs get fulfilled. Beyond this it remains more or less unchanged unless some other needs, which are considered indispensable for increasing well-being, are also satisfied. Most of these other needs are spiritual and non-material in character and need not necessarily become satisfied as a result of increase in income. Single-minded preoccupation with wealth has in fact hurt the satisfaction of spiritual and non-material needs. Some of these are leisure to attend to one's own relaxation, prayers and strengthening of family harmony, proper upbringing of children, and social solidarity. If the non-material needs are not fulfilled, real well-being may not be realized in spite of a rise in income and the society may ultimately start declining even in economic terms.

3.10 THE ISLAMIC WORLDVIEW

As a result of centuries of decline, Muslim countries are at present not in a position to serve as a model for any country. They face many of the same problems that other countries are facing, some more seriously and some less. This leads us to the question of whether the revival of Islam that is now taking place in Muslim societies can lead to a significant improvement in the future. It is in general the belief of Muslims that it can. What is needed is to raise human beings who have all the good qualities of character that are needed to make them a 'blessing' not only for themselves but also their society and do not have any of the bad qualities that would make them a source of harm and disgrace. The Qur'an and the *hadith* have indicated a number of these qualities. Moreover, in spite of the moral and material decline of Muslims over the centuries, Islam continues to be the only reality in the Muslim world that has the charisma to attract the masses, unite them in spite of their great diversity, and motivate them to improve their own selves and act righteously.[27] This is because the Islamic worldview gives primary importance to moral values, human brotherhood, socio-economic justice and family and social solidarity. Moreover, it does not rely primarily on either the state or the market for realizing its vision of human well-being and of becoming a blessing for mankind. It does not divide life into separate compartments, material and spiritual. It rather takes a comprehensive view of life and relies on the integrated roles of all variables, including the innate goodness of the individual himself, values and institutions, market, families, society, state and religion as well as intellectual and technological development to ensure the realization of its vision of well-being for all. It puts great emphasis on socio-economic justice and social change through a reform of the individual himself as well as his/her family, society and institutions, without which the market and the state could both perpetuate inequities.

The fundamental Islamic belief is, like that of some other revealed religions, that this universe and everything in it, including human beings, have been created by the One and Only God. All human beings are His vicegerents. Being the vicegerents of the Creator of this universe confers on them a great honour and dignity and makes them all equal in this honour and dignity. It does not, hence, grant anyone superiority over others because of his/her race, sex, nationality, wealth, or power. They all belong to the same family of God and are, thus, brothers or sisters with respect to each other.[28] This belief would not be very meaningful without accountability before someone who is Just, All-Knowing and Powerful. This comes from the belief that their sojourn in this world is temporary, and that their ultimate destination is the Hereafter where they will be accountable before Him. Their well-being in the Hereafter will depend essentially on whether or not they have lived in this world, and fulfilled their obligations towards themselves as well as others, in a way that would help ensure the well-being of all.[29]

One of the things that seriously affects the well-being of all is the way scarce resources are acquired and utilized.[30] For the efficient and equitable use of these resources, the Creator and Owner of these resources has provided certain values or rules of behaviour, to all people at different times in history through a chain of His Messengers (who were all human beings), including Abraham, Moses, Jesus and, the last of them, Muhammad, peace and blessings of God be on all of them. This is the reason why, as indicated earlier, there is a continuity and great deal of similarity in the value systems of all Revealed religions to the extent to which the Message has not been lost or distorted over the ages. Since all the resources provided by God are a trust, human beings are expected to use them, and to interact with each other, within the framework of the values provided by Him for the purpose of ensuring the well-being of all.

The Messengers did not, however, bring just the values. They also acted upon these themselves to serve as models and also struggled to reform the individuals and institutions of their societies in the light of these values. Individual, socio-economic and political reform was, therefore, the major thrust of the mission of all messengers including Muhammad (pbut). Without such reform, it is not possible to ensure the well-being of all. To accept *what is* and not to struggle for the realization of the vision, or *what ought to be*, is a vote in favour of the prevailing inequities and of doing nothing to remove them. Such an attitude cannot be justifiable within the perspective of the primary vision of all societies. The mission of human beings is not just to abide themselves by these values, but also to struggle peacefully for the reform of all aspects of their societies in accordance with these values. Without such reform, their societies would tend to gradually become more and more disgruntled and unhappy and ultimately decline.

Such reform would, it is believed, help promote a balance between individual and social interest and help actualize the *maqasid al-Shari'ah* (the goals of the *Shari'ah*),[31] or what may be referred to as the vision of Islam, two of the most important constituents of which are socio-economic justice and the well-being of all God's creatures (including not only human beings but also animals, birds and insects). Injustice cannot but thwart the realization of true well-being, accentuate tensions and social unrest, discourage individuals from rendering their best, and thus retard development. However, whereas conventional economics assumes the prevalence of self-interested behaviour on the part of individuals, Islam does not assume the prevalence of ideal behaviour. It believes that a constant struggle (*jihad*) needs to be made on the part of both individuals and society for the moral uplift and the well-being (*falah*) of all.

Islam, however, rules out the use of force for moral uplift: 'There shall be no compulsion in religion' (al-Qur'an, 2:256), and 'Say that the Truth has come from your Lord: Whoever wishes may either believe in it or reject it' (al-Qur'an, 18:29). It rather lays stress on a number of measures to motivate individuals to do what is right and to abstain from doing what is wrong. One of these is to create conviction in individuals through logical reasoning and friendly dialogue (al-Qur'an, 16:125). Another measure is to create an urge in the individual himself to abide by these values. This urge is expected to come from two sources. One of these is the innate goodness of the human being himself or herself. Within the framework of Islamic worldview, people are good by nature because God has created them in harmony with His own nature or disposition (*fitrat Allah*) (al-Qur'an, 30:30). They are not born sinners, or pawns on the chessboard of history. They are capable of having all the good qualities that can help them become a blessing for themselves as well as others and their environment. Accordingly they do not necessarily always act wrongly in their self-interest. They have the ability to act righteously under a feeling of moral obligation even if this hurts their self-interest and requires a certain degree of sacrifice from them. However, since individuals are also free, they may or may not preserve their innate goodness and may act in ways that are in conflict with their own innate nature (*fitrat*). Therefore, it is necessary to educate them and also provide material as well as spiritual incentives and deterrents to motivate them to do their best for their own good as well as that of others and to prevent them from causing harm to others. There can be several ways of doing this.

Market discipline, which has received a major emphasis in economics, is only one of these. While it can help promote efficiency in a competitive environment, it may not necessarily be able by itself to always safeguard social interest. This is because there are several clandestine ways of restraining competition and using unfair means to enrich oneself without getting detected and punished. Therefore, families, societies and governments have an important role to play. Families do this normally through proper upbringing while societies do it by resorting to what is essentially an invisible way of social control through disgrace or prestige. A crucial part of the governments' role is not only to pass regulations but also to enforce them. It is, however, not possible to pass regulations without having a vision and a perception of what is the right thing to do. It is generally the moral basis of society that serves as the foundation for regulations. Almost all major religions have provided such a moral basis of society. Moreover, it may not be realistic to depend primarily on regulations to safeguard social interest. This is because regulations need to be enforced. It is the job of the governments to enforce them. However, even governments may not succeed because there are so many different ways of resorting to corruption, cheating and exploiting others without being detected and caught that it may be difficult for governments to succeed unless there is an inner urge on the part of the people themselves to do what is right, to fulfil their contracts and other commitments faithfully, and to not undermine competition or resort to unfair means of earning.

It is, therefore, necessary to inculcate belief in the reward and punishment in the Hereafter. If a person abstains from wrongdoing and also sacrifices his/her self-interest in this world for the sake of others, he/she will substantially improve his/her well-being in the Hereafter. The concept of Hereafter thus gives a long-term perspective to self-interest by extending it beyond the individual's lifespan in this world. In the last analysis, therefore, it may not be possible to safeguard social interest effectively without the help of all familial, socio-economic, religious and political institutions, including proper upbringing of children in stable morally oriented families, proper education, effective market discipline, social vigilance and a prudent government role. The use of all these institutions may help realize human well-being better than reliance primarily on market discipline or the government. In addition, the Islamic worldview introduces three mechanisms into the market system to make it more effective in ensuring greater honesty and equity in the economy. These mechanisms are filtering, motivation, and socio-economic and political restructuring.[32]

Filtering refers to the removal of all those claims on resources that jeopardize the realization of comprehensive human well-being. This needs, however, to be done through a democratic and morally oriented process. Socialist central planning with a centralized filtering process did not prove to be an effective mechanism for this purpose. It was done by a centralized authority that did not necessarily reflect the wishes of the people. Accordingly, there used to be shortages or over-production and, almost all socialist countries were under constraint to abandon it. However, while the market mechanism helps filter out excess claims on resources and establish equilibrium between demand and supply through a democratic process, it has also not been able to succeed in fully safeguarding the social interest. This is because it is neutral with respect to the tastes and preferences and the purchasing power of buyers operating in the market. It, therefore, leads to a market equilibrium which is in line with the tastes and preferences of the rich, enabling them to tilt the production process in favour of goods and services that suit their tastes and preferences. Such market equilibrium may not necessarily be in harmony with the need fulfilment of the poor. It need not, therefore, be able to help realize comprehensive human well-being.

It is, therefore, necessary to reform the people's tastes and preferences and behaviour in a way that can help weed out all those claims on resources that unnecessarily drain the resources and thereby end up unconsciously in hurting the poor. The moral filter is capable of helping more effectively in such reform, particularly if the use of coercion is to be ruled out. Thus both the filters, the moral filter as well as the price filter, need to be utilized simultaneously to create the kind of equilibrium between supply and demand for resources that is necessary for actualization of the humanitarian goals of society. The moral filter weeds out excess claims on resources democratically even before the buyer goes to the market while the price filter accomplishes the job after he does so.

The moral filter may, however, be of little use if there is no mechanism to motivate people to faithfully observe its values. This is because, as already discussed, faithful observance of moral values, demands sacrifice of self-interest on the part of individuals. The moral filter needs, therefore, to be complemented by a motivating mechanism to ensure its effectiveness. This is supplied in the religious paradigm by belief in the Hereafter where a person will have to account for all his deeds, including how he earned his wealth and how he used it.

Since the physical, social, and political environment also influences human behaviour and the use of scarce resources, the religious world-view tries to complement the filter mechanism as well as the motivating system by socio-economic and political reform, which was one of the primary missions of all God's Messengers. The reform aims at making individuals, families, society and the government use the resources and interact with each other in a way that helps promote general well-being. In a paradigm that emphasises human brotherhood and mutual care, everyone is individually and collectively responsible for not just his own well-being but also that of others. Everyone needs to cooperate not only in promoting good behaviour but also in curbing 'nasty' behaviour that hurts others and frustrates the realization of general well-being (*amr bi al-ma'ruf wa nahi 'an al-munkar*).

If an effective system for detecting and punishing the culprits does not exist, then it may be possible for anyone to get away with dishonesty, bribery, and other unfair means of earning. Such practices may then become locked-in through the long-run operation of path dependence and self-reinforcing mechanisms. Everyone may then condemn the practice, but may not be able to eliminate it single-handedly by himself being honest and fair. It may not, then, be possible to eliminate the undesired practices by just giving sermons and not undertaking comprehensive reform through socio-economic and political restructuring. What Islam aims at doing, therefore, is to inject, like other major religions, a moral dimension into economics and society along with proper upbringing of children, moral education, social reform, family and social solidarity, good governance and accountability of all individuals in the Hereafter – the higher the position, the greater the accountability. This should help all sectors of the human society to play a positive role in the realization of human well-being.

It is heartening to note that the anti-religion stance of the Enlightenment Movement has now started being considered as a great mistake and the religious worldview is gradually gaining strength.[33] Accordingly, the editors of *Religion in Contemporary Europe* have clearly admitted that they are seeing the beginning of the end of 200 years of hostility towards religion.[34] The role of altruism, cooperation, moral values, and a host of social, economic and political institutions in furthering human well-being is being emphasized. A number of schools have appeared in economics which are no longer in favour of the unrealistic assumption that the serving of self-interest by the 'economic man' will necessarily lead to the serving of social interest. It is rather argued that altruistic behaviour is not necessarily an aberration from rationality and that the equating of rational behaviour with only self-interested behaviour was unrealistic.[35]

Commitment to the imperative of value neutrality, the sacred ideal of the Enlightenment scientists bequeathed by economists, has started being considered as both untenable and undesirable – untenable because scientific inquiry is based on assumptions which tacitly involve value judgments; undesirable because scientific inquiry cannot avoid addressing questions of social goals and priorities in resource allocation. It is acknowledged that any discipline committed to value neutrality cannot succeed in evaluating policies and recommendations for public choice. Such an evaluation necessarily involves value judgments. Hence according to Sen, 'the distancing of economics from ethics has impoverished Welfare Economics and also weakened the basis of a good deal of descriptive and predictive economics'. His conclusion is that economics 'can be made more productive by paying greater and more explicit attention to ethical considerations that shaped human behaviour and judgment'.[36] Hausman and McPherson have also concluded in their survey article in the *Journal of Economic Literature* on 'Economics and Contemporary Moral Philosophy' that: 'An economy that is engaged actively and self-critically with the moral aspects of its subject matter cannot help but be more interesting, more illuminating and ultimately more useful than one that tries not to be'.[37]

The problem, however, is how to derive values which command wide acceptance and are also observed with a sense of moral obligation such that anyone who violates them gets censured. Can conventional economics help bring about such a consensus? Probably not. 'Social morality', as Schadwick has aptly observed, 'depends on agreed standards, upon a consensus which is received as so axiomatic that it hardly ought to be discussed', and that, 'except in the case of a small number of exceptional groups of people, morality never had been separated from religion in the entire history of the human race'.[38] Utilitarianism and social contract theories do not carry the potential of providing values which everyone accepts as given and which no one challenges. Even Social Economics cannot be helpful because, in spite of its recognition of values, it is a 'highly pluralistic discipline inspired and enriched by several often radically different worldviews, Schumpeterian visions, and at times even quite antagonistic social doctrines'.[39] Conflict of views and interests may lead to differences of opinion which may be difficult to resolve. No wonder Minsky remarked: 'There is no consensus on what we ought to do'.[40]

Decline in the undue emphasis on 'self-interest' and the 'economic man' and recognition of the importance of value judgments, and the fulfilment of *all* essential human needs are certainly a welcome development. It shows that human beings are capable of rising to the occasion, of analyzing their problems, and of knowing what is wrong. However, what is not so easy is the remedy. It does not lie in a patchwork of cosmetic changes. It lies rather in reorganization of the whole society and the economic system in such a way that there is a transformation of the individual from the 'economic man' to a morally conscious human being who is willing to live up to the demands of brotherhood, socio-economic justice, and family solidarity. Once this happens, Islamic economics and conventional economics will become very close to each other and together lead to the solution of a number of problems that mankind is now facing.

NOTES

* This is the revised and enlarged version of a paper presented by the author at a seminar organized by the Goethe Institute, Munich, Germany, and the Dar al-Fikr, Damascus, Syria, in Damascus on 21 June 2007.

1. Some of the essential material needs are: food, clean water, adequate clothing, education, comfortable housing with proper sanitation and essential utilities, timely medical care, transport, and employment or self-employment opportunities.

2. The Qur'an does not mention the names of all Messengers of God. It rather mentions primarily those whose names were familiar people to the names of only those who came to the Middle East. The names of others were not familiar to the people in this area and the Qur'an is not intended to be an encyclopaedia. It, however, states clearly that: 'And indeed We have sent Our Messengers to every community in every period'

(al-Qur'an, 16:36). 'And We sent Messengers before you, some of them We have mentioned to you, while the others We have not mentioned' (al-Qur'an, 40:78). According to a *hadith* of the Prophet, peace and blessings of God be on him, there have come around 124,000 messengers at different times in history to all people in different parts of the world. Of these only 25 (including Mohammad) have been mentioned in the Qur'an (peace and blessings of God be on them all (Tafsir Ibn Kathir, see the commentary on verse 164 of Surah (4) al-Nisa').

3. Brinton (1967), p. 520.
4. Sartre (1957), pp. 38, 439 and 615. See also Stevenson (1974), and Manser (1966).
5. See Hausman and McPherson (1993); Wilson (1997).
6. See, for example, Dopfer (1976); Balogh (1982); Bell and Kristol (1981).
7. For a discussion of these concepts, see Chapra (2000), pp. 19–28.
8. Toynbee, Somervell's abridgement (1958), Vol. 2, p. 380, and Vol. 1, pp. 495–96.
9. Will and Ariel Durant (1968), p. 51.
10. Williams (1985), p. 174.
11. Fukuyama (1992), p. xi.
12. Fukuyama (1997), p. 8.
13. Lundberg and Pollak (2007), pp. 4 and 23.
14. Fukuyama (1997), p. 17; Buchanan (2002), pp. 25–49; Stevenson and Wolfers (2007), pp. 27 and 37.
15. Stevenson and Wolfers (2007), p. 49.
16. Ibid.
17. See Fukuyama (1997).
18. McLanahan and Sandefur (1994).
19. Daly and Wilson (1968), p. 63.
20. Stevenson and Wolfers (2007), p. 27.
21. *The Times*, 16 January 2000.
22. Buchanan (2002), p. 14.
23. Buchanan (2002), p. 15.
24. Buchanan (2002).
25. Hausman and McPherson (1993), p. 693.
26. Easterlin (2001), p. 472. See also Easterlin (1974 and 1995); Oswald (1997); Blanchflower and Oswald (2000); Diener and Oishi (2000); and Kerry (1999).
27. Marshall Hodgson (1977), has rightly indicated in his book, *The Venture of Islam: Conscience and History in a World Civilization*, that 'the vision has never vanished, the venture has never been abandoned; these hopes and efforts are still vitally alive in the modern world' (Vol. 1, p. 77).
28. The Prophet (pbuh) said, 'Mankind is the family of God and the most beloved of them before Him is the one who is best to His family' (Narrated on the authority of al-Bayhaqi's *Shu'ab al-Iman* by al-Tabrizi in his *Mīshkāt*, Vol. 2, p. 613:4998.
29. For greater detail on the fundamentals of Islamic worldview, see Chapra (1992), pp. 201–12.
30. It is for this reason that the Prophet (pbuh) said: 'A person will not be able to move on the Day of Judgment until he has been asked four questions: about his knowledge, how much he acted upon it; about his life, how he utilized it; about his wealth, how he earned it and where he spent it; and about his body, how he wore it out' (Narrated by Tirmidhi from Abu Barzah al-Aslami, see al-Mundhiri, 1986, Vol. 1, p. 115, No. 5).
31. The Qur'an repeats the same message in a number of other places. For example: 'Are you going to compel people to believe' (al-Qur'an, 10:99), and 'You are not there to force them to believe. Exhort through the Qur'an whoever takes heed of the Warning' (al-Qur'an, 50:45).
32. For further elaboration, see Chapra (1992), pp. 213–33, and Chapra (2000), p. 26.

33. The entire following section of this chapter has been adapted from Chapra (2000), pp. 45–49.
34. Fulton and Gee (1994).
35. See, Janos Horvath 'Foreword' in Solo and Anderson (1981), pp. ix–x. See also Hahn and Hollis (1979), p. 12; Lutz and Lux (1979), p. ix; Choudhury (1986), p. 12; Sen (1987), pp 78-79; Hausman and McPherson (1993), p. 723.
36. See Sen (1987), pp. 78 and 79.
37. Hausman and McPherson (1993), p. 723.
38. Schadwick (1975), pp. 229 and 234.
39. Lutz (1990), p. ix.
40. Minsky (1986), p. 290.

REFERENCES

Balogh, Thomas (1982), *The Irrelevance of Conventional Economics* (London: Weidenfeld & Nicolson).

Bell, David and Kristol, Irving (eds) (1981), *The Crisis of Economic Theory* (New York: Basic Books).

Blanchflower, David and Oswald, Andrew (2000), Well-being over time in Britain and the USA. NBER Working Paper 7487.

Brinton, Crane (1967), Enlightenment, in *The Encyclopedia of Philosophy*, Vol. 2, p. 521.

Buchanan, Patrick (2002), *The Death of the West: How Dying Populations and Immigrant Invasions Imperil our Country and Civilization* (New York: St Martin's Press).

Chapra, M. Umer (1992), *Islam and the Economic Challenge* (Leicester, UK: The Islamic Foundation).

Chapra, M. Umer (2000), *The Future of Economics: An Islamic Perspective* (Leicester, UK: The Islamic Foundation).

Choudhury, Masudul Alam (1986), The micro-economics foundations of Islamic economics: A study in social economics, *The American Journal of Islamic Sciences*, 2, 231–45.

Daly, Martin and Wilson, Margo (1968), *Homicide* (New York: Aldine de Gruyter).

Diener, E., and Shigehiro Oishi (2000), Money and happiness: Income and subjective well-being, in E. Diener and E. Suh (eds), *Culture and Subjective Well-being* (Cambridge, MA: The MIT Press).

Dopfer, Kurt (ed.) (1976), *Economics in the Future: Towards a New Paradigm* (London: Macmillan).

Durant, Will and Durant, Ariel (1968), *The Lessons of History* (New York: Simon and Schuster).

Easterlin, Richard (1974), Does growth improve the human lot?: Some empirical evidence, in Paul David and Melwin Reder (eds), *Nations and Households in Economic Growth: Essays in Honour of Moses Abramowitz* (New York: Academic Press).

Easterlin, Richard (1995), Will raising the income of all increase the happiness of all? *Journal of Economic Behaviour and Organization*, 27:1, 35–48.

Easterlin, Richard (2001), Income and happiness: Towards a unified theory, *Economic Journal*, 111: 473.

Fukuyama, Francis (1992), *The End of History and the Last Man* (London: Penguin Books).

Fukuyama, Francis (1997), *The End of Order* (London: The Social Market Foundation).

Fulton, John and Gee, Peter (eds) (1994), *Religion in Contemporary Europe* (Lampeter, Wales: Edward Mellen Press).

Hahn, F. and Hollis, M. (1979), *Philosophy and Economic Theory* (Oxford: Oxford University Press).

Hausman, Daniel and McPherson, Michael (1993), Taking ethics seriously: Economics and contemporary moral philosophy, *Journal of Economic Literature*, June, 671–731.

Hodgson, Marshall (1977), *The Venture of Islam: Conscience and History in a World Civilization* (Chigago: University of Chicago Press), Vol. 1, p. 77.

Kerry, Charles (1999), Does growth cause happiness, or does happiness cause growth? *Kyklos*, 52:1, 3–26.

Lundberg, Shelly and Pollak, Robert (2007), The American family and family economics, *Journal of Economic Perspectives*, 2:21, Spring, 3–26.

Lutz, Mark (ed.) (1990), *Social Economics: Retrospect and Prospect* (London: Kluwer Academic).

Lutz, Mark and Lux, Kenneth (1979), *The Challenge of Humanistic Economics* (Menlo Park, CA: Benjamin/Cummings).

Manser, Anthony (1966), *Sartre: A Philosophic Study* (London: Athlone Press).

Maslow, Abraham (1970), *Motivation and Personality* (New York: Harper & Row).

McLanahan, Sara and Sandefur, Gary (1994), *Growing Up With a Single Parent: What Hurts, What Helps* (Cambridge, MA: Harvard University Press).

Minsky, Hyman (1986), *Stabilizing an Unstable Economy* (New Haven: Yale University Press).

Mundhiri, 'Abd al-'Azim al-(d. 1258) (1986), *Al-Targhib wa al-Tarhib* (Mustafa al-Amarah (ed.) (Dar al-Kutub al-'Ilmiyyah).

Oswald, Andrew (1997), Happiness and economic performance, *Economic Journal*, 107:445, 1815–31.

Sartre, Jean-Paul (1957), *Being and Nothingness*, transl. by Hazel Barnes (London: Methuen).

Schadwick, Owen (1975), *The Secularization of the European Mind in the Nineteenth Century* (Cambridge: Cambridge University Press).

Sen, Amartya (1987), *On Ethics and Economics* (Oxford: Basil Blackwell).

Solo, Robert A. and Anderson, Charles W. (eds) (1981), *Value Judgment and Income Distribution* (New York: Praeger).

Stevenson, Besley and Wolfers, Justin (2007), Marriage and divorce, changes and their driving forces, *Journal of Economic Perspectives*, 2:21, Spring, 27–52.

Stevenson, Leslie (1974), *Seven Theories of Human Nature* (Oxford: Clarendon Press).

Tabrizi, Wali al-Din al- (1381AH), *Mīshkāt al-Masabih*), M. Nasir al-Din al-Albani (ed.) (Damascus: al-Maktabah al-Islami).

Toynbee, Arnold J. (1958), *A Study of History*, abridgement by D.C. Somervell (London: Oxford University Press).
Williams, Bernard (1985), *Ethics and the Limits of Philosophy* (Cambridge, MA: Harvard University Press).
Wilson, Rodney (1997), *Economics, Ethics and Religion* (London: Macmillan).

4. Ibn Khaldun's theory of development: does it help explain the low performance of the present-day Muslim world?*

4.1 INTRODUCTION

The development and decline of economies and societies has been of interest to scholars throughout history because of their desire to know the causes of these phenomena and to enable their society to continue the rise or to at least bring the decline to an end. The rise of Development Economics in modern times is, therefore, not something unique. The difference, however, is that development economists until recently took into account primarily the economic variables that affected development. They considered the major institutional, psychological, social, historical and political forces in a given society to be exogenous and did not, therefore, analyze the impact of these on the endogenous economic variables that they take into account. It was generally assumed that a positive change in the economic variables would be sufficient to lead to development.

However, other scholars have been oriented towards a multidisciplinary approach which considers economic development to be a part of overall human development. Positive change in one or a few economic variables may not necessarily make a significant difference in development unless this is also accompanied by a positive development-oriented change in other sectors of the society. Accordingly, overall human development is also not considered by them to be indicated by merely a rise in real per capita income, literacy, and life expectancy at birth, as is assumed to be the case in the UNDP's Human Development Index.[1] They take into account all or most of the relevant, socio-economic and political variables that affect human well-being and the rise and fall of societies. A number of scholars, including Ibn Khaldun (1332–1406) and Gibbon (1737–1794) in the past, and Spengler (1926 and 1928), Schweitzer (1949), Sorokin (1951), Toynbee (1935), Myrdal (1968 and 1979), North and

Thomas (1973), Kennedy (1987) and some others in modern times have discussed the rise and fall of civilizations within this multidisciplinary framework. This chapter is intended to show the contribution made to the discussion by Ibn Khaldun more than 600 years ago to explain the causes of Muslim decline which had been under way during his lifetime. Even though a substantial part of what Ibn Khaldun wrote has become a part of conventional wisdom by now, it is still relevant because most of the Muslim world, and not just the area he was concerned with at that time, has been unable until now to get rid of what he considered to be the primary cause of the decline.

Ibn Khaldun, whose family had been forced by political upheavals in Spain to migrate to Tunis, was born in 1332 in Tunis, where he received thorough education from reputed scholars. At a very young age, the Black Death of the 1340s claimed the life of his parents as well as a large number of relatives, friends of the family, teachers, and others in his society. Consequently, he had to undergo a great deal of suffering. However, even Tunis, like other neighbouring countries, was not spared by political upheavals. These forced him to move from place to place until 1382 when he finally settled down in Egypt and spent the rest of his life there before his death in 1406 at the age of 74.

'The Muslim civilization was in the process of decline during his lifetime. The Abbasid Caliphate (750–1258) had come to an end around three quarters of a century before his birth, after the pillage, burning and near destruction of Baghdad and its surrounding areas by the Mongols. A number of other historical events, including the Crusades (1095–1396), Mongol invasions (1258–1355), and the Black Death (1340s) had also weakened most of the central Muslim lands. In addition, the Circassian Mamluks (1382–1517), during whose period Ibn Khaldun spent nearly a third of his life, were corrupt and inefficient and followed policies that could not but accelerate the decline.

PART I
IBN KHALDUN'S THEORY OF DEVELOPMENT

Under these circumstances, it would be strange if a man of Ibn Khaldun's moral and mental calibre would not be in search of an effective strategy to bring about a reversal of the tide (Talbi, 1986, p. 808). As a man of extraordinary intellectual capabilities (Toynbee, 1935, Vol. 3, pp. 321–22), he was well aware that the reversal could not be dreamed of without first drawing lessons from history and determining the factors that had led the Muslim civilization to bloom out of humble beginnings and to decline thereafter. He, therefore, constructed a model that could help explain the rise and fall of civilizations or the development and decline of economies, both of which are interdependent phenomena in his model.

The model that he developed is powerful enough to enable us to answer some of the most crucial questions that Development Economics needs to answer – questions about why the Muslim world rose rapidly and continued to rise for several centuries, and why it declined thereafter to the extent that it lost its *élan vital*, and did not only become largely colonized but is also unable to respond successfully to the challenges that it is now faced with'?

A number of scholars[2] have emphasized different internal as well as external factors that led to the decline of Muslims, particularly after the 12th century. Some of the most important of these are moral degenera- tion, loss of dynamism in Islam after the rise of dogmatism and rigidity; decline in intellectual and scientific activity; internal revolts and disunity along with continued external invasions and warfare which ravaged and weakened the country, created fiscal imbalances and insecurity of life and property, and reduced investments and growth; decline in agriculture, crafts and trade; exhaustion or loss of mines and precious metals; and natural disasters like plague and famine which led to a decline in the overall population and demand followed by the weakening of the economy.

While the adverse impact of all these internal as well as external factors cannot be denied, it is expected that a living and dynamic society would be able to discuss and analyze freely all these factors, and to develop and implement a proper strategy for effectively offsetting their adverse effects at least in the long-run, if not in the short-run. Why were the Muslims unable to do this? Was there something that prevented them from responding successfully to the internal as well as external chal- lenges that they faced? What was that something? What Ibn Khaldun's theory does is to weave all these factors together, as an interrelated chain of events, into a philosophy of development to show how most of them were activated by what he considers to be the trigger mechanism in a manner that made it difficult for the society to stop the decline without coming to grips with the primary cause.

4.2 MULTIDISCIPLINARY AND DYNAMIC

Ibn Khaldun tried to address all these questions in the *Muqaddimah* which literally means 'introduction' and constitutes the first volume of a seven-volume history, briefly called *Kitab al-Ibar* or the 'Book of Lessons [of History]'.[3] It is an attempt to explain the different events in history through a cause and effect relationship and to derive scientifically the principles that lie behind the rise and fall of a ruling dynasty or state (*dawlah*) *or* civilization (*umran*). Even though he benefited in this venture from the contributions made by his predecessors and contemporaries in the Muslim world, the *Muqaddimah* is extremely rich in a great deal of his own original and penetrating analysis. His entire model is condensed to a substantial extent, even though not fully, in the following advice extended by him to the sovereign:

- The strength of the sovereign (*al-mulk*) does not materialize except through the implementation of the *Shari'ah*;[4]
- The *Shari'ah* cannot be implemented except by the sovereign (*al-mulk*);
- The sovereign cannot gain strength except through the people (*al-rijal*);
- The people cannot be sustained except by wealth (*al-mal*);
- Wealth cannot be acquired except through development (*al-imarah*);
- Development cannot be attained except through justice (*al-adl*);
- Justice is the criterion (*al-mizan*) by which God will evaluate mankind; and
- The sovereign is charged with the responsibility of actualizing justice (Muqaddimah (M), p. 39; Rosenthal's translation (R): I, p. 80).[5]

The entire *Muqaddimah* is an elaboration of this advice which consists of, in Ibn Khaldun's own words: 'eight wise principles (*kalimat hikami-yyah*) of political wisdom, each one dovetailed with the other for mutual strength, in such a circular manner that the beginning or the end is indistinguishable' (M, p. 403; R: I, p. 82).

   The strength of Ibn Khaldun's analysis lies in its multidisciplinary and dynamic character. It is multidisciplinary because it links all important socio-economic and political variables, including the sovereign or political authority (*G*), beliefs and rules of behaviour or the *Shari'ah* (*S*), people (N), wealth or stock of resources (*W*), development (g), and justice (j), in a circular and interdependent manner, each influencing the others and in turn being influenced by them (see Figure 4.1).[6] Since the operation of this cycle takes place in his model through a chain reaction over a long period of three generations or almost 120 years, a dimension of dynamism gets introduced into the whole analysis and helps explain how political, moral, institutional, social, economic, demographic, and economic factors interact with each other over time to lead to the development and decline, or the rise and fall, of an economy or civilization. In a long-term analysis of this kind, there is no *ceteris paribus* clause because none of the variables is assumed to remain constant. One of the variables acts as the trigger mechanism.[7] If the other sectors react in the same direction as the trigger mechanism, the decay will gain momentum through an interrelated chain reaction such that it becomes difficult over time to identify the cause from the effect. If the other sectors do not react in the same direction, then the decay in one sector may not spread to the others and either the decaying sector may be reformed over time or the decline of the civilization may be much slower.

4.2.1   The Role of the Human Being (N)

The centre of Ibn Khaldun's analysis is the human being (Rosenthal, 1967, p. 19) because the rise and fall of civilizations is closely dependent on the well-being or misery of the people. This is, in turn, dependent not just on economic variables but also on the closely interrelated role of moral, institutional, psychological, political, social, and demographic factors through a process of circular causation extending over a long period of history (M, pp. 39 and 287; R: I, p. 80 and II, p. 105). This emphasis on the human being is in keeping with the Qur'anic teaching which states that: 'God does not change the condition of a people until they change their own innerselves' (13:11) and that 'Corruption has appeared everywhere because of what *people* have done' (30:41, italics added). These two verses along with many others emphasize the role of human beings themselves in their rise and fall. This is why all the messengers of God (including Abraham, Moses, Jesus and Muhammad) came to this world to reform human beings and the institutions that affect their behaviour.

4.2.2   The Role of Development (g) and Justice (j)

If human beings are the centre of analysis, then development and justice become the most crucial links in the chain of causation. Development is essential because unless there is a perceptible improvement in the well-being of the people, they will not be motivated to do their best (M, p. 287; R: II, p. 109). Moreover, in the absence of development, the inflow of scholars, artisans, labour and capital that need to take place from other societies to boost development further may not take place (M, pp. 362–63; R: II, pp. 271–76). This may make it difficult to sustain development and may lead ultimately to a decline (M, p. 359; R: II, p. 270).

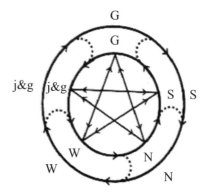

Figure 4.1   Ibn Khaldun's model of socio-economic and political dynamics

Development in Ibn Khaldun's model does not refer to merely economic growth (M, pp. 39 and 347–49; R: I, p. 39 and II, pp. 243–49). It encompasses all-round human development such that each variable enriches the others (G, S, N, W, j, and g) and is in turn enriched by them, contributing thereby to the true well-being or happiness of people and ensuring not only the survival but also the rise of the civilization. Economic development cannot be brought about by economic forces alone in isolation of non-economic sectors of the society. It needs moral, social, political and demographic support. If this support does not become available, economic development may not get triggered, and if it does, it may not be sustainable.

Development is, however, not possible without justice. However, justice, like development, is also not conceived by him in a narrow economic sense but rather in the more comprehensive sense of justice in all spheres of human life. He clearly states that

> Do not think that injustice consists in only taking money or property from its owner without compensation or cause, even though this is what is commonly understood. Injustice is more comprehensive than this. Anyone who confiscates the property of someone or forces him to work for him, or presses an unjustified claim against him, or imposes on him a duty not required by the *Shari'ah*, has committed injustice. Collection of unjustified taxes is also injustice; transgression on another's property or taking it away by force or

theft constitutes injustice; denying other people their rights is also injustice. (M, p. 288; R: II, pp. 106–7)

'One of the greatest injustices and the most destructive of development is the unjustified imposition of tasks on people and subjecting them to forced labour' (M, p. 289; R: II, pp. 108–9). Justice is considered so crucial by Ibn Khaldun for development that he has a whole section entitled 'injustice triggers the destruction of civilization' (M, pp. 286–90; R: II, pp. 103–11). This is the reason why j and g have been juxtaposed in the above diagram. 'The extent to which property rights are infringed determines the extent to which the incentive to earn and acquire it goes'. 'If the incentive is gone, they refrain from earning' (M, p. 286, R: II, p. 103). This adversely affects their efficiency, innovativeness, entrepreneurship, drive and other qualities, ultimately leading to the society's disintegration and decline.

Justice in this comprehensive sense cannot be fully realized without *asabiyyah*, which has been varyingly translated as 'social solidarity', 'group feeling' or 'social cohesion'. It 'provides protection, makes possible mutual defence as well as the settlement of claims and performance of all agreed activities' (M, p. 139; R: I, p. 284). It helps create the mutual trust and cooperation, without which it is not possible to promote division of labour and specialization, which are necessary for the accelerated development of any economy (M, pp. 41–43; R: I, pp. 89–92). The crucial role that trust plays in development is now being rightly emphasized by economists (Arrow, 1973, Etzioni, 1988; Fukuyama, 1995; Hollingsworth and Boyer, 1998) and has become a part of 'conventional wisdom' or 'embeddedness'. Ibn Khaldun has used the word, '*asabiyyah*' for what is, to a great extent, currently referred to as 'social capital' or 'social infrastructure' (see Dasgupta and Serageldin, 2000). However, some scholars have raised objections against the use of the word 'capital' for something that is abstract and cannot be possessed like physical capital by individuals (see, for example, Arrow, 2000; Solow, 2000; and Bowles and Gintis, 2002). Therefore, Ibn Khaldun's use of the expression *asabiyyah* or 'social solidarity' seems to be a better alternative.

4.2.3 The Role of Institutions (S) and the State (G)

Justice, however, necessitates certain rules of behaviour called institutions in Institutional Economics and moral values in religious worldviews. They are the standards by which people (N) interact with, and fulfil their obligations towards, each other (M, pp. 157–58; R: I, pp. 319–21). All societies have such rules based on their own worldview. The primary basis of these rules in a Muslim society is the *Shari'ah (S)*. 'Divine Laws command the doing of good and prohibit the doing of what is evil and destructive' (M, p. 304; R: II, p. 142). They are, therefore, according to Ibn Khaldun, 'for the good of human beings and serve their interests' (M, p. 143; R: I, p. 292). Their Divine origin carries the potential of helping promote their willing acceptance and compliance and of serving as a powerful cement for holding a large group together (M, pp. 151–52; R: I, pp. 305–8 and 319–22). This can help curb socially harmful behaviour, ensure justice (j), and enhance solidarity and mutual trust among the people, thereby promoting development (g).

The *Shari'ah(S)* cannot, however, play a meaningful role unless it is implemented fairly and impartially (M, pp. 39 and 43; R: I, pp. 80 and 91–92). The *Shari'ah* can only give rules of behaviour, it cannot itself enforce them. It is the responsibility of the political authority (G) to ensure compliance through incentives and deterrents (M, pp. 127–28; R: I, pp. 262–63). The Prophet clearly recognized this by saying: 'God restrains through the sultan (sovereign) what he cannot restrain through the Qur'an' (al-Bayhaqi, 1990, from Anas ibn Malik, Vol. 5, 267, No. 6612). For Ibn Khaldun, political authority has the same relationship to a civilization as form has to matter (M, pp. 371 and 376; R: II, pp. 291 and 300). 'It is not possible to conceive of political authority without civilization and of civilization without political authority' (M, p. 376; R: II, p. 300). However, Ibn Khaldun clearly emphasizes that 'good ruler-ship is equivalent to gentleness' (M, p 188; R: I, p. 383). 'If the ruler is tyrannical and harsh in punishments … the people become fearful and depressed and seek to protect themselves by means of lies, ruses and deception. This becomes their character trait. Their perceptions and character become corrupted … . They may conspire to kill him' (M, p. 188; R: I, p. 383).

While Ibn Khaldun emphasizes the role of the state in development, he does not, in step with other classical Muslim scholars, support a totalitarian role for the state. He stands for what has now become characterized as 'good governance'. Recognition of private property and respect for individual freedom within the constraints of moral values is a part of Islamic teachings and has always been prevalent in Muslim thinking. The job of the state in the writings of almost all classical Muslim scholars, including Ibn Khaldun, is, in addition to defence and maintenance of law and order, to ensure justice, fulfilment of contracts, removal of grievances, fulfilment of needs, and compliance with the rules of behaviour.[8] In other words, the state must do things that help people carry on their lawful businesses more effectively and prevent them from committing excesses and injustices against each other.

Ibn Khaldun considers it undesirable for the state to get directly involved in economic activity (M, p 281; R: II, p. 93). Doing so will not only hurt the people (N) by reducing their opportunities and profits (now termed as crowding out of the private sector) but also reduce the state's tax revenue (M, pp. 281–83; R: II, pp. 93–96). Thus the state is visualized by Ibn Khaldun as neither a laissez-faire state nor a totalitarian state. It is rather a state which ensures the prevalence of the *Shari'ah* (S) and serves as an instrument for accelerating human development and well-being.[9] The slant towards nationalization came in the thinking of some Muslim writers under the influence of socialism, and was exploited by ambitious generals and politicians in several Muslim countries to serve their own vested interest. Socialism, however, brought nothing but misery to nearly all those Muslim countries where it was imposed through military coups (Desfosses and Levesque, 1975).

4.2.4 The Role of Wealth (W)

Wealth (W) provides the resources that are needed for ensuring justice (j) and development (g), the effective performance of its role by the government (G), and the well-being of *all* people (N). Wealth does not depend on the stars (M, p. 366; R: II, p. 282), or the existence of gold and silver mines (ibid.). It depends rather on economic activities (M, pp. 360 and 366; R: II, pp. 271 and 282), the largeness of the market (M, p. 403; R: II, p. 351), incentives and facilities provided by the state (M, p 305; R: II, pp. 143–44), and tools (M, pp. 359 and 360; R: II, pp. 270–72), which in turn depend on saving or the 'surplus left after satisfying the needs of the people' (M, p 360; R: II, p. 272). The greater the activity, the greater will be the income. Higher income will contribute to larger savings and greater investment in tools (M, p. 360; R: II, pp. 271–72) which will in turn contribute to greater development (g) and wealth (W) (ibid.). He emphasized the role of investment further by saying: 'And know that wealth does not grow when hoarded and amassed in safes. It rather grows and expands when it is spent for the well-being of the people, for giving them their rights, and for removing their hardships' (M, p. 306; R: II, p. 146). This makes 'the people better off, strengthens the state, makes the times prosperous, and enhances the prestige [of the state]' (M, p. 306; R: II, p. 146). Factors that act as catalysts are low rates of taxes (M, pp. 279–81; R: II, pp. 89–91), security of life and property (M, p. 286; R: II, p. 103), and a healthy physical environment amply provided with trees and water and other essential amenities of life (M, pp. 347–49; R: II, pp. 243–48).

Wealth also depends on division of labour and specialization, the greater the specialization the higher will be the growth of wealth:

> Individual human beings cannot by themselves satisfy all their needs. They must cooperate for this purpose in their civilization. The needs that can be satisfied by the cooperation of a group exceed many times what they can produce individually. ... [The surplus] is spent to provide the goods of luxury and to satisfy the needs of inhabitants of other cities. They import other goods in exchange for these. They will then have more wealth ... . Greater prosperity enables them to have luxury and the things that go with it, such as elegant houses, clothes and utensils, and the use of servants and carriages ... . Consequently, industry and crafts thrive. (M, pp. 360–61; R: II, pp. 271–72)

Human beings do not allow their labour to be used free (M, p. 402; R: II, p. 351). Therefore, division of labour will take place only when exchange is possible (M, p. 380; R: II, p. 311). This requires well-regulated markets which enable people to exchange and fulfil their needs (M, pp. 360–62, R: II, pp. 271–76).

A rise in incomes and wealth contributes to a rise in tax revenues and enables the government to spend more on the people's well-being. This leads to an expansion in economic opportunities (M, p. 362; R: II, p. 275) and greater development, which, in turn, induces a natural rise in population and also the immigration of skilled and unskilled labour and scholars from other places (M, pp. 362–63; R: II, pp. 271–76), thus further strengthening the human and intellectual capital of that society. Such a rise in population boosts the demand for goods and services, and thereby promotes industries (*al-sanai*), raises incomes, promotes sciences and education (M, pp. 359 and 399–403; R: II, pp. 270 and 346–52), and further accelerates development (M, pp. 363 and 403; R: II, pp. 277 and 351–52). In the beginning, prices tend to decline with the rise in development and production. However, if demand keeps on rising and the supply is unable to keep pace with it, scarcities develop, leading to a rise in the prices of goods and services. The prices of necessities tend to rise faster than those of luxuries, and prices in urban areas rise faster than those in rural areas. The cost of labour also rises and so do taxes. These lead to a further rise in prices, which creates hardship for people and leads to a reversal in the flow of population. Development declines and along with it prosperity and civilization (M, pp. 168 and 363–65; R: I, pp. 339–42 and II, pp. 276–85).

The decline in income leads to a decline in tax revenues which are no longer sufficient to cover state spending. The state tends to impose more and more taxes and also tries to gain excessive control over all sources of power and wealth. The incentive to work and earn is adversely affected among the farmers and the merchants, who provide most of the tax receipts. Hence when incomes decline, so do the tax revenues. The state is in turn unable to spend on development and well-being. Development declines, the recession deepens further, the forces of decay are accelerated and lead to the end of the ruling dynasty (M, pp. 168 and 279–82; R: I, pp. 339–42 and II, pp. 89–92).

If one were to express Ibn Khaldun's analysis in the form of a functional relationship, one could state that:

$$G = f(S, N, W, j \text{ and } g) \tag{4.1}$$

This equation does not capture the dynamics of Ibn Khaldun's model, but does reflect its interdisciplinary character by taking into account *all* of the major variables discussed by him. In this equation, G or the political authority has been shown as a dependent variable because one of the main concerns of Ibn Khaldun was to explain the rise and fall of dynasties, states or civilizations. According to him the strength or weakness of the dynasty depends on the strength or weakness of the political authority which it embodies. The survival of the political authority (G) depends ultimately on the well-being of the people (N) which it (G) must try to ensure by providing a proper environment for actualizing development (g) as well as justice (j) through the implementation of the *Shari'ah* (S). If the political authority (G) is corrupt and incompetent and not accountable before the people, it will not perform its functions conscientiously. Consequently, the resources at its disposal will not get effectively utilized and the services that need to be provided to facilitate development will not become available. Development as well as well-being will then suffer. Unless there is development (g), the resources needed to enable the society as well as the government to meet the challenges that they face and to actualize their socio-economic goals will not expand.

4.2.5 The Role of the Trigger Mechanism

However, while a normal cause and effect relationship is not necessarily reversible, the circular and interdependent causation in human societies emphasized by Ibn Khaldun generally tends to be so. This is indicated in Figure 4.1 by means of arrows and dots. Any one of the independent variables and, in particular, development (g), which is the main theme of this chapter, may be treated as a dependent variable with the others being considered independent. This implies that the trigger mechanism for the decline of a society may not necessarily be the same in all societies. In Muslim societies, with which Ibn Khaldun was concerned, the trigger mechanism was the failure of the political authority (G) which, unfortunately, continues in most Muslim countries until the present time (as will be seen in Part II of this chapter), and has led to the misuse of public resources and their non-availability for the realization of justice, development and general well-being.

Therefore, while all factors play an important role in the development and decline of a society, the trigger mechanism has a crucial role. The trigger mechanism in other societies may be any of the other variables in Ibn Khaldun's model. It could, for example, be the disintegration of the family, which was not a problem in Ibn Khaldun's time and which he did not, therefore, mention in his analysis. It is, however, an integral part of N and is now having a greater manifestation in the Western world even though all societies are affected by it in varying degrees. Such disintegration, if it continues unchecked, may first lead to a lack of proper upbringing of children and then to a decline in the quality of human beings (N), who constitute the bedrock of any civilization. It may not, then, be possible for that society to sustain its economic, scientific, technological and military supremacy. The trigger mechanism could also be the weakness of the economy resulting from a faulty economic system based on unhelpful values and institutions (S), as happened in the Soviet Union. It could also be the absence of justice, educational and health facilities, and access to venture capital, which may lead to the inefficient performance of human resources (N) and thereby to sluggish development, as the case is in many developing countries, of which the Muslim world is an integral part.

Ibn Khaldun did not, thus, commit the mistake of confining himself to economic variables alone to explain development and decline. He rather adopted a multidisciplinary and dynamic approach to show how the interrelated relationship of social, moral, economic, political, historical and demographic factors leads to the rise and fall of societies. This is what can also explain why some countries develop faster than others, what makes development sustainable, and when people realize true well-being. Fortunately, Development Economics has gradually started taking into account the roles of almost all these variables as well as their mutual interaction through circular causation.

Nevertheless, his concept of trigger mechanism has not become fully utilized. Without this concept even the stress on property rights by North and Thomas (1973), to explain the rise of the Western world does not take us very far. Property rights have been there in most societies, and particularly so in the Muslim World because of the Islamic stress on them. However, all societies do not necessarily develop. The reason is that property rights, like other institutions, carry no weight unless they are enforced. What is it that led to their enforcement in Western societies? It was perhaps the emergence of democracy which led to political accountability. This led to the enforcement of institutions, of which property rights are a crucial part. It is, therefore, political accountability resulting from democracy which acted as the trigger mechanism for the enforcement of property rights and justice. This led to development. North and Thomas perhaps realize this themselves to a certain extent when they state that innovation, economies of scale, education, capital accumulation, and so on, are not causes of growth; they are growth (North and Thomas, 1973, p. 3). Using the same logic, one could argue that enforcement of property rights, is also an effect rather than a cause. Property rights were enshrined in Christian values but were not enforced. If it was not for democracy, property rights may not have been enforced.

Ibn Khaldun also did not commit the neoclassical economists' mistake of being concerned primarily with short-term static analysis by assuming other factors to be constant when changes are taking place in these factors in all human societies through a chain reaction even though these changes may be so small as to be imperceptible. Nevertheless, their influence on economic variables continues to be significant and cannot be ignored. Therefore, even though economists may adopt the *ceteris paribus* assumption for convenience and ease of analysis, multidisciplinary dynamics of the kind used by Ibn Khaldun also needs to be simultaneously utilized because of the help it can give in formulating socio-economic policies that help improve the overall long-run performance of an economy and raise the well-being of its people. Neoclassical Economics is unable to do this because, as North has rightly asked: 'How can one prescribe policies when one doesn't understand how economies develop?' He, therefore, considers Neoclassical Economics to be 'an inappropriate tool to analyze and prescribe policies that will induce development' (North, 1994, p. 359). Since Ibn Khaldun formulated a brilliant model for explaining the rise and fall of a society, Toynbee was right in declaring that in terms of 'both breadth and profundity of vision as well sheer intellectual power', Ibn Khaldun, in his *Muqaddimah* to his *Universal History*, 'conceived and formulated a philosophy of history which is undoubtedly the greatest work of its kind that has ever been created by any mind in any time or place' (Toynbee, 1935, Vol. 3, pp. 321 and 322).

With some variations in the definitions and the content of each variable according to the change in environment and analytical framework, his model can still be very useful today. For example, 'N' need not be taken as a solid aggregate but rather as the sum of different components, including men and women, scholars, political elite and the lay people; and families, social and economic groups, and society as a whole. Ibn Khaldun took some of these into account but not all. Moreover, the role of women is much greater now than in Ibn Khaldun's times and it may not be possible to exploit their potential unless families, society and the government all join hands. Even without nationalization and central planning, the role of governments is much greater now and they are required to contribute more effectively to justice (j) and development (g). While it is necessary to take W into account, it is also necessary to take into account all economic variables like saving, investment, capital accumulation, and technology, which Development Economics does but which Ibn Khaldun did only indirectly.

PART II
APPLYING IBN KHALDUN'S MODEL TO MUSLIM COUNTRIES

4.3   THE CONTRIBUTION OF ISLAM

While applying Ibn Khaldun's model to the present-day Muslim world, the first question that one is confronted with is about which of the variables included in his model (G, S, N. W, j and g) has triggered the Muslim decline and continues to be responsible for the inferior performance of most of these countries. As far as Islam (S) is concerned, it is itself a victim rather than the trigger mechanism. A number of Western scholars, including Toynbee (1935), Hitti (1958), Hodgson (1977), Baeck (1994), and Lewis (1995) have argued that Islam played a positive role in the development of Muslim societies in the past. It is only the factor of Islam which can help answer the question of why a Bedouin society, which was characterized by internecine feuds, paucity of resources, and a harsh climate, and which had hardly any of the requisites for growth, was able to develop so rapidly against all odds and stand firmly against the intellectually and materially far superior Byzantine and Sassanian empires. It started blooming in the 7th century while, according to North and Thomas, Western Europe 'was mainly a vast wilderness' even in the 10th century (North and Thomas, 1973, p. 28). If it was not for Islam, there would not have been, in the words of Toynbee, that 'extraordinary deployment of latent spiritual forces by which Islam transformed itself, and thereby transfigured its mission, in the course of six centuries' (Toynbee, 1957, Vol. 2, p. 30).

What Islam (S) did was to activate all the developmental factors in a positive discretion. It contributed to the moral and material uplift of individuals (N), who constitute the primary force behind the rise or fall of a society. It changed their outlook towards life by injecting a meaning and purpose into it. It provided development-friendly institutions or moral values (S) and also created a proper climate for their observance in a way that helped change the character of that society. It established a morally oriented political system where the *Khalifah* (caliph) was elected by the people, ruled in keeping with the decisions of the *Shura* (advisory council), and was accountable before the people. It thereby created a framework for what is now called 'good governance' (G) to ensure justice, dignity, equality, self-respect and sharing of the benefits of development by all, particularly the poor and the downtrodden (j). It established rule of law and ensured sanctity of life, individual honour, and property. It gave a higher and more respectable status to the farmer, craftsman and merchant as compared with what they enjoyed under the Mazdean or the then-prevailing Christian traditions.

The prevalence of justice and security of life and property strengthened the motivation for honesty, integrity, hard work, accumulation of capital, entrepreneurship and technological progress. It created a vast common market with free movement of goods, capital and labour, and low rates of tariffs in an area which had been previously vitiated by tribal feuds, continued wars between the Byzantine and Sassanian empires, waylaying of caravans, and extortionate taxes. Consequently, there was a revolutionary rise in agricultural and manufacturing output as well as long distance trade.[10]

'This was the classic age of Islam, when a new, rich and original civilization, born of the confluence of many races and traditions, came to maturity' (Lewis, 1960, p. 20). The institutional requirements for development emphasized by North and Thomas (1973, pp. 2–3) and North (1990, pp. 3–10) were satisfied. Schatzmiller acknowledges this by stating that 'all the factors which enabled Europe to succeed were available to Islam much earlier'. (Schatzmiller, 1994, p. 405). As a result of this, there was all-round economic development (g) embracing agriculture, crafts and trade. This led to a substantial rise in the incomes of all people (N) as well as the state (G).

There was great public support for education and research. This led not only to improvements in human skills and technological and intellectual development but also provided a favourable climate for what Hitti calls a 'momentous intellectual awakening' in which scholars of all fields of learning and faiths participated without discrimination. (Hitti, 1958, p. 306; Saunders, 1966, p. 24; and Lewis, 1960, p. 20). This enabled the Muslim civilization, to achieve and maintain supremacy in nearly all fields of science and technology for almost four centuries from the middle of the 8th to the middle of the 12th century. Even after the loss of the top place, substantial contributions continued to be made for at least two more centuries (see Sarton, 1927, particularly Vol. 1 and Book 1 of Vol. 2).

The position of women (N) also improved significantly. The Qur'an prescribed for them rights equal to those of men (2:228) and enjoined men to fulfil their obligations towards them graciously (2:237). No wonder, Umar, the second Caliph (d. 644), felt prompted to say that: 'During the pre-Islamic period (*al-Jahiliyyah*), we did not consider women to be anything. However, after the coming of Islam, when God himself expressed His concern for them, we realized that they also had rights over us' (al-Bukhari, 1987, Vol. 7, p. 281:735). During the Prophet's days, they played an important role in all different activities, including the war effort. (Abu Shuqqah, 1990, Vol. 3, pp. 132–233; See also Roded, 1994, p. 35). They 'were accorded property rights not equalled in the West until modern times' (Lewis, 1995, p. 72).

They are well represented in the biographical literature devoted to the Prophets' companions; about 1,200 female companions are included in it, roughly 10 to 15 per cent of the total entries. (Roded, 1994, p. 19). After reading the biographies of thousands of women in 40 bibliographical collections dating from the 9th century, Ruth Roded, lecturer at the Hebrew University of Jerusalem, did not find any evidence to support the view that Muslim women were 'marginal, secluded and restricted' (Roded, 1994, pp. viii and ix). While studying charitable endowments (*awqaf*) in Ottoman Aleppo, she was 'astounded to discover that 41 per cent of the endowments were founded by women and that women's endowments differed little from those of men'. (Roded, 1994, p. vii). Women also acted as farmers, merchants, artisans and landlords (Faroghi, 1994, pp. 599 and 605) and 'courts were active in safeguarding women's rights in conformity with the *Shari'ah*'. (Schatzmiller, 1994, p. 362).

4.3.1   The Trigger Mechanism of Muslim Decline

If Islam played a catalytic role in Muslim development in the earlier centuries by bringing about the orientation of all factors included in Ibn Khaldun's model in the positive direction, then there arises the question of what is it that triggered the decline later on? As indicated earlier, the trigger mechanism of Muslim decline was, according to Ibn Khaldun, political illegitimacy, which started when Mu'awiyah, the fifth Caliph, initiated hereditary succession by appointing his son, Yazid, to the Caliphate in 679. This was in clear violation of Islamic teachings with respect to statecraft. Democracy is not only in harmony with Islam but also a part of its mandatory ethical values. (al-Qur'an, 3:159 and 42:38). Just like democracy, there is no Church in Islam to create a conflict between the Church and the state. However, moral values are eternal in Islam while they can be relative in a secular democracy. Nevertheless, even though it is theoretically possible for a secular democracy to violate or ignore the moral code of the society, this does not normally happen. If there is a deviation, it would essentially reflect a change in the society's values, which does not happen suddenly, but rather gradually over a long period of time. The legal blessing given to gambling, drinking, homosexuality, lesbianism, prostitution and the cohabitation of unmarried couples in some secular democracies may be instances of change in values. In an Islamic democracy, these would remain illegal as long as the state claims to be Islamic.

After the introduction of hereditary succession, Islamic teachings with respect to statecraft gradually became less and less reflected in the political institutions of the Muslim world. Nevertheless, Political authority (G) did not deteriorate into despotism immediately after the abolition of the Caliphate. Since the *Shari'ah* (S) continued to be a source of inspiration for the people (N), the government was under constraint to ensure not only law and order but also justice and socio-economic uplift. The judicial system operated effectively and honestly, security of life and property was ensured, rules of behaviour were generally observed, and social and contractual obligations continued to be fulfilled.

Unfortunately, the governments became more and more absolute and arbitrary with the passage of time. The trend was 'towards greater, not lesser, personal authority for the sovereign and his agents' (Lewis, 1995, p. 144). Accountability of the rulers and the political elite, equality before law, and freedom of expression began to decline in clear violation of the *Shari'ah*. Even though lip service continued to be paid to Islam, state resources began to be misused for the luxury of the royal court and taxes rose gradually beyond the ability of the people to bear.[11] Justice (j) and development (g) accordingly became the worst victims, and solidarity, which previously prevailed between the people (N) and the government (G), deteriorated. The people suffered, and their incentive to work, produce and innovate was adversely affected. The position of women also declined gradually as a result of the overall decline within the framework of circular causation. They are now illiterate, secluded, and generally deprived of the rights that Islam has given them. Any society where nearly half of the population becomes marginalized and is unable to play its potential role in keeping with its talents is bound to have stunted growth. Hodgson is perhaps right in saying that the 'civilization of Islam as it has existed is far from a clear expression of the Islamic faith'. (Hodgson, 1977, Vol. 1, p. 71).

The non-implementation of Islamic values in the highly crucial political field, always remained a source of contention between the rulers and the *sufis* and religious scholars (*ulama*). The more conscientious of them, who also happened to be the most vocal, began to be persecuted. Consequently, they started avoiding the royal courts and became confined to their monasteries (*khanqahs*) or religious schools (*madrasahs*). This had a far-reaching adverse impact on Muslim society. The *sufis* and the *ulama* lost touch with the realities of a rapidly changing environment and *fiqh* (Islamic jurisprudence) could not, accordingly, develop with the needs of the time. It became nearly stagnant. This deprived Islam of the dynamism which it reflected in the earlier centuries. The seclusion of the *ulama* also deprived the rulers of the restraint that existed previously on their arbitrariness. Sycophants, who did not and could not make any worthwhile contribution to the society, began surrounding the rulers and scooped all the benefits by telling them what they wished to hear.

A crucial question that arises here is, why did the *sufis* and the *ulama* not struggle for political reform and supremacy of human rights, as enshrined in the Islamic value system, instead of getting themselves secluded in their monasteries and religious schools. They did. There were a number of revolts, starting with the Prophet's own grandsons against Yazid, the first to succeed on the basis of heredity. However, all these revolts were suppressed ruthlessly. This is because such revolts were generally localized. The slow means of communication and transport at that time did not make it possible to organize a widespread revolt.

When the procedure for peaceful succession of rulers through the consensus of the community got removed, succession generally took place through court conspiracies, internecine wars of succession, and military coups, which drained the resources of Muslims, sapped their creative energies, and led to their overall decline. Transfer of power even among members of the same family was not always without bloodshed and the army seems to have played a decisive role in such acquisition and transfer. Succession wars almost always heightened insecurity, which in turn adversely affected production and trade, particularly when taxes already paid to the previous regime had to be repaid to the new regime to help it solve its financial problems. Sanctity of individual life, honour, and property, which Islam had guaranteed, became violated.

The influence of Islam reversed the decline during a number of periods when honest and far-sighted rulers took over the helm of affairs. Even though they were not elected by the people, they pursued the right policies which enabled Muslim countries to develop rapidly. However, all these intermittent periods of movement in the positive direction helped reduce only the pace of decline. They could not reverse the long-run declining trend. The corrupt and incompetent rulers who succeeded them could not be removed as they can be in a democratic environment. The virus of political illegitimacy gradually infected all other aspects of the society and the economy (S, N. W, j and g) through circular causation. The Muslim world started losing the momentum of development that had been triggered by Islam to the extent that it could not successfully address the external shocks that it encountered. It could not, therefore, prevent its colonization by the European countries. Kramer has, hence, rightly pointed out, in step with Ibn Khaldun, that 'the causes of the decline were to be sought mainly within the body politic' (Kramer et al., 1993, p. 197).

4.3.2   Is Islam an Impediment to Growth?

Some scholars have argued that even though Islam may have promoted development in the past, the Muslim world is poor and underdeveloped today as a result of certain Islamic institutions that were 'designed to serve laudable economic objectives', but had the unintended effect of serving as 'obstacles to economic development' (Kuran, 2004, pp. 71–72). Noland has, however, concluded in a recent unpublished study that 'in general this is not borne out by econometric analysis either at the cross-country or within-country level' and that 'Islam does not appear to be a drag on growth or an anchor on development as alleged. If anything, the opposite appears to be true' (Noland, n.d., pp. 26–27).

Nevertheless, it should be worthwhile looking at the three Islamic intuitions which, have, according to Kuran, proved to be inimical to growth. These are:

1. Islam's egalitarian inheritance system, which did not allow primo-geniture to take root in Muslim societies;
2. Absence of the concepts of limited liability and juridical or legal personality in Islam; and
3. The Islamic institution of *waqf* (philanthropic trust) (Kuran, 2004, pp. 71–72).

The first two of these are claimed to have hindered accumulation of capital and the formation of corporations, both of which are essential for accelerated development. The third institution is alleged to have blocked vast resources into projects which became dysfunctional over time (Kuran, 2004).

4.3.3 Absence of Primogeniture

There is no doubt that Islam does stand for an egalitarian inheritance system in which there can be absolutely no room for primogeniture. However, Kuran has not substantiated his contention that primogeniture contributed to the development of large enterprises in the West. Primogeniture served primarily the needs of feudalism by ensuring that the fief did not get broken up among the many sons of the vassal or tenant and that only one person remained responsible for providing the required military and other services to the lord (Rheinstein and Glendon, 1994, p. 641). Feudalism, however, enabled the lords 'to extract a rent by extra-economic coercion' as a result of which the peasant labourers had 'no *economic* incentive to work diligently and efficiently for the lords'. This 'limited the agricultural economy's capacity to improve' (Brenner, 1987, pp. 309 and 311, italics in the original). Consequently, feudalism got buried in Western Europe by 1500, 'when capitalism as it is known today was not yet born and the industrial revolution was fully two-and-a-half centuries into the future' (North and Thomas, 1973, p. 102). The demise of feudalism weakened primogeniture except among ruling families. In America, it was swept away during the course of the American Revolution while in Europe, it collapsed during the French Revolution. The Napoleonic Code took care to prevent its reestablishment (Rheinstein and Glendon, 1994, p. 642). If primogeniture had been a useful institution, it would not have been swept away in both Europe and America.

The onset of economic development in Europe depended rather on 'the transformation of the feudal property relations into capitalistic property relations' (Brenner, 1987, p. 133; Dobb, 1946; Hilton, 1969). Hardly any scholar, therefore, mentions primogeniture among the causes of the industrial revolution. The causes that are emphasised include the enforcement of property rights by democratic governments and the boost that the spread of education, research and technology provided to development (see North, 1990, pp. 130–40; and Checkland, 1987). Arnold Toynbee, uncle of the great historian Arnold J. Toynbee, has placed great stress on the inventions that helped provide the technology needed for the revolution in agriculture, manufacturing, and transport (Toynbee, 1961). In the agricultural sector, the steam plough helped bring about the consolidation of small farms into large ones and also made possible the tillage of inferior soils through the enclosure system. In the manufacturing sector, the spinning jenny, steam engine and power loom facilitated the establishment of large factories. In the transport sector, the coming of the railroad in 1830 brought about a substantial expansion in the market as well as trade (pp. 58–66). 'The new class of great capitalist employers made enormous fortunes' (p. 65). It was this fortune, along with the technology, and not primogeniture, that made the establishment of large businesses possible, and thereby, created a need for the corporation.

However, even if it is assumed that primogeniture did play a role in the development of Europe and America, there is no reason to assume that it is indispensable for the development of all countries. Japan and East Asian tigers have developed without primogeniture having played any role in their development. Some of the factors that played a crucial role in their development were good governance, land reforms, social equality, and cultural values (see Chapra, 1992, pp. 173–81). Of these, land reforms had an effect which was the opposite of primogeniture. They reduced the average family holding in Japan to about 2.5 acres of arable land (Jansen, 1973–74, p. 88). Even in 1985, the average farm size amounted to 1.2 acres in Japan, with only 4 per cent of all farms operating on land of more than 3 hectares (7.41 acres) (Australian Bureau of Agricultural and Research Economics, 1988). According to Sachs, 'land reforms in these countries were more extensive than in any other case in modern history' (Sachs, 1987, p. 301). These reforms destroyed the power base of the feudal lords and virtually eliminated farm tenancy, which was widespread before the reforms, and had the far-reaching effect of substantially reducing income and wealth inequalities. The higher income of small farmers plus the cultural values of simple living enabled them to save more. The high rate of saving kept inflation and interest rates at a relatively lower level and enabled rural as well as urban development without unduly large monetary and credit expansion and external borrowing (for details, see Chapra, 1992, pp. 173–81).

4.3.4 Juridical Entity and Limited Liability

Kuran is certainly right in asserting that a legal entity with limited liability of shareholders is indispensable for large-scale investment. However, the seeds of both these concepts existed in the classical discussions of Islamic jurisprudence. The closest approximation to the corporate legal entity were the *bayt al-mal* (public treasury), mosque property, and *waqfs* (al-Khafif, 1962, pp. 22–27, Udovitch, 1970, p. 99; and Abdullah, n.d., pp. 235–39). Even the concept of limited liability existed in the *mudarabah* (commenda) form of business organization (Chapra, 1985, pp. 255–56; Usmani, 1998, pp. 221–28), and has been extended without any difficulty to the corporation in modern times (Abdullah, n.d., p. 239).

It is unrealistic to expect that everything necessary for development would be specified in the Qur'an or the *Sunnah* (the Prophetic traditions). One of the most important and well-known principles of Islamic jurisprudence is that whatever is not specifically prohibited is allowed. Since very few things have been specifically prohibited, there is a great potential for the evolution of institutions needed for promoting development. This did take place in Muslim societies, as Kuran has himself acknowledged by stating that: 'the distinguishing economic features of classical Islamic civilization evolved over the next three centuries' (Kuran, 2004, p. 72). Such evolution took place in accordance with need. This was in keeping with the natural evolutionary process in the development of institutions in human societies. There is hardly any society where all the institutions needed for development in the future evolved together in the very initial phase of development. This raises the question of why the need for corporate form did not arise earlier in Muslim societies.

The answer to this question needs to be found not in Islamic teachings but rather in political illegitimacy as a result of which the property rights enshrined in Islamic teachings did not get effectively enforced. North has rightly argued that insecure property rights 'result in using technologies that employ little fixed capital and do not entail long-term agreements. Firms will typically be small' (North, 1990, p. 65). This is what happened in the Muslim world. If property rights had been secure, the momentum of development that had become built up from the 8th to the 14th centuries would perhaps have continued, creating the need for replacing small firms by large business organizations.

There is no reason to assume that the increased need for finance that this would have created may not have led to the development of the corporation, the seeds for which, as indicated earlier, were already present in Islamic jurisprudence. In the 20th century when development started once again in the Muslim world, the need arose for large business establishments and the jurists had no difficulty in approving the corporate form of business organization. If there was anything in Islam against it, there would not have been such great unanimity in its acceptance. Lal has rightly observed that 'it is not Islamic institutions themselves that have hindered development but dysfunctional etatism and dirigisme which, when reversed in the Muslim parts of Southeast Asia, have developed Promethean intensive growth' (Lal, 1998, p. 66).

Even in medieval England, the earliest corporations were boroughs, guilds, churches and charities (Hessen, 1987, p. 675). This is similar to what happened in Islam. These earlier corporations in medieval England did not, however, become the forerunners of today's corporations until they became fully private, which happened at the end of the 17th century (Hessen, 1987, p. 678), long after the death of feudalism and the weakening of primogeniture. Nevertheless, it was not until the 19th century that the limited liability principle got established in both the US and the UK (Oesterle, 1994, pp. 590–91).

The agricultural and scientific revolution that took place in early Islam could not get transformed into the industrial revolution because of a number of factors, the most important of which was political illegitimacy. Insecure property rights resulting from this forced people to hide their wealth to avoid its becoming subject to unjust taxation and outright confiscation. Firms remained small. It was not possible for large business enterprises to develop in such an environment. If this had not been the case, the absence of primogeniture should have in fact had the effect of leading to the establishment of corporations by motivating people to put together their capital as shares to form bigger and viable business enterprises.

4.3.5 *Waqf* (Philanthropic Trust)

As far as the institution of *waqf* is concerned, it developed in the Muslim world during the early days of Islam, long before it did in the West, and made a significant contribution to the development of Muslim societies. As Kuran has himself acknowledged, the *waqfs* supplied a vast array of social services (Kuran, 2004, p. 754). These included education, health, science laboratories, the construction and maintenance of mosques, orphanages, lodging for students, teachers and travellers, bridges, wells, roads and hospitals (see for example Makdisi, 1981, pp. 35–74; Hodgson, 1977, Vol. 2, p. 124; Kahf, 2004; and Ahmed, 2004). This happened when the *waqfs* were properly regulated and supervised (Inalcik, 1970, p. 307). However, when effective regulation and supervision did not continue and led to corruption, loss of the original deeds, lack of proper maintenance, and misuse and misappropriation of *waqf* properties (Ahmed, 2004, pp. 42–44), they became dysfunctional as Kuran has rightly pointed out. The tax system also played a significant role in hindering the further development of the *waqf* system. Islam cannot be blamed for what happened. However, the *waqf* institution is once again getting an impetus in the Muslim world because of the recognition of property rights and the renewed private initiative along with government support, regulation and supervision (Ahmed, 2004, pp. 42–44). It is hoped that it will once again start playing the same crucial role in the development of social and physical infrastructure through private philanthropy as it did in the past.

The gist of this whole analysis is that it is not Islam which has led to the relative poverty and underdevelopment of Muslim societies. It is rather the violation of property rights and the decline in official support for education, research and development of technology, that were prevalent in the earlier centuries of Islam and that democratic governments have ensured in the West. It is this that made large-scale business possible in the West and, thereby created the need for the corporation. Illegitimate governments, not accountable before the people, are generally not under pressure to enforce property rights and serve the interests of the people. Development, therefore, suffers. Hardly anyone would agree with Kuran's contention that 'such [authoritarian] governments were all governed at least until the nineteenth century, and in some cases until more recently, by Islamic law' (Kuran, 2004, p. 83).

4.4   THE PRESENT POSITION

4.4.1   Absence of Democracy

Six hundred years have passed since Ibn Khaldun wrote. The overall Muslim decline has continued persistently relative to major industrial countries even though it has not been a straight line phenomenon and some Muslim countries have done better than others. The primary reason for this overall decline is that political illegitimacy, which had triggered the decline, has continued until today in most Muslim countries. The Muslim world, which is much larger and diversified now than what it was in Ibn Khaldun's times, has not been able until now to establish a procedure for the orderly transfer of the reins of power to the most upright and competent in the eyes of the people as desired by the Qur'an (49:13), the efficient and equitable use of public resources in accordance with the *Shari'ah*, and the free and fearless criticism of government policies. Only 13, or a little less than 23 per cent, of the 57 member countries of the Organization of the Islamic Conference (OIC) had democracy in 2002,[12] while 44, or 77 per cent, did not. Of these 44 countries, 31 have pseudo-democracy, five have absolute monarchy, three have dictatorship, and five are in transition (based on data given in the Index of ElectionWorld.org).

However, even the Muslim countries that do have democracy, have it only in a formal sense: they hold elections and the democratic structures provide an alternance of power. Powerful vested interests, nevertheless, succeed in getting elected and re-elected. The poor and disadvantaged are in most cases not free to vote as they wish and are poorly represented in the echelons of power (see Besley and Burgess, 2003, p. 17). Democracy has, thus, not been able to take hold in a real sense. While effective democratic processes have gone a long way in ensuring good governance and effective use of public resources for development in the Western world, the Muslim world has lagged behind because of the near absence of accountability of the rulers and of good governance which democracy tends to bring.[13]

4.4.2 Low Economic Performance

The absence of democracy has led to a number of evils. One of these is lack of freedom of the press. Only four Muslim countries[14] are free, 14 are partly free and 39 are not free (based on data given in Freedom of the Press 2004, www.freedomhouse.org).[15] The inability to criticize the government in the news media or other forums like the parliament (*shura*) contributes to poor governance, lack of transparency and unhealthy policies. It also promotes corruption and misuse of public resources for the private benefit of the rich and the powerful. Empirical studies have led to a consensus in economic literature that corruption and poor governance have substantial adverse effects on development (Kaufmann, Kraay, and Zoido-Lobaton, 1999; Knack and Keefer, 1995; and Mauro, 1995 and 2004).

The Corruption Perceptions Index for the year 2002 prepared by the Berlin-based Transparency International includes 133 countries and ranges from 10 (least corrupt) to zero (most corrupt).[16] A score of 5 on this index indicates a borderline country. (www.transparency international corruption perception index). Only five Muslim countries are above this borderline with scores ranging from 5.2 to 6.3. Twenty-seven countries fall below this borderline. No data are available for the rest. The likelihood, however, is that most of these other countries for which no data are available may also lie below the borderline. This is so in spite of the fact that the Qur'an emphatically prohibits wrongful acquisition of wealth and the taking of bribes (2:188 and 4:29).

Corruption, combined with lack of freedom of expression, tends to corrupt the courts as well, in which case, there is little likelihood that the power elite will get punished. When the wrongdoers do not get punished, the vice tends to spread until it becomes locked-in through the operation of path dependence and self-reinforcing mechanisms. It then becomes difficult to root out the evil. If only the poor get punished, then there is a rise in discontent and a decline in solidarity between the government (G) and the people (N). This contributes to social and political instability, which is among the major factors that hurt economic development.

As a result of corruption, a substantial amount of the scarce public resources of these countries gets diverted to the building of palaces and the financing of luxury and conspicuous consumption of the power elite, making the governments unable to spend adequately on education, health, infrastructure construction and the provision of public services needed for accelerated development. Corruption also raises the trans-actions costs of the private sector. Savings, therefore, go abroad and domestic investment tends to decline. This is bound to affect growth as is confirmed by the inferior performance of most Muslim countries. Even though the total population of the 57 Muslim countries is 1,331 million and constitutes a little over 21 per cent of the world population of 6,199 million,[17] their total PPP adjusted GNP is only \$3,993 billion which is only 8.2 per cent of the world PPP adjusted GNP of \$48,462 billion (World Bank, 2004, p. 253). Only four Muslim countries, all of whom happen to be oil-producing, are able to get into the high income category (HIC) and only six into the upper middle income (UMC) category. Eighteen fall into the low middle income category (LMC) and 29 fall into the low income category (LIC) (World Bank, 2004, p. 251).

Education, which received high priority in the early history of Islam and which was one of the causes of its rise, has not received the emphasis it needs in government budgets. Accordingly, the average adult illiteracy rate in these countries was 32 per cent in 2002 (Islamic Development Bank, 2005, p. 13). This means that around 426 million people are illiterate and unable to contribute their full potential to development. All these countries together have only 600 universities whereas the US alone has 1975, or more than three times as many, when its population is less than one-quarter (www. universities worldwide). Democracy, education and development reinforced each other in the Western world. Education promoted development and development led to a rise in the demand for education, which it was possible to satisfy because of state support for it as a result of the rise in its revenue. Education and development together helped reinforce democracy.

4.4.3 Human Development Index

No wonder only five Muslim countries score high on the UNDP Human Development Index (HDI), while 31 and 21 get medium and low scores respectively (UNDP, 2003, pp. 237–40). However, the problem with HDI is that it incorporates only three variables: life expectancy at birth, literacy, and GDP per capita adjusted for purchasing power parity. It thus reflects the restricted framework of Development Economics before it recognized the crucial role played in development by social, cultural and political institutions, which Ibn Khaldun emphasized in his model and which Development Economics has now belatedly come to recognize.

It is, therefore, necessary to prepare a more comprehensive index. This would lead to the inclusion of a number of other variables, including justice, family integrity, social harmony, mental peace, reward for merit and hard work, and minimization of crime, tension and anomie. Also important are democracy, freedom of expression, equitable distribution of income and wealth, and an honest and effective judiciary. Data may not be available about all of these. It is, nevertheless, important to construct as comprehensive an index as possible and to strive for the collection of data not available now. It may not be surprising if Muslim countries, which do not score high on the existing HDI, may perhaps turn out to be even more so on the scale of a more comprehensive index. The primary reason for this in Ibn Khaldun's model is political illegitimacy which has gradually vitiated all the socio-economic and political institutions of these countries over the last several centuries through the operation of circular causation so that it is now difficult to distinguish the cause from the effect. There is, therefore, need for comprehensive reform. Paying attention to only economic or even political variables for promoting economic development in Muslim countries may not be enough.

4.5 THE NEED FOR REFORM

The question is: where to start? While all socio-economic and political factors need to be given attention, maximum stress needs to be given to the reform of human beings, who are the main locomotive behind the rise or fall of any civilization and whom Ibn Khaldun made the centre of his analysis. This is in keeping with the teachings of Islam as well as most major religions. They can help promote the development of their society only if their upbringing, character, ability, and mental outlook are right.

It is, therefore, necessary to transform the individual into a better human being. Maximum attention needs to be given to his education and socio-economic uplift. Merely a rise in literacy and income may not be sufficient. It is also necessary to raise the individuals' moral calibre, which neoclassical economics generally tends to ignore, but which is absolutely indispensable, as Nigel Lawson has rightly acknowledged: 'no political or economic order can long survive except on a moral base' (Lawson, 1995, p. 35). Rasing the moral calibre will help create the qualities of honesty, integrity and conscientiousness which are necessary for promoting development. It may, however, be difficult to raise the moral calibre unless poverty is also addressed simultaneously and justice, dignity, equality and self-respect are ensured for every individual in society. These are all interrelated and it may be difficult to bring about a sustained improvement in one without an improvement in the others.

4.5.1 Need for Political Reform

Reform and socio-economic uplift of human beings would, however, be relatively less difficult if the political system is also supportive. The political illegitimacy now prevailing in the Muslim world is a great stumbling block. Political reform, along with freedom of expression, honest judiciary and accountability of the power elite is, therefore, one of the dire needs of most Muslim countries. It would help reduce, with some time lag, corruption and mismanagement, and ensure the efficient use of public resources for education, health, and rural as well as urban development, leading thereby to socio-economic uplift. It would also help in the introduction of land reforms, thereby not only enabling the peasant to get a just share of his existing output but also providing him with the resources that he needs to acquire training along with better seeds, tools and fertilizers to raise his future output. The Muslim world would then be able to generate the kind of agricultural surplus needed for investment in technological, industrial and infrastructure development – the surplus that the Muslim world was able to generate in the earlier centuries and which Japan, South Korea and Taiwan were able to generate in recent history. The land reforms introduced in these countries by the Occupation Authorities helped destroy the power base of the feudal lords (see Chapra, 1993, pp. 175–77).

   The crucial question, however, is how to bring about political reform in countries where illegitimacy is well-entrenched, and where the governments use all forms of repression to curb any struggle for political reform. Armed struggle has, nevertheless, to be ruled out. Armed struggle has, rarely succeeded in Muslim countries in the past, and is even less likely to succeed now, when the governments have more sophisticated means of suppressing it and of torturing and impoverishing those involved. Any effort to overthrow prevailing governments by resort to force and violence may lead to enormous losses in terms of life and property. It may also destabilize the societies, slow down development and reform, and accentuate the existing problems. The suffering of the poor and the underprivileged may be unbearably high.

4.5.2 Can Peaceful Struggle be Successful?

The best strategy for political reform is peaceful and non-violent struggle, even though this may appear to be time-consuming. This brings to mind a number of questions. One of these is whether there is any hope of success through peaceful struggle. There are a number of factors that inspire one's confidence in the future. The international environment is now unfriendly towards illegitimate governments and these have been gradually falling.[18] The international environment is also against corruption and money laundering, making it difficult to hide ill-gained wealth. Moreover, domestic pressures for the introduction of democracy are also gaining momentum in practically all Muslim countries. The spread of education and the gradual improvement in the economic condition of the poor will help weaken the existing power structures which thrive on the illiteracy and poverty of the masses. Establishment of democratic governments, even if they are initially dominated by feudal lords, may tend to weaken the power structures over time because of the voting power of the electorate. The pressures on elected governments to fulfil their promises, may also help reduce corruption and military spending,[19] divert more resources to education, health and development, and also make possible the introduction of land reforms. The resulting improvement in the socio-economic condition of the rural poor, which is already taking place to some extent as a result of the remittances of expatriate labour, will give rise to a broader and healthier middle class willing and able to fight for its rights democratically.

Globalization is also acting as a check on despotic governments. Absence of freedom of expression domestically has become substantially offset by criticism in the international news media. The spread of news through radio and satellite television, fax machines, and the Internet has frustrated the efforts of repressive governments to censor external criticism and to prevent its circulation among the people inside the repressed country. Therefore, even if governments are not accountable domestically, they have become accountable internationally for their corruption and human rights violations. Though this is not sufficient, it will tend to exercise a healthy influence on the future course of events.

Making democracy successful in these countries may not, however, be an easy task. This is because of the die-hard autocratic attitude of the present ruling elite, who will perhaps continue to use all means at their disposal to win elections. Their attitudes may not change easily and they may try to use a number of contrivances to avoid true accountability. There may not, hence, be a significant difference between the behaviour of dictators and elected rulers in the initial phase. The real difference will, however, come gradually with the success of the struggle to get democracy buttressed by international monitoring of elections and a free press as well as a number of badly needed legal, political and judicial reforms. One of the most important of these reforms will have to be a restructuring of the election process, to remove, or at least minimize, the influence of money, power, and manipulation in the choice of political leadership. Excessive campaign spending works in favour of the wealthy and the powerful and against the worthy middle class candidates. It also invites corruption by the post-election effort of successful candidates to recover the amount spent or to provide benefits to the financiers. Such reform may, however, meet great resistance and take time to be put in place successfully. Incompetent and corrupt political authority accentuates injustice, impoverishes the people, and retards development.

The historically inherited land holding and land tenure systems are also a great hindrance to democracy by being among the primary causes of inequities and underdevelopment and of several economic, social and political problems. Exploitation of the peasants renders them incapable of even feeding themselves and their families, leave alone generation of the surplus needed for investment in improved seeds, fertilizers and tools, and the establishment of micro industries in rural as well as urban areas to increase output and income. Such exploitation tends to weaken their moral fibre and induces them to lie and cheat. It hurts their pride and their incentive to work. Their low productivity and output further reduces their ability to save and invest. It also deprives them of the education and training that they need to raise their productivity and economic condition. The peasants, who constitute a preponderant majority of the population, are unable to vote freely to choose political representatives of their own choice. The feudal lords are also able to influence the armed forces and the government bureaucracy as well as the judiciary and the police through their sons and relatives, who occupy important positions in these institutions, and the use of their power and resources to suppress all opposition. The entire government machinery thus becomes their handmaid to serve their vested interest. The deprivation of the peasantry does not lead to higher savings on the part of the feudal lords, who either fritter away their income on luxury and conspicuous consumption or invest it abroad. This forces the country to resort to large doses of external borrowing which raises the debt-servicing burden and reduces the resources available for development.

4.5.3 Can the Western World Help?

The West can play a catalytic role in the restoration of democracy in Muslim countries. It cannot, however, play this role by the use of force. Force has never worked and will never work. The use of force can only create hatred for the West and lead to a clash of civilizations which will be bad for all, but in particular for the Muslim world because it will slow down not only its development but also the pace of badly needed socio-economic and political reforms. The best strategy for the West would be to help in the field of education and socio-economic uplift which it is capable of doing. It can also help in monitoring elections and promoting legal and institutional reform. This will help create a better climate not only for accelerated reform and development but also for mutual cooperation and globalization.

4.5.4 Can Islam Play a Catalytic Role Once Again?

A crucial question which arises here is whether the revival of Islam that is now taking place in the Muslim world can be of any help in reforming and developing Muslim societies. Can it help them realize justice and socio-economic and political reform as it did in the classical period? The general consensus in the Muslim world seems to be in favour of a positive answer. This was also acknowledged by Ramsey Clark, US Attorney General in the Lyndon Johnson Administration, when he stated that Islam 'is probably the most compelling spiritual and moral force on earth today' (Clark, 1997).

This may perhaps be because Islam is the only living reality in the Muslim world that has the charisma to attract the masses, unite them in spite of their great diversity, and motivate them to act righteously in spite of centuries of degeneration (see Etzioni, 2004). It has its own programme for comprehensive moral, social, economic and political reform which is more suitable for these countries than any programme that may be imported from abroad. Its strong stress on socio-economic justice, accountability of the political authority, rule of law, moral values, and character building, combined with its strategy of using education and dialogue for bringing about change, should prove to be a great blessing for the Muslim world. It encourages simple living, which would help reduce conspicuous consumption and thereby weaken one of the major causes of corruption and low saving and investment. It can also help inculcate in the people a number of other desirable qualities like honesty and integrity, punctuality, conscientiousness, diligence, frugality, self-reliance, and concern for the rights and well-being of others – qualities which are necessary to raise efficiency as well as equity. It places a strong stress on family and social solidarity, which are essential for even the survival of a society, leave alone its development.

Since Islamic revival has become a deeply rooted phenomenon in the Muslim world, any effort to undo Islam and transplant secularism in its place would necessitate the use of force. This would have tragic results in the Muslim world. It would accentuate social conflict and instigate violence, which may be difficult to bring under control. What may take its place is the prevailing materialist and hedonist philosophy, which would promote conspicuous consumption, sexual promiscuity, and self-gratification. This will tend to further weaken the moral fibre, encourage living beyond means, reduce saving and investment, worsen imbalances, aggravate inequities, and weaken family and social solidarity. The consequence of this for development and socio-economic uplift should not be difficult for anyone to figure out (see also Richards, 2003, and Etzioni, 2004).

The first ruthless effort to undo Islam by a Muslim government in a Muslim country took place in Turkey. This led to an excessive role in the government for the military, which exercised real authority in spite of an outward facade of democracy and removed duly elected governments four times over the last forty years; 1960, 1971, 1981 and 1997. In spite of the ruthless use of force by the army to undo Islam it could not succeed and Islam is having a revival even in Turkey. 'If ever there was a Kemalist wish for Islam to wither away, it has not done so and is unlikely to do so in the future when human rights are expected to flourish rather than diminish' (Mehmet, 1990, p. 125).

This does not, of course, mean that there is no need for reform in the present-day understanding of Islam. The Islamic stress on justice, brotherhood of mankind, and tolerance seems to have in general become substantially diluted over the centuries in certain sectors of Muslim societies and so is its emphasis on character building. Instead, there is greater emphasis on appearances and trivialities. Some of the socio-economic and political institutions which Islam came to abolish have become a part of the Islamic panorama through lack of proper education, path dependence, and self-reinforcing mechanisms. This is due largely to historical factors arising from centuries of degeneration and inequities followed by foreign occupation. It may not be possible to correct the situation without creating a proper understanding of Islam. This would demand a substantial change in the curricula of all educational institutions, including the *madrasahs*. Murad Hofmann has rightly emphasized: 'I know of nothing better to propose than to urge the Muslim world to become 'fundamentalist' in the original sense of the word – to go back to the real foundations of our Islamic creed, and to analyze the factors which were instrumental for the Madina, Andalus and Abbasid experiments' (Hofmann, 1966, p. 86).

4.6 PROSPECTS FOR THE FUTURE

Prospects for the future seem to be bright because the reversal of the tide desired by Ibn Khaldun 600 years ago seems to be taking place now after the independence of most Muslim countries from foreign domination in the middle of the 20th century. Political illegitimacy, nevertheless, continues but is losing ground. Even the major industrial countries, with whose moral and material support it has thrived, seem to have now realized that the spread of democracy and the socio-economic uplift of the masses is also in their own long-run interest. The writing on the horizon clearly indicates a movement in the direction of democracy, along with land reforms, a free press, a strong and independent judiciary, and the growth of effective and impartial institutions for detecting and punishing corruption and inefficiency. This will ultimately promote the use of public resources for development and well-being of the people through the elimination of illiteracy, provision of better quality education, improvement of health facilities, construction of infrastructure beyond the showpiece highways and buildings, and the development of these countries. Female education is also spreading. This will enable women to not only assert for their rights more successfully but also to ensure proper upbringing of their children and to contribute richly to the development of their societies. Democracy will force political as well as religious parties to moderate their views to make themselves acceptable to broader sectors of the population, thus increasing tolerance and reducing extremist views. Moreover, the ongoing revival of Islam may make it possible to have material advance accompanied by moral uplift, justice and social harmony, which are important for providing the needed social and ethical capital for sustained development. In other words, a number of indicators point toward the reversal of Ibn Khaldun's cycle of circular causation from the negative to the positive direction.

NOTES

* The first part of this chapter draws heavily from Chapra (2000). The views expressed in this chapter do not necessarily reflect the views of IRTI/IDB. He is grateful to Drs Ausaf Ahmad, Sami Al-Suwailem, Tariqullah Khan, Habib Ahmed and Salman Syed Ali and two anonymous referees for their valuable comments on an earlier draft and

to Shaikh Muhammad Rashid and Muhammad Rasul Haque for the efficient secretarial assistance provided by them in the preparation of this chapter.

1. For details of this Index, see the United Nation's Development Program (UNDP) (1990), pp. 1–16.

2. Some of these include: Hitti (1958), Arsalan (1962), Issawi (1966 and 1970); Lambton (1970); Saunders (1966); Inalcik (1970); Inalcik and Quataert (1994); Musallam (1981); Imam (1977); Najjar (1989); and Kuran (1997). Lewis (1962) gives the views of Lutfi Pasha, Kochu Bey, Hajji Khalifah, Huseyn Hazarfenn and Sari Mehmed Pasha on the causes of Ottoman decline.

3. The full name of the book in Arabic (given in the list of References) may be freely translated as 'The Book of Lessons and Record of Cause and Effect in the History of Arabs, Persians and Berbers and their Powerful Contemporaries'. Several different editions of the *Muqaddimah* are now available in Arabic. The one I have used in writing this chapter is that published in Cairo by al-Maktabah al-Tijariyyah al-Kubra without any indication of the year of publication. It has the advantage of showing all vowel marks which makes the reading relatively easier. The *Muqaddimah* was translated into English in three volumes by Franz Rosenthal. Its first edition was published in 1958 and the second in 1967. Selections from the *Muqaddimah* by Charles Issawi were published in 1950 under the title, *An Arab Philosophy of History: Selections from the Prolegomena of Ibn Khaldun of Tunis* (1322–1406). Even though I have given the reference to Rosenthal's translation (R) wherever I have referred to Ibn Khaldun's *Muqaddimah* (M), the translations used in this chapter are my own.

4. The term *Shari'ah* refers literally to the beliefs and institutions or rules of behaviour of any society, but has now become associated with those prescribed by Islam.

5. The same advice is repeated on p. 287 (R: II, p. 105). Ibn Khaldun himself says that his book is a *tafsir* (elaboration) of this advice (p. 40), which was given by Mobedhan, a Zoroastrian priest, to Bahram ibn Bahram and reported by al-Mas'udi in his *Muruj al-Dhahab*, 1988 (Vol. 1, p. 253). Ibn Khaldun acknowledges this fact (p. 40), but also simultaneously clarifies that 'We became aware of these principles with God's help and without the instruction of Aristotle or the teaching of Mobedhan' (p. 40).

6. For a more detailed picture of Ibn Khaldun's model, see Chapra (2000, pp. 145–172). See also Spengler (1964); Boulakia (1971); and Mirakhor (1987).

7. The words used by Ibn Khaldun throughout the *Muqaddimah* are *mu'dhin* and *mufdi*; which mean 'inviting' or 'leading' towards something. However, I have used the expression 'trigger mechanism' which is now used more commonly in English to convey the same meaning.

8. The functions of the state are discussed by him in a number of places in the *Muqaddimah*. He states in one place, for example, that: the ruler 'must defend and protect the subjects, whom God has entrusted to him, from their enemies. He must enforce restraining laws and prevent them from committing aggression against each other's person and property. He must ensure the safety of roads. He must enable them to serve their interests. He must supervise whatever affects their livelihood and mutual dealings, including food stuffs and weights and measures, to prevent cheating. He must look after the mint to protect the currency used by people from forgery ... . A noble wiseman has said that "moving mountains from their places is easier for me than winning the hearts of people"' (M, p 235; R: II, p. 3).

9. Ibn Khaldun classifies political authority into three kinds. The first is the 'natural or normal' (*tabi'i*) authority which enables everyone to satisfy self-interest (*al-ghard*) and sensual pleasures (*al-shahwah*); the second is the rational political authority (*siyasah aqliyyah*), which enables everyone to serve this-worldly self-interest and to prevent harm in accordance with certain rationally derived principles; and the third is

the morally based political authority (*siyasah diniyyah* or *khilafah*) which enables everyone to realize well-being in this world as well as the Hereafter in accordance with the teachings of the *Shari'ah* (M, pp. 190–91; R: I, pp. 387–88). If one were to use modern terminology for these three different forms of governments, one could perhaps call them the secular laissez-faire or passive state, the secular welfare state, and the Islamic welfare state or *khilafah*. (For the Islamic welfare state, see Chapra 1979 and 1992 (Chapters 1, 3 and 5).

10. For some details on these revolutions, see Watson (1981 and 1983); and Sarton (1927).

11. After discussing the transformation of *khilafah* into royal authority or kingship in a whole chapter (M, pp. 202–8; R: I, pp. 414–28), Ibn Khaldun concludes; 'you have seen how the form of government got transformed into kingship. Nevertheless, there remained [in the beginning] the meaning of *khilafah* which required observance of religious teachings and adherence to the path of truth … . Then the characteristic traits of *khilafah* disappeared and only its name remained. The form of government became kingship pure and simple. Acquisition of power reached its extreme limit and force came to be used for serving self-interest through the arbitrary gratification of desires and pleasures' (M, p. 208; R: I, p. 427).

12. Democracy is defined by the Index of ElectionWorld as a country in which democratic structures provide an alternance of power. Pseudo-democracy is defined as a country having democratic structures but without a real chance for an alternance of power.

13. There is a great deal of literature available now on the positive effect of democracy on good governance and of good governance on development (see, for example, Mulligan et al., 2004; Kaufmann and Kraay, 2002; Hall and Jones, 1999; and Kaufmann et al., 1999). A few authors have, however, argued that democracy hinders economic growth, particularly, in less developed countries, because democratic governments are unable to implement vigorously policies which are necessary for accelerated development (Sirowy and Inkles, 1990; Johnson, 1964; and MacIntyre, 1996). This line of thinking gained prominence during the heyday of the Soviet Union and of China's great leap forward, but seems to have fewer followers now.

14. Wherever the term Muslim countries is used in this chapter, it refers to the 57 members of the Organization of the Islamic Conference (OIC), which is like the United Nations of Muslim Countries.

15. The definition of free, partly free and not free is based on each country's prevailing legal (0–30 points), political (0–40 points) and economic (0–30 points) environment affecting the press. The higher the restrictions, the higher the number of points the country gets. A country's final score is based on the total of these three criteria. A score of 0 to 30 places the country in the free press group; 31 to 60 in the partly free group, and 61 to 100 in the not free group.

16. Corruption is defined by the Transparency International 'as the abuse of public office for private gain, and measures the degree to which corruption is perceived to exist among a country's public officials and politicians'.

17. There are Muslims in non-Muslim countries and non-Muslims in Muslim counties. This figure does not, therefore, indicate the total number of Muslims all over the world. The total number of Muslims is estimated to be somewhere between 1.3 and 1.8 billion.

18. In 1974, only 39 countries – one in every four – were democratic worldwide. Today 115 countries – a little more than two in three – use open elections to choose their national leadership. (The figure for 1974 is from the World Bank, 1997, p. 111, while the latest data are as of 14 January 2004 from www.ElectionWorld.org).

19. Global military spending had fallen significantly from $1.2 trillion in 1985 to $809 billion in 1998. However, it rose to $950 billion in 2003. This is unfortunate but is

supposed to be primarily due to the US attack on Iraq. However, the rise may not
continue because of the public criticism of the unproved assumptions on which the
pre-emptive strike policy was based and the huge budgetary deficits it has caused
(World Military Spending, 16 June 2004 www.globalissues.org/geopolitics/armstrade/
spending.asp#world military spending).

REFERENCES

Abdullah, Ali Ahmed (n.d.), *Al-Shakhsiyyah al-I'tibariyyah fi al-Fiqh al-Islami*
(Legal Personality in Islamic Jurisprudence) (Khartoum, Sudan: Al-Dar
al-Sudaniyyah li al-Kutub).
Abu Shuqqah, 'Abd al-Halim M. (1990), *Tahrir al-Mar'ah fi 'Asr al-Risalah*
(The Liberation of Women during the Prophet's Time) (Dar al-Qalam,
Kuwait), 6 volumes.
Ahmed, Habib (2004), Role of Zakah and Awqaf in poverty alleviation. Occa-
sional Paper No. 8. Islamic Research and Training Institute/Islamic Develop-
ment Bank, Jeddah.
Arrow, Kenneth J. (1973), Social responsibility and economic efficiency, *Public
Policy*, 21, 303–17.
Arrow, Kenneth J. (2000), Observations on social capital, in Dasgupta and
Serageldin (2000), pp. 3–5.
Arsalan, Shakeb Amir (1962), *Our Decline and its Causes*. M.A. Shakoor, transl.
(Lahore: Shaikh Muhammad Ashraf).
Australian Bureau of Agricultural and Research Economics (1988), *Japanese
Agricultural Policies*. Policy Monograph No. 3. Canberra, Australia.
Baeck, Louis (1994), *The Mediterranean Tradition in Economic Thought* (Lon-
don: Routledge).
Bayhaqi, Imam Abu Bakr al- (d. 1065) (1990), *Shuab al-Imam*, Muhammad
al-Sa'id Bisyuni Zaghlul (ed.) (Beirut: Dar al-Kutub al-Ilmiyyah).
Besley, Timothy and Burgess, Robin (2003), Halving global poverty, *Journal of
Economic Perspectives*, Summer, 17:3, 3–22.
Boulakia, Jean David C. (1971), Ibn Khaldun: A fourteenth century economist,
Journal of Political Economy, September/October, 1105–18.
Bowles, Samuel and Gintis, Herbert (2002), Social capital and community
governance, *The Economic Journal*, November, F419–F436.
Brenner, Robert (1987), Feudalism, *The New Palgrave Dictionary of Economics*
(London: Macmillan), Vol. 2, pp. 309–16.
Bukhari, Ismail al- (d. 869) (1987), *Sahih al-Bukhari*, Al-Shaykh Qasim
al-Shamma'i al-Rifa'I (ed.) (Beirut: Dar al-Qalam).
Chapra, M. Umer (1979), *The Islamic Welfare State and its Role in the Economy*
(Leicester, UK: The Islamic Foundation).
Chapra, M. Umer (1985), *Towards a Just Monetary System* (Leicester, UK: The
Islamic Foundation).
Chapra, M. Umer (1992), *Islam and the Economic Challenge* (Leicester, UK:
The Islamic Foundation).
Chapra, M. Umer (1993), *Islam and Economic Development* (Islamabad: Inter-
national Institute of Islamic Thought and Islamic Research Institute).

Chapra, M. Umer (1998), Islam and economic development: A discussion within the framework of Ibn Khaldun's philosophy of history, *Proceedings of the Second Harvard University Forum on Islamic Finance*, October. Harvard University, Cambridge, MA.

Chapra, M. Umer (2000), *The Future of Economics: An Islamic Perspective* (Leicester, UK: The Islamic Foundation).

Checkland, S.G. (1987), Industrial Revolution, *The New Palgrave Dictionary of Economics* (London: Macmillan), Vol. 2, pp. 811–15.

Clark, Ramsey (1997), Interview with *Impact International*, London: UK, 10 December.

Dasgupta, Partha and Serageldin, Ismail (2000), *Social Capital: A Multifaceted Perspective* (Washington, DC: World Bank).

Desfosses, Helen and Levesque, Jacques (eds) (1975), *Socialism in the Third World* (New York: Praeger).

Dobb, M. 1946. *Studies in the Development of Capitalism* (London: Routledge and Kegan Paul).

Etzioni, Amitai (1988), *The Moral Dimension: Towards a New Economics* (New York: The Free Press).

Etzioni, Amitai (2004), Religious civil society is antidote to anarchy in Iraq and Afghanistan, *The Christian Science Monitor*, 1 April (www.csmonitor.com/2004/0401/p09501-coop.html).

Faroghi, Suraiya (1994), Crisis and change, in Inalcik and Quataert (1994), pp. 411–36.

Fukuyama, Francis (1995), *Trust, Social Virtues and the Creation of Prosperity* (New York: The Free Press).

Gibbon, Edward (1960), *History of the Decline and Fall of the Roman Empire*, J.B. Bury's edition, in 7 volumes. Abridged in 1 volume by D.M. Low (New York: Brace Harcourt).

Hall, Robert and Jones, Charles (1999), Why do some countries produce so much more output per worker than others? *Quarterly Journal of Economics*, 114:1, 83–116.

Hessen, Robert (1987), Corporation, *The New Palgrave Dictionary of Economics* (London: Macmillan), Vol. 1, pp. 675–77.

Hilton, R.H. (1969), *The Decline of Serfdom* (London: Macmillan).

Hitti, Philip (1958), *History of the Arabs* (London: Macmillan).

Hodgson, Marshall (1977), *The Venture of Islam: Conscience and History in a World Civilization* (Chicago: University of Chicago Press).

Hofmann, Murad Wilfried (1966), Backwardness and the rationality of the Muslim world, *Encounter*, March, 76–87.

Hollingsworth, J. Rogers and Boyer, Robert (1998), *Contemporary Capitalism: The Embeddedness of Institutions* (Cambridge: Cambridge University Press).

Holt, P.M., Lambton, Anne and Lewis, Bernard (eds) (1970), *The Cambridge History of Islam* (Cambridge: Cambridge University Press).

Ibn Khaldun, Abd al-Rahman (n.d.), *Muqaddimah* (referred to in the text references of this paper as M) (Cairo: Al-Maktabah al-Tijariyyah al-Kubra). For its English translation, see Rosenthal (1976), and for selections from it, see Issawi (1950).

Ibn Khaldun, Abd al-Rahman (n.d.), *Kitab al- Ibar wa Diwan al- Mubtada wa al- Khabar fi Ayyam al-Arab wa al- Ajam wa al- Barbar wa man Asharahum min Dhawi al-Sultan al-Akbar* (Beirut: Maktabah al-Madrasah wa Dar al-Kitab al-Lubnani).

Imam Zakariyyah Bashir (1977), *Tariq al-Tatawwur al-Ijtima'i al-Islami* (Jeddah: Dar al-Shuruq).

Inalcik, Halil (1970), The rise of the Ottoman Empire, and The heyday and decline of the Ottoman Empire, in Holt et al. (1970), Vol. 1, pp. 295–323 and 324–31.

Inalcik, Halil and Qarataert, Donald (eds) (1994), *An Economic and Social History of the Ottoman Empire in 1300–1914* (Cambridge: Cambridge University Press).

Islamic Development Bank (2005), *Key Socio-Economic Statistics on IDB Member Countries: Statistical Mimeograph No. 25* (Jeddah: IDB).

Issawi, Charles (1950), *An Arab Philosophy of History: Selections from the Prolegomena of Ibn Khaldun of Tunis (1332–1406)* (London: John Murray).

Issawi, Charles (1966), *The Economic History of the Middle East, 1800–1914* (Chicago, IL: Chicago University Press).

Issawi, Charles (1970), *The Decline of Middle Eastern Trade, 1100–1850*, in Richards (1970).

Jansen, Marius B. (1973–74), Japan, history of, *The New Encyclopedia Britannica*, 15th edn, Vol. 10.

Johnson, John W. (1964), *The Military and Society in Latin America* (Stanford, CA: Standford University Press).

Kahf, Monzer (2004), *Shari'ah* and historical aspects of *Zakah* and *Awqaf*. Background Paper prepared for the Islamic Research and Training Institute/ Islamic Development Bank, Jeddah.

Kaufmann, Daniel and Kraay, Aart (2002), Growth without governance. World Bank Policy Research Paper 2928, Washington, DC (http://www. worldbank.org/wbi/governance/pubs/growthgov/html).

Kaufmann, Daniel, Kraay, Aart and Zoido-Lobaton, Pablo (1999), Governance matters. World Bank Policy Research Working Paper 2196, Washington, DC (http://www.worldbank.org/wbi/governance/pubs/growthgov/html).

Kennedy, Paul (1987), *The Rise and Fall of the Great Powers: Economic Change and Military Conflict from 1500–2000* (New York: Random House).

Khafif, Ali al- (1962), *Al-Shirkat fi al-Fiqh al-Islami* (Corporations in Islamic Jurisprudence) (Cairo: Ma'had al-Dirasat al-Arabiyyah al-'Aliyah).

Knack, Stephen and Keefer, Philip (1995), Institutions and economic performance: Cross-country tests using alternative intuitional measures, *Economics and Politics*, 7:3, 207–27.

Kramer, J.H. et al. (1993), Othmanli, *The Encyclopedia of Islam*, Vol. 8, pp. 190–231.

Kuran, Timur (1997), Islam and underdevelopment: An old puzzle revisited, *Journal of Institutional and Theoretical Economics*, March, 41–71.

Kuran, Timur (2004), Why the Middle East is economically underdeveloped: Historical mechanisms of institutional stagnation, *The Journal of Economic Perspectives*, Summer, 18:3, 71–90.

Lal, Deepak (1998), *Unintended Consequences: The Impact of Factor Endowments, Culture, and Politics on Long-Run Economic Performance* (Cambridge, MA: The MIT Press).

Lambton, Ann K.S. (1970), Persia: The breakdown of society, in Holt et al. (1970), Vol. 1, pp. 430–67.

Lawson, Nigel (1995), Some reflections on morality and capitalism, in Samuel Brittan and Alan Hamlin (eds), *Market Capitalism and Moral Values: Proceedings of Section (Economics) of the British Association for the Advancement of Science, Keele* (Aldershot, UK and Brookfield, VT, USA: Edward Elgar Publishing).

Lewis, Barnard (1960), Abbasids, in *The Encyclopedia of Islam*, Vol. 1, pp. 15–26.

Lewis, Bernard (1962), Ottoman observers of Ottoman decline, *Islamic Studies*, 1, 71–87.

Lewis, Bernard (1995), *The Middle East: 2000 Years of History from the Rise of Christianity to the Present Day* (London: Weidenfeld and Nicholson).

MacIntyre, Andrew (1996), Democracy and markets in Southeast Asia, in *Constructing Democracy and Markets: East Asia and Latin America*, International Forum for Democratic Studies and Pacific Council on International Policy, Pacific Council, Los Angeles, pp. 39–47.

Makdisi, G. (1981), *The Rise of Colleges: Institutions of Learning in Islam and the West* (Edinburgh: Edinburgh University Press).

Mas'udi, Abu al-Hasan 'Ali (1988), *Muruj al-Dhahab wa Ma'adin al-Jawhar*, M. Muhy al-Din 'Abd al-Hamid (ed.) (Beirut: Al-Maktabah al-'Asriyyah).

Mauro, Paolo (1995), Corruption and growth, *Quarterly Journal of Economics*, 110:3, 681–712.

Mauro, Paolo (2004), The persistence of corruption and slow economic growth, *IMF Staff Papers*, 51:1, 1–18.

Mehmet, Ozay (1990), *Islamic Identity and Development: Studies in the Islamic Periphery* (London: Routledge).

Mirakhor, Abbas (1987), The Muslim scholars and the history of economics: A need for consideration, *The American Journal of Islamic Social Sciences*, December, 245–76.

Mulligan, Casey, Gil, Richard and Sal-i-Martin, Xavier (2004), Do democracies have different public policies than non-democracies?, *Journal of Economic Perspectives*, Winter, 51–74.

Musallam, B.F. (1981), Birth control and Middle Eastern history: Evidence and hypotheses, in Udovitch (1981), pp. 419–70.

Myrdal, Gunnar (1968), *Asian Drama* (New York: The Twentieth Century Fund).

Myrdal, Gunnar (1979), Need for reforms in underdeveloped countries, *Quarterly Economic Journal*, National Bank of Pakistan, January–March.

Najjar, Zaghlul Raghib al- (1989), *Qadiyyah al-Takhalluf al-' lmi wa al-Taqani fi al- Alam al-Islami* (Qatar: Ri'asah al-Mahakim al-Shar'iyyah wa al-Shu'un al-Diniyyah).

Noland, Marcus (n.d.), Religion, culture, and economic performance. Unpublished Paper.

North, Douglass C. (1990), *Institutions, Institutional Change, and Economic Performance* (Cambridge: Cambridge University Press).

North, Douglass C. (1994), Economic performance through time, *The American Economic Review*, June, 359–68.

North, Douglass C. and Thomas, Robert Paul (1973), *The Rise of the Western World: A New Economic History* (Cambridge: Cambridge University Press).

Oesterle, Dale Arthur (1994), Limited liability, *The New Palgrave Dictionary of Money and Finance* (London: Macmillan), Vol. 2, pp. 590–91.

Rheinstein, Max and Glendon, Mary (1994), Inheritance and succession, *The New Encyclopaedia Britannica*, 15th edn, pp. 638–47.

Richards, Alan (2003), Explaining the appeal of Islamic radicals, Centre for Global Economic and Regional Studies, January, No. 1.

Richards, D.S. (ed.) (1970), *Islam and the Trade of Asia* (Oxford, UK: Bruno Cassirer, and Philadelphia, USA: University of Pennsylvania Press).

Roded, Ruth (1994), *Women in Islamic Bibliographical Collections from Ibn Sa'ad to Who's Who* (Boulder, CO, and London: Lynne Rienner Publishers).

Rosenthal, Franz (1967) (referred to in this chapter as R), *Ibn Khaldun: The Muqaddimah, An Introduction to History* (London: Routledge and Kegan Paul, 1st edn, 1958; 2nd edn, 1967), 3 volumes.

Sachs, Jeffrey D. (1987), Trade and exchange rate policies in growth oriented adjustment, in Carlos Vittoria, Goldstein, Morris and Khan, Mohsin (eds), *Growth-Oriented Adjustment Programmes: Proceedings of a Symposium Held in Washington, DC, 25–27 February 1986* (Washington, DC: IMF/IBRD).

Sarton, George (1927–48), *Introduction to the History of Science* (Washington, DC: Carregie Institute, 3 volumes issued between 1927 and 1948, the 2nd and the 3rd volumes have two parts each).

Saunders, John J. (ed.) (1966), *The Muslim World on the Eve of Europe's Expansion* (Englewood Cliffs, NJ: Prentice Hall).

Schatzmiller, Maya (1994), *Labour in the Medieval Islamic World* (Leiden: Brill).

Schweitzer, Alfred (1949), *The Philosophy of Civilization* (New York: Macmillan).

Sirowy, Larry and Inkles, Alex (1990), The effects of democracy on growth and inequality: A review, *Studies in Comparative International Development*, 25, 125–6.

Solow, Robert M. (2000), Notes on social capital and economic performance, in Dasgupta and Serageldin (2000), pp. 6–10.

Sorokin, Pitirim (1951), *Social Philosophies of an Age of Crisis* (Boston, MA: Beacon).

Spengler, Joseph (1964), Economic thought in Islam: Ibn Khaldun, *Comparative Studies in Society and History*, April, 268–306.

Spengler, Oswald (1926 and 1928), *Decline of the West* (Vol. 1, 'Form and Actuality'; Vol. 2, 'Perspective of World History') (New York: Alfred Knopf).

Talbi, M. (1986), Ibn Khaldun, *in The Encyclopedia of Islam* (Leiden: Brill), Vol. 3, pp. 825–31.

Toynbee, Arnold (uncle of the great historian Arnold J. Toynbee) (1961), *Industrial Revolution*. First published in 1884 as *Lectures on the Industrial Revolution in England* (Boston, MA: The Beacon Press).

Toynbee, Arnold J. (1935), *A Study of History*, 2nd edn (London: Oxford University Press), abridgement by D.C. Somervell (1957), London: Oxford University Press.

Udovitch, Abraham L. (1970), *Partnership and Profit in Medieval Islam* (Princeton, NJ: Princeton University Press).

Udovitch, Abraham L. (1981), *The Islamic Middle East, 700–1900: Studies in Economic and Social History* (Princeton, NJ: The Darwin Press).

United Nations Development Programme (UNDP) (1990 and 2003), *Human Development Report* (Oxford: Oxford University Press).

Usmani, Muhammad Taqi (1998), *An Introduction to Islamic Finance* (Karachi: Idarah al-Ma'arif).

Watson, Andrew M. (1981), A medieval green revolution: new crops and farming techniques in the early Islamic world, in Abraham Udovitch, *The Islamic Middle East, 700–1900: Studies in Economic and Social History* (Princeton, NJ: The Darwin Press), pp. 29–58.

Watson, Andrew M. (1983), *Agricultural Innovation in the Early Islamic World: The Diffusion of Crops and Farming Techniques: 700–1100* (Cambridge: Cambridge University Press).

World Bank (1997 and 2004), *World Development Report* (Washington, DC: World Bank, www.worldbank.org/wdr).

World Bank (2004), *World Development Indicators Online*, May.

World Military Spending (2004), accessed at: www.globalissues.org/geopolitics/armstrading spending.asp #world military spending.

PART II

Islamic finance

5. The case against interest: is it compelling?

5.1 INTRODUCTION

Four of the world's major religions (Judaism, Christianity, Hinduism, and Islam), having a following of more than two-thirds of the world's population, have prohibited interest.[1] In sharp contrast with this prohibition, the entire international financial system is now based on interest and has been so for more than 200 years. However, protests have been, and continue to be, made against interest.[2]

These protests have been particularly prominent in the Muslim world, where an effort is under way to replace the interest-based system of financial intermediation with the profit-and-loss-sharing (PLS) system.

The introduction of a new model of financial intermediation based on PLS is not an easy task. The difficulties involved in the changeover justifiably raise the question of why should anyone try to replace the conventional system, which has been in existence for such a long time and has by now become highly sophisticated. Is the case against interest so compelling that a change needs to be considered seriously? One reason for the change is the imperative of abiding by a religious edict. This reason, though of prime importance to committed believers in Islam and other religions, may not have any appeal for those who are not so highly committed. It is, therefore, necessary to see whether the effort to remove interest from the financial system has any economic rationale. Such a rationale would exist if the PLS system can be shown to be capable of improving the realization of both efficiency and equity, the two criteria on the basis of which any economic or financial system needs to be evaluated.

The interest-based system was generally assumed superior to the interest-free system on the criterion of efficiency. It was, however, normally considered to be inferior on the criterion of equity or socio-economic justice. The persistent instability and crises to which the international financial system has become exposed over the last few decades and the problems that this has created have, however, raised doubts about its superiority on the efficiency criterion. This chapter is an attempt to discuss the primary cause of the crises and to show the contribution that a risk–reward sharing system can make toward greater financial stability as well as socio-economic justice.

5.2   THE FINANCIAL CRISES

The efficiency argument in favour of the conventional interest-based system of financial intermediation has been substantially weakened by the crises it has experienced over the last few decades.[3] There is not a single geographical area or major country that has been spared the effect of these crises. Hence there is an uneasy feeling that 'something is wrong with the global financial system' (Stiglitz, 2003, p. 54). This has led to a call for comprehensive reform of the financial system to help prevent the outbreak and spread of financial crises or, at least, minimize their frequency and severity. The needed reform has come to be labelled 'the new architecture'.

There is perhaps no one who has challenged this call for a new architecture for the financial system. However, as Andrew Crockett, General Manager of the Bank for International Settlements and Chairman of the newly created Financial Stability Forum, has rightly pointed out: 'a grand new design for the international financial system has still to be devised' (Crockett, 2000, p. 13). What could be the reason for the inability to prepare a convincing reform program in spite of so much investment in terms of time and effort? Could it be the failure to determine the ultimate cause of the crises?

5.3   THE ROOTS OF THE CRISES

A number of economists have made an effort to determine the causes of the crises. Some consider financial liberalization to be the cause in an environment where financial systems of many countries are not sound as a result of improper regulation and supervision (Bisignano, 1999; Glick, 1998). Others feel that the ultimate cause is the bursting of the speculative bubble in asset prices driven initially by the excesses of financial intermediaries (Krugman, 1998). It has also been argued that the root cause of the crises was the maturity mismatch: short-term international liabilities were far greater than short-term assets (Chang and Velasco, 1998; Radelet and Sachs, 1998). The available literature indicates a number of other causes as well.

Even though all these factors had some role to play in the crises, no consensus seems to have developed so far in pinpointing the ultimate cause or the cause of all causes. In the absence of a proper understanding of the ultimate cause, conflicting remedies have been proposed. This makes it difficult to lay down an effective reform program. Hence the proposals for the new architecture have been unable to step beyond the basic principles of conventional wisdom, which emphasize sound macroeconomic policies along with sustainable exchange rates, proper regulation and supervision, and greater transparency (Camdessus, 2000, pp. 1, 7–10). These principles are undoubtedly indispensable because, in the last analysis, all crises have their roots in unhealthy fiscal, monetary, and exchange rate policies. Hence no one has ever denied the need for their honest implementation. Nevertheless, these principles have been, and continue to be, violated.

The violation of these principles brings to mind a number of questions. The first is about what is it that enables the continuation of macroeconomic imbalances, unsustainable exchange rates, and unhealthy financial practices over a prolonged period. One would expect that market discipline would normally be able to bring about a correction in these by ensuring honest and effective implementation of the basic principles of conventional wisdom. Why is it that market discipline is unable to prevent macroeconomic imbalances in the public sector and living beyond means in the private sector? What is it that makes it possible to have excessive leverage, which is one of the major factors that leads speculative bubbles to the point of bursting? Is it because there is inadequate market discipline?

A second related question is about why some of the countries that have followed sound fiscal and monetary policies have also faced crises. The European Exchange Rate Mechanism (ERM) crisis of the early 1990s challenges the view that foreign exchange market crises stem from undisciplined fiscal and monetary policies. Many of the countries caught up in the crisis did not have overly expansionary policies (International Monetary Fund [IMF], 1999, p. 67). Even the East Asian countries do not convincingly fit into the mold of unhealthy macroeconomic policies.

A third but equally important question is about why some of the apparently well-regulated financial systems like those of the US and the UK have also faced crises and whether greater regulation, supervision, and transparency will by themselves help avoid such crises.

5.4   THE INADEQUATE MARKET DISCIPLINE: IS THIS THE ROOT CAUSE?

It may not be possible to answer these questions without looking at the underlying reason for the failure to implement the basic principles of the new architecture in spite of their being a part of conventional wisdom. The primary cause in our view is the inadequate market discipline in the conventional financial system. Instead of making the depositors and the bankers share in the risks of business, it assures them of the repayment of their deposits or loans with interest. This makes the depositors take little interest in the soundness of the financial institution. It also makes the banks rely on the crutches of the collateral to extend financing for practically any purpose, including speculation. The collateral cannot, however, be a substitute for a more careful evaluation of the project financed. This is because the value of the collateral can itself be impaired by the same factors that diminish the ability of the borrower to repay the loan. The ability of the market to impose the required discipline thus gets impaired and leads to an unhealthy expansion in the overall volume of credit, to excessive leverage, and to living beyond means. This tendency of the system gets further reinforced by the bias of the tax system in favour of debt financing – dividends are subject to taxation while interest payments are allowed to be treated as a tax-deductible expense.

The system's inadequate market discipline is, however, not something new. It has existed all along with the development and spread of the conventional financial system. Then, why, one may ask, has there been greater volatility in the last two decades compared with what prevailed before? What has created the difference is the rise in the volume of funds as a result of rapid economic development after the Second World War, the revolution in information and communications technology, and the liberalization of foreign exchange markets. These developments are, however, a manifestation of human progress and cannot be blamed for the crises. When the volume of funds was small and there were also controls on their free movement, inadequate market discipline was not able to create havoc. However, now the position is different.

Therefore, instead of blaming the new developments, it would be more appropriate to examine carefully the fault line in the international financial system resulting from the lack of adequate market discipline because of the absence of explicit risk sharing. It is this fault line that makes it possible for the financier to lend excessively and also to move funds rapidly from place to place at the slightest change in the economic environment. A high degree of volatility thus gets injected into interest rates and asset prices. This generates uncertainty in the investment market, which in turn discourages capital formation and leads to mis-allocation of resources (BIS, 1982, p. 3). It also drives the borrowers and lenders alike from the long end of the debt market to the shorter end. Consequently, there is a steep rise in highly leveraged short-term debt, which has accentuated economic and financial instability. The IMF has acknowledged this fact in its May 1998 *World Economic Outlook* by stating that countries with high levels of short-term debt are 'likely to be particularly vulnerable to internal and external shocks and thus suscepti-ble to financial crises' (IMF, 1998a, p. 83).

One may wish to pause here to ask why a rise in debt, and particularly short-term debt, should accentuate instability? One of the major reasons for this is the close link between easy availability of credit, macro-economic imbalances, and financial instability. The easy availability of credit makes it possible for the public sector to have a high debt profile and for the private sector to live beyond its means and to have a high leverage. If the debt is not used productively, the ability to service the debt does not rise in proportion to the debt and leads to financial fragility and debt crises. The greater the reliance on short-term debt and the higher the leverage, the more severe the crises may be. This is because short-term debt is easily reversible as far as the lender is concerned, but repayment is difficult for the borrower if the amount is locked up in loss-making speculative assets or medium-and-long-term investments with a long gestation period. While there may be nothing basically wrong in a reasonable amount of short-term debt that is used for financing the purchase and sale of real goods and services by households, firms, and governments, an excess of it tends to get diverted to unproductive uses as well as speculation in the foreign exchange, stock, and property markets. Jean Claude Trichet, president of the European Central Bank, has rightly pointed out that 'a bubble is more likely to develop when investors can leverage their positions by investing borrowed funds' (Trichet, 2005, p. 4).

The following discussion of the primary factors responsible for the (1) East Asian crisis, (2) collapse of the Long-term Capital Management (LTCM) hedge fund, (3) foreign exchange market instability, and (4) the prevailing imbalances in the US economy will help explain why the easy availability of credit and the resultant steep rise in debt, particularly short-term debt, are the result of inadequate market discipline in the financial markets due to the absence of risk sharing.

5.4.1 The East Asian Crisis

The Eastern tigers had been considered to be among the global economy's shining success stories. They had high domestic saving and investment rates coupled with low inflation. They also pursued healthy fiscal policies that could be the envy of a number of developing countries. Since one of the major causes of financial instability is the financing of government deficit by bonds or fixed-interest-bearing assets (Christ, 1979; Scarth, 1979), the fiscal discipline of these countries should have helped save them from such instability. However, it did not. The rapid growth in bank credit in local currency to the private sector by domestic banks on the basis of easily available short-term inflows in foreign currency loans from abroad created speculative heat in the stock and property markets and generated a mood of 'irrational exuberance' that pushed up asset prices far beyond what was dictated by fundamentals.

The large foreign exchange inflows from abroad also enabled the central banks to peg exchange rates. This helped provide the assurance needed by foreign banks for lending and, along with relatively high domestic interest rates, attracted further inflows of funds from abroad in foreign currencies to finance direct investment as well as the ongoing boom in the assets markets. Since about 64 per cent, of the inflows in the five seriously affected countries (South Korea, Indonesia, Thailand, Malaysia, and the Philippines) were short-term (BCBS, 1999, p. 10), there was a serious maturity and currency mismatch. This joined hands with political corruption and ineffective banking regulation to lend heavily to favoured companies, which became highly over-leveraged.

The fast growth of these companies was thus made possible by the availability of easy money from conventional banks who do not generally scrutinize the projects minutely because of, as indicated earlier, the absence of risk sharing. It was the old mistake of lending on collateral without adequately evaluating the underlying risks. Had there been risk sharing, the banks would have been under a constraint to scrutinize the projects more carefully, and would not have yielded even to political pressures if they considered the projects to be too risky. Therefore, there is a strong rationale in drawing the conclusion that one of the most important underlying causes of excessive short-term lending was the inadequate market discipline resulting from the absence of risk sharing on the part of banks as well as depositors. It is very difficult for regulators to impose such a discipline unless the operators in the market are themselves rightly motivated. The assurance of receiving the deposits or the principal amount of the loan with the predetermined rate of return stands in the way.

There was a reverse flow of funds as soon as there was a negative shock. Shocks can result from a number of factors, including natural calamities and unanticipated declines in the economies of borrowing countries due to changes in interest rates or relative export and import prices. Such shocks lead to a decline in confidence in the borrowing country's ability to honour its liabilities in foreign exchange. The rapid outflow of foreign exchange, which would not have been possible in case of equity financing or even medium- and long-term debt, led to a sharp fall in exchange rates and asset prices, along with a steep rise in the local currency value of the debt. Private sector borrowers who were expected to repay their debts in the local currency were unable to do so on schedule. There was a domestic banking crisis, which had its repercussions on foreign banks because of the inability of domestic banks to meet their external obligations.

Governments have only two options in such circumstances. The first is to bail out the domestic banks at a great cost to the taxpayer, and the second is to allow the problem banks to fail. The second alternative is not generally considered to be politically feasible in spite of the recent calls to the contrary (Calomiris, 1998; Meltzer, 1998; Schwartz, 1998). In a financial system that assures, in principle, the repayment of deposits with interest, it would be a breach of trust on the part of the governments to allow the violation of this principle. Moreover, there is also a presumption, right or wrong, that if the big problem banks are allowed to fail, the financial system will break down and the economy will suffer a severe setback as a result of spillover and contagion effects – hence, the 'too big to fail' doctrine. The governments, therefore, generally feel politically safer in choosing the first alternative of bailing out the banks.

Since the domestic banks' external liabilities were in foreign exchange and the central banks' foreign exchange reserves had declined steeply, a bail out of external banks was not possible without external assistance, which the IMF came in handy to provide. This has, as indicated earlier, raised a storm of criticism and a call for the reform of the IMF itself by reducing its role (Meltzer, 1998; Schwartz, 1998). The IMF did not perhaps have a choice. Not having any way of assuring its influential members that its refusal to provide resources would not destabilize the entire international financial system, it chose the safer way out. The IMF bail out, however, got the debt unintentionally transferred from the private foreign banks to the central banks and the governments of the affected countries. Joseph Stiglitz, a Nobel Laureate, has, however, rightly observed that 'private-debts should not be converted into public debts – a mistake that was made in many instances as a result of pressure from Western banks and governments' (Stiglitz, 2003, p. 58). Professor James Tobin, another Nobel Laureate, has also concluded that 'when private banks and businesses can borrow in whatever amounts, maturities and currencies they choose, they create future claims on their country's reserves' (World Bank, 1998, p. 3).

Discussion of the role of excessive reliance on short-term credit or inflow of funds in the Asian crisis need not lead to the false impression that this is not possible in industrial countries with properly regulated and supervised banking systems. The IMF has clearly warned of the existence of such a possibility by stating that 'whatever their causes the market dynamics of surges and reversals are not peculiar to emerging markets and it is unrealistic to think that they will ever be completely eliminated' (IMF, 1998b, p. 98). The continued rise in the US public- as well as private sector spending has been possible because of short-term flows of funds from abroad, just as it had been in East Asia.

5.4.2   The Collapse of LTCM

The collapse of the US hedge fund LTCM in 1998 was also due to highly leveraged short-term lending. Even though the name hedge fund brings to mind the idea of risk reduction, 'hedge funds typically do just the opposite of what their name implies: they speculate' (Edwards 1999, p. 189). They are 'nothing more than rapacious speculators, borrowing heavily to beef up their bets' (*The Economist*, 1998, p. 21). These hedge funds are left mostly unregulated and are not encumbered by restrictions on leverage or short sales and are free to take concentrated positions in a single firm, industry, or sector – positions that might be considered 'imprudent' if taken by other institutional fund managers (Edwards, 1999, p. 190). They are, therefore, able to pursue the investment or trading strategies they choose in their own interest without due regard to the impact that this may have on others.

There is a strong suspicion that these hedge funds do not operate in isolation. If they did, they would probably not be able to make large gains, and the risks to which they are exposed would also be much greater. They therefore normally tend to operate in unison. This becomes possible because their chief executives often go to the same clubs, dine together, and know each other very intimately (Plender, 1998). On the strength of their own wealth and the enormous amounts that they can borrow, they are able to destabilize the financial market of any country around the world whenever they find it to their advantage. Hence they are generally blamed for manipulating markets from Hong Kong to London and New York (*The Economist*, 1998). Mahathir Muhammad, Malaysia's ex-prime minister, charged that short-term currency speculators, and particularly large hedge funds, were the primary cause of the collapse of the Malaysian Ringgit in summer 1997, resulting in the collapse of the Malaysian economy (Muhammad, 1997, p. C1). It is difficult to know whether this charge is right or wrong because of the skill and secrecy with which these funds collude and operate. However, if the charge is right, then it is not unlikely that these funds may also have been instrumental in the collapse of the Thai Bhat and some other South Asian currencies.

The LTCM had a leverage of 25:1 in mid-1998 (BIS, 1999, p. 108), but the losses that it suffered reduced its equity (net asset value) from the initial $4.8 billion to $2.3 billion in August 1998. Its leverage, therefore, rose to 50:1 on its balance-sheet positions alone. However, its equity continued to be eroded further by losses, reaching just $600 million, or one-eighth its original value, on 23 September 1998. Since its balance-sheet positions were in excess of $100 billion on that date, its leverage rose to 167 times capital (IMF, 1998c, p. 55). There was, thus, tier upon tier of debt, which became difficult to manage. The Federal Reserve had to come to its rescue because its default would have posed risks of systemic proportions. Many of the top commercial banks, which are supervised by the Federal Reserve and considered to be healthy and sound, had lent huge amounts to these funds. If the Federal Reserve had not come to their rescue, there may have been a serious crisis in the US financial system, with spillover and contagion effects around the world.[4] If the misadventure of a single hedge fund with an initial equity of only $4.8 billion could take the US and the world economy to the precipice of a financial disaster, then it would be perfectly legitimate to raise the question of what would happen if a number of the 6,000 or so hedge funds got into trouble.[5]

A hedge fund is able to pursue its operations in secrecy because, as explained by former Chairman of the Board of Governors of the Federal Reserve System, Alan Greenspan, it is 'structured to avoid regulation by limiting its clientele to a small number of highly sophisticated, very wealthy individuals' (Greenspan, 1998b, p. 1046). He did not, however, explain how the banks found it possible in a supposedly very well-regulated and supervised banking system to provide excessively lever-aged lending to such 'highly sophisticated, very wealthy individuals' for risky speculation when it is well known that the higher the leverage, the greater the risk of default. The unwinding of leveraged positions can cause major disruption in financial markets by exaggerating market movements and generating knock-on effects (IMF, 1998c, pp. 51–53).

This shows that a crisis can come not merely because of improper regulation of banks, as it did in East Asia, but also in a properly regulated and supervised system, as it did in the United States. Even though the hedge funds were not regulated, the banks were. Then why did the banks lend huge amounts to the LTCM and other funds? What were the supervisors doing, and why were they unable to detect and correct this problem before the crisis? Is there any assurance that the regulation of hedge funds would, without any risk sharing by banks, stop excessive flow of funds to other speculators?

5.4.3   Foreign Exchange Market Instability

The heavy reliance on short-term borrowing has also injected a substantial degree of instability into the international foreign exchange markets. According to a survey conducted by the Bank for International Settlements, the daily turnover in traditional foreign exchange markets, adjusted for double-counting, had escalated to $1,830 billion in April 2004, compared with $1,200 billion in April 2001, $1,490 billion in April 1998, and $590 billion in April 1989 (BIS, 1998 and 2004).[6] The daily foreign exchange turnover in April 2004 was more than 37 times the daily volume of world merchandise trade (exports plus imports).[7] Even if an allowance is made for services, unilateral transfers, and nonspeculative capital flows, the turnover is far more than warranted. Only 35 per cent of the 2004 turnover was related to spot transactions, which have risen at the compounded annual rate of about 1.9 per cent per annum over the 15 years since April 1989. The balance of the turnover (65 per cent) was related largely to outright forwards and foreign exchange swaps, which have registered a compounded growth of 11.8 per cent per annum, far more than the growth of 7.6 per cent per annum in world trade over this period.[8] If the assertion normally made by bankers that they give due consideration to the end use of funds had been correct, such a high degree of leveraged credit extension for speculative transactions may not have taken place. High leverage has had the effect of driving foreign exchange markets by short-term speculation rather than long-run fundamentals. This has made them highly volatile, injected excessive instability into them, and adversely affected the efficient operation of these markets. The effort by central banks to overcome this instability through small changes in interest rates or the intervention of a few hundred million dollars a day has generally not proven to be significantly effective.

The dramatic growth in speculative transactions, of which derivatives are only the latest manifestation, has also resulted in an enormous expansion in the payments system. Accordingly, Crockett has been led to acknowledge that 'our economies have thus become increasingly vulnerable to a possible breakdown in the payments system' (Crockett, 1994, p. 3). Even Greenspan, sitting at the nerve centre of international finance, himself finds this expansion in cross-border finance relative to the trade it finances as startling (Greenspan, 1998a, p. 3). Such a large expansion implies that if problems were to arise, they could quickly spread throughout the financial system, exerting a domino effect on financial institutions.

The Tobin tax on foreign exchange transactions has, therefore, been suggested to reduce the instability. This proposal needs to be reviewed against the ineffectiveness of the securities transaction tax, which is levied on the sale of stocks, bonds, options, and futures by a number of major industrial countries, including the United States, the United Kingdom, France, Germany, and Japan. This tax proved to be ineffective in preventing or even diluting the October 1998 stock market crash (Hakkio, 1994). Is there any guarantee that the foreign exchange transactions tax would fare any better? Critics of the Tobin tax have accordingly argued that even this tax would be ineffective. One of the reasons given for this is that the imposition of such a tax would be impractical. Unless all countries adopt it and implement it faithfully, trading would shift to tax-free havens. However, even if all countries complied, experienced speculators may be able to devise ways of evading or avoiding the tax because all countries do not have an effective tax administration.[9]

5.4.4 The Prevailing Imbalances in the US Economy[10]

The United States has been doing well over the past few years by most measures of overall economic performance. Nevertheless, the large and growing discrepancy between what it produces and what it consumes rings a worrisome note not only for the United States but also for the world economy. The US trade account has been persistently in deficit since the late 1970s, and the current account has also been in a similar state since the mid 1980s. The current account deficit has reached a record of 6.3 per cent, of GDP. As a result of these persistent deficits, the US net foreign indebtedness has reached a record high in both absolute terms as well as a percentage of GDP.

The current account deficit is a reflection of the public sector budgetary deficit and the private sector saving deficiency. The federal government has spent more than what it has taken in every year since 1970, except for a brief respite between 1998 and 2001. The budget has moved from a surplus of $236 billion in fiscal year 2000 to a deficit of $400 billion in 2004 (Kohn, 2005, pp. 1–2). The US private sector net saving (saving by households and businesses minus investment) has been negative since the mid-1990s as a result of the borrowing and spending spree by both households and firms. The personal saving rate has been declining since the mid-1990s (*The Economist*, 2005b, p. 87) and in 2004, the households saved only 1 per cent of the after-tax income, compared with 8 per cent on average from 1950 to 2000 (Kohn, 2005, p. 1). Nevertheless, investment in real estate and plant and equipment is high. This has generated a savings discrepancy that should have pushed up interest rates. This has not happened because of the inflow of funds from abroad, particularly from China and Japan. Low interest rates have generated a boom in residential real estate prices. The resultant increase in household net worth, combined with low interest rates, has had the effect of boosting consumer spending further at the cost of saving.

This raises the question of why has it been possible for the imbalances to persist for such a long period without an early correction being brought about by market forces. The reason, as discussed earlier, is the lack of adequate market discipline in the financial system. Why should the public and private sectors curtail spending when interest rates are low and it is easy to borrow? Borrowing is easy because of the absence of risk sharing by both the depositors and banks in the risks of banking business. Even if market forces are unable to impose fiscal discipline on the US government, it can at least lead to a decline in lending to the private sector. The resultant rise in saving might be able to offset the impact of public sector deficits.

This brings into focus the crucial issue of how long the foreigners will be willing to continue lending. Confidence in the strength and stability of the dollar is necessary to enable it to serve as a reserve currency. What will happen if the deficits continue, create loss of confidence in the dollar, and lead to an outflow of funds from the United States? This is not just a theoretical question. In the last 30 years, the dollar has experienced four bouts of marked depreciation. Since nearly two-thirds of the world's foreign exchange holdings are still in dollars, a movement out of the dollar into other currencies and commodities, as happened in the late 1960s, could lead to a sharp fall in the exchange rate of the dollar, a rise in interest rates and commodity prices, and a recession in the US economy. This might lead the whole world into a prolonged recession. The correction would then come with a vengeance when market discipline could have led to it much earlier with significantly less suffering.

5.5 THE REMEDY

If heavy reliance on short-term debt is desired to be curbed, then the question is about the best way to achieve this goal. One of the ways suggested, as already indicated, is greater regulation (Calomiris, 1999; Edwards, 1999; Stiglitz, 1999). Regulations, even though unavoidable, cannot be relied upon totally because they may not be uniformly applied in all countries and to all institutional money managers because of the off-balance-sheet accounts, bank secrecy standards, and the difficulty faced by bank examiners in accurately evaluating the quality of banks' assets. In such a situation, there will be a flight of funds to offshore havens where almost half of all hedge funds are already located (Edwards, 1999, p. 1919). Emerging market banking crises provide a number of examples of how apparently well-capitalized banks were found to be insolvent as a result of the failure to recognize the poor quality of their loan portfolio. Even the LTCM crisis shows how banks in an apparently well-regulated system can become entangled in a speculative spree. Third, bringing banks under a watertight regulatory umbrella may not only raise the costs of enforcement but also mislead depositors into thinking that their deposits enjoy a regulatory stamp of security.

    This does not mean that regulation is not necessary. However, regulation and supervision would be more effective if they are complemented by a paradigm shift in favour of greater discipline in the financial system by making investment depositors, as well as the banks, share in the risks of business. Just the bailing in of banks, as is being suggested by some analysts (Calomiris, 1998; Meltzer, 1998; Yeager, 1998), may not be able to take us far enough. What is necessary is not just to make the shareholders suffer when a bank fails, but also to strongly motivate even the depositors to be cautious in choosing their bank and the bank management to be more careful in making their loans and investments. Bank managers are better placed to evaluate the quality of their assets than regulators and depositors, and risk sharing would motivate them to take the decisions that they feel are in the best interest of banks and depositors.

    Therefore, it is necessary to reinforce regulation and supervision of banks by the injection of self-discipline into the financial system. This could be accomplished by making banks as well as shareholders and investment depositors (those who wish to get a return on their deposits) share in the risks of banking by increasing the reliance on equity and reducing that on debt, as is desired by the major religions. It would also be necessary to confine the availability of credit to the financing of real goods and services, with some risk sharing by the lender as well. Making the depositors as well as banks participate in the risk of business would motivate the depositors to take greater care in choosing their banks, and the bank management to assess the risks more carefully and to monitor the use of funds by the borrowers more effectively. The double assessment of investment proposals by both the borrower and the lender would help raise market discipline and introduce greater health into the financial system. The IMF has also thrown its weight in favour of equity financing by arguing that:

> foreign direct investment, in contrast to debt-creating inflows, is often regarded as providing a safer and more stable way to finance development because it refers to ownership and control of plant, equipment, and infrastructure and therefore funds the growth-creating capacity of an economy, whereas short-term foreign borrowing is more likely to be used to finance consumption. Furthermore, in the event of a crisis, while investors can divest themselves of domestic securities and banks can refuse to roll over loans, owners of physical capital cannot find buyers so easily. (IMF, 1998a, p. 82)

This may raise an objection that investment depositors are generally risk-averse and, unlike equity investors, would not like to expose their capital to risk. Forcing them to take risk may create insecurity and difficulty for them and their families. To avoid such a problem, it should be possible for banks to invest the funds provided by risk-averse investment depositors in less risky assets. The banks may also be required to build adequate loss-offsetting reserves so that the depositors do not have to suffer losses. Such an approach should have the added advantage of making the banks more effective in managing their risks and, thereby, making the banking system safer and healthier.

Moreover, as Hicks has argued, interest has to be paid in good or hard times alike, but dividends can be reduced in bad times and, in extreme situations, even passed. So the burden of finance by shares is less. There is no doubt that in good times an increased dividend would be expected, but it is precisely in such times that the burden of higher dividend can be borne. 'The firm would be insuring itself to some extent', to use his precise words, 'against a strain which in difficult conditions can be serious, at the cost of an increased payment in conditions when it would be easy to meet it. It is in this sense that the riskiness of its position would be diminished' (Hicks, 1982, p. 14). This factor should tend to have the effect of substantially reducing business failures and, in turn, dampening, rather than accentuating, economic instability.

Greater reliance on equity financing has supporters even in mainstream economics. Rogoff, a Harvard professor of economics, states, 'In an ideal world equity lending and direct investment would play a much bigger role'. He further asserts, 'With a better balance between debt and equity, risk-sharing would be greatly enhanced and financial crises sharply muted' (Rogoff, 1999, p. 40). However, if, in addition to a better balance between debt and equity, the debt is also linked to the purchase of real goods and services, as required by Islamic teachings, it would take us a step further in reducing instability in the financial markets by curbing excessive credit expansion for speculative transactions. Thus it is not necessary to be pessimistic and to join Stiglitz in declaring that 'volatile markets are an inescapable reality' (Stiglitz, 1999, p. 6). The introduction of greater discipline in the financial system, which the prohibition of interest has the potential of ensuring, along with a more effective regulation and supervision, should go a long way in substantially reducing volatility in the financial market and promoting faster development.[11]

5.6 SOCIO-ECONOMIC JUSTICE

The above discussion has indicated that the absence of risk–reward sharing, which is an intrinsic characteristic of the interest-based financial system, has aggravated financial crises by adversely affecting discipline in the system. Since stability of the financial system is indispensable for promoting trade and development and since the interest-free risk–reward sharing system has a clear advantage here, it may be considered superior to the interest-based system on the criterion of efficiency. This is, however, only one of the advantages of the interest-free financial system. It was not discussed in the earlier Islamic literature because excessive volatility in the financial markets is a more recent phenomenon.

It is now important to see whether the assumption about the superiority of the interest-tree system with respect to the contribution that it can make to the realization of the universally cherished goal of socio-economic justice is realistic. Supporters of an interest-based financial system argue that interest was prohibited to prevent the exploitation of the poor resulting from the usurious rates of interest prevailing in those days. In addition, they argue that rates of interest are now much lower, and the modern welfare state has also introduced a number of measures that fulfil the needs of the poor and prevent them from resorting to exploitative borrowing. Even though this is true to a certain extent, the living beyond means that the interest-based system has the tendency to promote in both the public and private sectors leads to an indirect exploitation of the poor in different ways, two of which are their inadequate need fulfilment and insufficient employment opportunities for them.

5.6.1 Need Fulfilment

Financial intermediation on the basis of interest tends to allocate financial resources among borrowers primarily on the basis of their having acceptable collateral to guarantee the repayment of principal and sufficient cash flow to service the debt. End use of financial resources does get considered but does not constitute the main criterion. Even though collateral and cash flow are both indispensable for ensuring repayment of loans, giving them undue weight leads to a relative disregard of the purpose for which borrowing takes place. Hence financial resources go mainly to the rich, who have the collateral as well as the cash flow, and to governments, who, it is assumed, will not go bankrupt. However, the rich borrow not only for productive investment but also for conspicuous consumption and speculation, while the governments borrow not only for development and public well-being, but also for excessive defence build-up and unproductive projects. This does not merely accentuate macroeconomic and external imbalances, but also squeezes the resources available for need fulfilment and development. A decline in bank lending for speculative and unproductive projects, which a PLS system carries the potential of bringing about, can therefore be very healthy.

The ease of borrowing has enabled a number of developing countries to borrow excessively large amounts. This would not be possible in a risk–reward sharing system. Borrowing, however, does not eliminate the ultimate sacrifice; it only postpones it. The debt-servicing burden continues to rise with the rise in debt and becomes unbearable, particularly if the borrowed amount is not used productively. A number of developing countries have a debt-servicing burden exceeding 50 per cent of their total budgetary spending. The result is that they are unable to provide adequate budgetary resources for some of the most important national needs like education, health, and rural and urban development. It is primarily the poor and the lower middle classes who suffer as a result of this. Poverty does not get reduced, and inequalities of income and wealth continue to rise.

Ease of borrowing also creates problems for rich countries. The squeezing of resources for need fulfilment and productive investment resulting from conspicuous consumption and speculation has made it difficult for even rich countries like the United States to fulfil the essential needs of all their people in spite of their desire to do so and the abundant resources at their disposal. The continued US budgetary deficits in the 1950s and 1960s, made possible by the interest-based system, led to an international financial crisis in the late 1960s and the early 1970s and the breakdown of the Bretton Woods system. The after-effects of that crisis have continued to plague the world until now. There is a lurking fear that the reemergence of budgetary deficits in the United States in recent years during the tenure of President Bush might lead to a destabilization of the international financial system in the same way as it did in the late 1960s.

5.6.2 Full Employment

One of the most important requisites for generating full employment is the rise in a country's ability to invest. If this is to be achieved in a non-inflationary manner and without a rise in foreign debt, then it is necessary to have a rise in domestic savings. Unfortunately, there has been a decline in savings in almost all countries around the world. Gross domestic saving as a percentage of GDP has registered a worldwide decline over the last quarter century from 26.2 per cent in 1971 to 23.2 per cent in 2002. The decline in industrial countries has been from 23.6 per cent to 19.3 per cent. The drop in developing countries, which need higher savings to accelerate development without a significant rise in inflation and debt-servicing burden, has been even steeper, from 34.2 per cent to 28.1 per cent over the same period.[12]

There are a number of reasons for this decline in saving. One of these is the living beyond means by both the public and the private sectors. This saving shortfall has been responsible for persistently high levels of real interest rates. This has led to lower rates of rise in investment, which have joined hands with structural rigidities and some other socio-economic factors to reduce the rates of growth in output and employment.

Unemployment has hence become one of the most intractable problems of many developing as well as industrial countries. Unemployment stood at 8.8 per cent in the European Union in January 2005, more than three times its level of 2.9 per cent in 1971–73.[13] It may not be expected to fall significantly below this level in the near future, because the real rate of growth in these countries has been consistently lower than what is necessary to reduce unemployment significantly.[14] Even more worrying is the higher than average rate of youth unemployment because it hurts their pride, dampens their faith in the future, increases their hostility toward society, and damages their personal capacities and potential contribution. The problem is even more serious in developing countries, where the proportion of the population below the age of 18 is relatively high. These boys and girls will soon enter the labour market. If employment opportunities are not created for them, these countries may experience a rise in social turmoil as well as crime.

A decline in speculation and wasteful spending, along with a rise in saving and productive investment, could be very helpful. But this may not be possible when the value system encourages both the public and the private sectors to live beyond their means and the interest-based financial intermediation makes this possible by making credit easily available without due regard to its end use. If, however, banks are required to share in the risks and rewards of financing and credit is made available primarily for the purchase of real goods and services, which the Islamic system tries to ensure, the banks will be more careful in lending and credit expansion will tend to be in step with the growth of the economy. Unproductive and speculative spending may consequently decline and make it possible for more resources to become available for productive investment and development. This should help realize a higher rate of growth in output and employment and a decline in unemployment.

5.7   THE ISLAMIC FINANCIAL SYSTEM[15]

It is these weaknesses of the interest-based financial system that create a strong rationale for the introduction of a new architecture for the international financial system. This brings us to Islamic banking, which tries to remove interest and introduce in its place the principle of risk–reward sharing. Since demand deposits do not participate in the risks of financing by the financial institutions, they do not earn any return and must, therefore, be guaranteed. However, investment deposits do participate in the risks and must share in the profits or losses in agreed proportions. What this will do is turn investment depositors into temporary shareholders. Placing investment deposits in financial institutions will be like purchasing their shares, and withdrawing them will be like redeeming these shares. The same would be the case when these institutions lend to, and get repaid by, businesses. They will be sharing in the risks of businesses they finance. This will raise substantially the share of equity in total financing and reduce that of debt. Equity will take the form of either shares in joint stock companies and other businesses or of PLS in projects and ventures through the *mudarabah* and *musharakah* modes of financing.[16]

Greater reliance on equity does not necessarily mean that debt financing is totally ruled out. This is because all financial needs of individuals, firms, or governments cannot be made amenable to PLS. Debt is, therefore, indispensable. Debt, however, gets created in the Islamic financial system through the sale or lease of real goods and services via the sales-based modes of financing (*murabahah, ijarah, salam,* and *istisna*). In this case, the rate of return gets stipulated in advance and becomes a part of the deferred payment price. Since the rate of return is fixed in advance and the debt is associated with real goods or services, it is less risky as compared with equity or PLS financing. The predetermined rate of return on sales-based modes of financing may, however, make them appear like interest-based instruments. They are, however, not so because of significant differences between the two for a number of reasons.

First, the sales-based modes do not involve direct lending and borrowing. They are rather purchase and sale or lease transactions involving real goods and services. The *Shari'ah* has imposed a number of conditions for the validity of these transactions. One of these conditions is that the seller (financier) must also share a part of the risk to be able to get a share in the return. He cannot avoid doing this because of the second condition that requires that the seller (financier) must own and possess the goods being sold. The *Shari'ah* does not allow a person to sell what he does not own and possess.[17] Once the seller (financier) acquires ownership and possession of the goods for sale on credit, he/she bears the risk. All speculative short sales, therefore, get ruled out automatically. Financing extended through the Islamic modes can thus expand only in step with the rise of the real economy and thereby help curb excessive credit expansion, which is one of the major causes of instability in the international financial markets.

Second, it is the price of the good or service sold, and not the rate of interest, that is stipulated in the case of sales-based modes of finance. Once the price has been set, it cannot be altered, even if there is a delay in payment due to unforeseen circumstances. This helps protect the interest of the buyer in strained circumstances. However, it may also lead to a liquidity problem for the bank if the buyer willfully delays payment. This is a major unresolved problem in Islamic finance and discussions are in progress among the jurists to find a solution that is *Shari'ah*-compliant.[18]

The share of PLS modes is so far relatively small in the financing operations of Islamic banks, and that of sales-based modes is predominantly high. The reason may perhaps be that the task is difficult and in the initial phase of their operations these banks do not wish to get exposed to risks that they cannot manage effectively. They are not properly equipped for this in terms of skilled manpower as well as the needed institutional infrastructure.[19] Most scholars, however, feel that, even though the sales-based modes are different from interest-based financing and are allowed by the *Shari'ah*, the socio-economic benefits of the prohibition of interest argued above may not be realized fully until the share of PLS modes rises substantially in total financing. It would hence be desirable for the use of PLS modes to gain momentum.

Substantial progress has been made by Islamic banks worldwide, even though the niche that they have been able to create for themselves in the total volume of international, or even Muslim world, finance is very small. This was to be expected because they are trying to make headway in a new system of financial intermediation without the help of trained staff and of auxiliary or shared institutions that are needed for their successful operation. What counts, however, is not the volume of their deposits and assets, but rather the respectability that the interest-free financial intermediation has attained around the world and the positive evidence that it has provided about the workability and viability of this new system. While in the 1950s and 1960s Islamic banking was only an academic dream of which few people were aware even among educated Muslims, it has now become a practical reality. It has also attracted the attention of Western central banks like the Federal Reserve Board and the Bank of England, international financial institutions like the IMF and the World Bank, and prestigious centres of learning like Harvard and Rice Universities in the US and the London School of Economics and Loughborough and Durham Universities in the UK. It has also received favourable coverage in the Western press. Prospects for the future are expected to be better, particularly if the instability that now prevails in the international financial system continues to accentuate. This may lead to a realization that the instability may be difficult to remove by making cosmetic changes in the system. It is rather necessary to inject greater market discipline into the system. The interest-free risk–reward sharing system can help inject such a discipline.

5.8 CONCLUSION

Thus, we see that there is a strong rationale behind the prohibition of interest by the major religions of the world. The rationale is not merely to prevent the exploitation of the poor but also to make the financial system healthier and more stable by injecting greater discipline into it. If the share of equity is increased and that of debt is reduced substantially, the volatility now prevailing in the international financial markets will hopefully be substantially reduced. The result may be even better if credit is confined primarily to the purchase or lease of real goods and services. As a result of this, a great deal of the speculative expansion of credit may be eliminated. The ultimate outcome may be not only reduction in financial instability and greater socio-economic justice but also better allocation of resources and faster economic growth.

NOTES

1. For the Judaic and Christian views on interest, see Johns, Dow, Bennett, and Abelson (n.d.) and Noonan (1957); for the Hindu view, see Bokare (1993, p. 168); and for the Islamic view, see Chapra (1985, pp. 55–66) and M.N. Siddiqi (2004, pp. 35–64).
2. For some of these protests, see Mills and Presley (1999, pp. 101–13).
3. By some reckonings, there have been 100 crises in the past 35 years (Stiglitz, 2003, p. 54). The more important of these crises are the US stock market crash in October 1987, the bursting of the Japanese stock and property market bubble in the early 1990s, the breakdown of the European Exchange Rate Mechanism (ERM) in 1992–93, the bond market crash in 1994, the Mexican crisis in 1995, the East Asian crisis in 1997, the Russian crisis in August 1998, the breakdown of the US hedge funds in 1998, the Brazilian exchange rate crisis in 1999, and the steep decline in US stock prices in 2002.
4. This was clearly acknowledged by Greenspan in the following words: 'Had the failure of the LTCM triggered the seizing up of markets, substantial damage could have been inflicted on many market participants, including some not directly involved with the firm, and could have potentially impaired the economies of many nations, including our own' (Greenspan, 1998b, p. 1046).
5. The figure for hedge funds is from *The Economist* (2004, p. 72).
6. The Bank for International Settlements (BIS) conducts a survey of foreign exchange markets every three years in the month of April. The daily global foreign exchange turnover has increased continuously since the first survey in April 1989, except in 2001. The major reasons for this tail in 2001 were, according to the BIS, the introduction of the euro, the growing share of electronic banking in the spot inter-bank market, and the consolidation in the banking industry (BIS, 2001, p. 1).
7. World trade (exports plus imports) rose from $499.0 billion in April 1989 to $1,489.7 billion in April 2004 (IMF, International Financial Statistics, CD-ROM, and September 2004). The average value of daily world trade in the month of April during these two years comes to $16.6 and $49.7 billion, respectively.
8. The decline in average daily turnover in April 2001, as indicated in Note 6, was most pronounced in spot markets, where average daily turnover fell from $568 billion to $387 billion. Trading in forwards rose from $128 billion to $131 billion while that in swaps dropped from $734 billion to $656 billion (BIS, 2001, p. 1 and Table 1 on p. 3).
9. See the arguments in favour of and against the feasibility of the Tobin tax by various writers in Haq, Kaul and Grunberg (1996).
10. See the address entitled 'Imbalances in the US Economy' by Donald Kohn, member of the Board of Governors of the US Federal Reserve System, at the 15th Annual Hyman Minsky Conference, the Levy Economics Institute of Bard College, Annandale-on-Hudson, New York, 22 April 2005 (BIS Review, 28/2005).

11. A number of Islamic economists have argued this point. See, for example, M.N. Siddiqi (1983); Chapra (1985, pp. 117–122); Chishti (1985); Khan (1987); Mirakhor and Zaidi (1987); S. Siddiqi and Fardmanesh (1994); and a number of others.
12. Figures have been derived from the table on 'Final Consumption Expenditure as Percent of GDP' in IMF (2000; pp. 177–179; 2004, pp. 121–122). See also *The Economist* (2005a).
13. OECD (1991. Table 2, p. 7) and OECD website on Main Economic Indicators, March 2005.
14. A question may be raised here about the current low rate of unemployment in the United States in spite of a substantial decline in household saving. There are a number of reasons for this. One of the most important of these is the large inflow of foreign funds that 'has helped to fund a pronounced increase in the rate of growth of the nation's capital stock' (Peach and Steindel, 2000, p. 11). Once there is a reversal of, or even a decline in, this inflow, it may be difficult to sustain the high rate of growth in output and employment. In addition, the stock market may also experience a steep decline, creating a spillover effect for the whole world economy.
15. This section is based on Chapra and Khan (2000, pp. 11–15).
16. For a description of these and other Arabic terms used in this article, see the Appendix.
17. Exceptions to this rule are *salam* and *istisna* (see the Appendix).
18. For a discussion of this problem, see Section 3.1 on the 'Late Settlement of Financial Obligations' in Chapra and Khan (2000).
19. For the needed institutional infrastructure, see Chapra and Ahmed (2002, pp. 79–84).

REFERENCES

Bank for International Settlements (BIS). (1982), Annual report (Basel, Switzerland: Author).
Bank for International Settlements (BIS). (1998), Giving preliminary results of the Triennial Central Bank survey of foreign exchange and derivative market activity. Press release.
Bank for International Settlements (BIS). (1999), Annual report (Basel, Switzerland: Author).
Bank for International Settlements (BIS). (2001), Giving preliminary results of the Triennial Central Bank survey of foreign exchange and derivative market activity. Press release.
Bank for International Settlements (BIS). (2004), Giving preliminary results of the Triennial Central Bank survey of foreign exchange and derivative market activity. Press release.
Basel Committee on Banking Supervision (BCBS), Bank for International Settlements (BIS). (1999), Supervisory lessons to be drawn from the Asian crisis. Working Paper 2.
Bisignano, J. (1999, March), Precarious credit equilibria: Reflections on the Asian financial crisis. Paper presented at Asia: An Analysis of Financial Crises. BIS Working Paper 64.
Bokare, G.M. (1993), *Hindu-economics: Eternal Economic Order* (New Delhi: Janaki Prakashan).

Calomiris, C. (1998), The IMF's imprudent role as lender of last resort, *Cato Journal*, 17:3, 275–95.

Calomiris, C. (1999), *How to Invent a New IMF* (Washington, DC: American Enterprise Institute).

Camdessus, M. (2000), Main principles for the future of the International Monetary Financial System, International Monetary Fund Survey.

Chang, R. and Velasco, A. (1998), The Asian liquidity crisis., Working Paper. National Bureau of Economic Research.

Chapra, M.U. (1985), *Towards a Just Monetary System* (Leicester, UK: Islamic Foundation).

Chapra, M.U. (2000), Why has Islam prohibited interest? Rationale behind the prohibition of interest in Islam, *Review of Islamic Economics*, 9, 5–50.

Chapra, M.U. (2001), Alternative versions of international monetary reform, in M. Iqbal and D. Llewellyn (eds), *Islamic Banking and Finance: New Perspectives on Project-Sharing and Risk* (Cheltenham, UK and Northampton, MA, USA: Edward Elgar Publishing), pp. 219–40.

Chapra, M.U. and Ahmed, H. (2002), *Corporate Governance in Islamic Financial Institutions* (Jeddah: Islamic Research and Training Institute, Islamic Development Bank).

Chapra, M.U. and Khan, T. (2000), *Regulation and Supervision of Islamic Banks* (Jeddah: Islamic Research and Training Institute, Islamic Development Bank).

Chishti, S.U. (1985, Summer), Relative stability of an interest-free economy, *Journal of Research in Islamic Economics*, pp. 3–11.

Christ, C. (1979), On fiscal and monetary policies and the government budget restraint, *American Economic Review*, 69, 526–38.

Crockett, A. (1994), Address at the 24th International Management Symposium Review. St. Galen: Bank for International Settlements.

Crockett, A. (2000, March), A pillar to bolster global finance, *Financial Times*, p. 13.

Edwards, F.R. (1999, Spring), Hedge funds and the collapse of long-term capital management, *Journal of Economic Perspectives*, pp. 189–210.

Glick, R. (1998), Thoughts on the origins of the Asian crisis: Impulses and propagation mechanisms. Working Paper Series. Federal Reserve Bank of San Francisco.

Greenspan, A. (1998a), The globalization of finance, *Cato Journal*, 17:3, 1–7.

Greenspan, A. (1998b, December), Statement before the Committee on Banking and Financial Services, US House of Representatives, 1 October 1998. *Federal Reserve Bulletin*, pp. 1046–50.

Hakkio, C.S. (1994), Should we throw sand in the gears of financial markets? Federal Reserve Bank of Kansas City, *Economic Review*, Second Quarter, pp. 17–30.

Haq, M., Kaul, L. and Grunberg, I. (eds) (1996), *The Tobin Tax: Coping with Financial Volatility* (Oxford, UK: Oxford University Press).

Hicks, J. (1982), Limited liability: The pros and cons, in T. Orhnial (ed.), *Limited Liability and the Corporation* (London: Croom Helm), pp. 11–21.

International Monetary Fund. (1998a, May), *World Economic Outlook* (Washington, DC: Author).

International Monetary Fund. (1998b, September), *World Economic Outlook* (Washington, DC: Author).

International Monetary Fund. (1998c, December), *World Economic Outlook and International Capital Markets* (Washington, DC: Author).

International Monetary Fund. (1999, May), *World Economic Outlook* (Washington, DC: Author).

International Monetary Fund. (2000), *International Financial Statistics Yearbook* (Washington, DC: Author).

International Monetary Fund. (2004), *International Financial Statistics Yearbook* (Washington, DC: Author).

Johns, C.H.E., Dow, J., Bennett, W.H. and Abelson, J. (n.d.), On the Babylonian, Christian, Hebrew and Jewish views respectively in 'Usury', in *Encyclopedia of Religion and Ethics* (New York: Charles Scribner's Sons), Vol. 12, pp. 548–58.

Khan, M.S. (1987), Islamic interest-free banking: A theoretical analysis, in *Theoretical Studies In Islamic Economics* (Houston, TX: Institute for Research and Islamic Studies), pp. 15–35, 201–6.

Kohn, D.I. (2005), Imbalances in the US economy, *BIS Review*, Vol. 28.

Krugman, P. (1998), What happened to Asia?, accessed at: http://web.mit.edu/krugman/www/DISINTER.html.

Meltzer, A. (1998), Asian problems and the IMF, *Cato Journal*, 17:3, 267–74.

Mills, P.S., and Presley, J. (1999), *Islamic Finance: Theory and Practice* (London: Macmillan).

Mirakhor, A. and Zaidi, I. (1987), Stabilization and growth in an open economy. Working Paper. Washington, DC: International Monetary Fund.

Muhammad, M. (1997, September), Highwaymen of the global economy, *Wall Street Journal*, p. CI.

Noonan, J.T. (1957), *The Scholastic Analysis of Usury* (Cambridge, MA: Harvard University Press).

Organisation for Economic Co-operation and Development (OECD). (1991, December), *Economic Outlook* (Paris, France: OECD).

Organisation for Economic Cooperation and Development (OECD). (2005, March), *Main Economic Indicators* (Paris, France: OECD).

Peach, R. and Steindel, C. (2000), A nation of spendthrifts? An analysis of trends in personal and gross savings, *Current Issues in Economic and Finance* (Federal Reserve Bank of New York), 6:10, 1–6.

Plender, J. (1998, 31 October), Western crony capitalism, *Financial Times*.

Radelet, S. and Sachs, J. (1998), The East Asian financial crises: Diagnosis, remedies, prospects. Brookings Papers on Economic Activity.

Rogoff, K. (1999), International institutions for reducing global financial instability, *Journal of Economic Perspectives*, 4:13, 21–46.

Scarth, W. (1979), Bond-financed fiscal policy and the problem of instrument instability, *Journal of Macroeconomics*, 1, 107–17.

Schwartz, A. (1998), Time to terminate the ESF and the IMF. Foreign Policy Briefing No. 48. The Cato Institute.

Siddiqi, M.N. (1983), *Issues in Islamic Banking* (Leicester, UK: Islamic Foundation).

Siddiqi, M.N. (2004), *Riba, Bank Interest and the Rationale of its Prohibition* (Jeddah: Islamic Research and Training Institute, Islamic Development Bank).

Siddiqi, S.A. and Fardmanesh, M. (1994), Financial stability and a share economy, *Eastern Economic Journal*, Spring.

Stiglitz, J. (1998, 25 March), Boats, planes and capital flows, *Financial Times*, p. 32.

Stiglitz, J. (1999, 10–11 April), Bleak growth prospects for the developing world, *International Herald Tribune*, p. 6.

Stiglitz, J. (2003, Spring), Dealing with debt: How to reform the global financial system, *Harvard International Review*, pp. 54–9.

The Economist. (1998, 17 October), The risk business, p. 21.

The Economist. (2004, 12 June), Funds of hedge funds: Borrowing and betting, pp. 72–3.

The Economist. (2005a, 9 April), The great thrift shift, pp. 3–26.

The Economist. (2005b, 23 June), America's economy: American private-sector borrowing is heading back into uncharted territory, p. 87.

Trichet, J.C. (2005), Asset price bubbles and monetary policy. MAS Lecture, Monetary Authority of Singapore.

World Bank. (1998, April–June), *Policy and Research Bulletin*.

Yeager, I.B. (1998), How to avoid international financial crises, *Cato Journal*, 17:3, 257–65.

APPENDIX: GLOSSARY OF ARABIC TERMS

Given below is the basic sense in which some Arabic terms are generally used:

Ijara   Leasing.

Istisna   Refers to a contract whereby a manufacturer (contractor) agrees to produce (build) and deliver a certain good (or premise) at a given price on a given date in the future. This is an exception to the general *Shari'ah* ruling that does not allow a person to sell what he does not own and possess. As against *salam* (q.v.), the price here need not be paid in advance. It may be paid in installments in step with the preferences of the parties or partly at the front end and the balance later on as agreed.

Mudarabah   An agreement between two or more persons whereby one or more of them provide finance, while the others provide entrepreneurship and management to carry on any business venture whether trade, industry, or service, with the objective of earning profits. The profit is shared by them in an agreed proportion. The loss is borne only by the financiers in proportion to their share in total capital. The entrepreneur's loss lies in not getting any reward for his/her services.

Murabahah   Sale at a specified profit margin. The term is, however, now used to refer to a sale agreement whereby the seller purchases the goods desired by the buyer and sells them at an agreed marked-up price, the payment being settled within an agreed timeframe, either in installments or lump sum. The seller bears the risk for the goods until they have been delivered to the buyer. *Murabahah* is also referred to as *bay mu'ajjal Musharakah*, an Islamic financing technique whereby all the partners share in equity as well as management. The profits can be distributed among them in accordance with agreed ratios. However, losses must be shared according to the share in equity.

Salam   Sale in which payment is made in advance by the buyer and the delivery of goods is deferred by the seller. This is also, like *Istisna,* an exception to the general *Shari'ah* ruling that you cannot sell what you do not own and possess.

Shari'ah   Refers to the divine guidance as given by the Qur'an and the *Sunnah* and embodies all aspects of the Islamic faith, including beliefs and practices.

Sunnah   The *Sunnah* is the most important source of the Islamic faith after the Qur'an and refers essentially to the Prophet's example as indicated by his practice of the faith. The only way to know the *Sunnah* is through the collection of *ahadiths*, which consist of reports about the sayings, deeds, and reactions of the Prophet, peace and blessings of God be on him.

6. Innovation and authenticity in Islamic finance

6.1 INTRODUCTION

Dr Muhammad Iqbal, poet-philosopher of the Indo–Pakistan subcontinent, says in a Persian couplet:

I am, as long as I move;
Not moving, I am not. (Iqbal, 1954, p. 150)

This implies that forward movement through progress and development is the lifeblood of societies. If societies do not move forward, they will not be able to remain stagnant for a long time; they will ultimately start declining. One of the essential requisites to enable societies to move forward is innovation. A well-known legal maxim of Islamic jurisprudence states that 'something without which an obligation cannot be fulfilled is also obligatory'. (Shatibi, n.d., p. 394; Zarqa, 1967, pp. 784 and 1088; and Nadvi, 2000, p. 480).

If it is necessary for a society to move forward to prevent stagnation and decline, innovation is also, therefore, indispensable. Don Sheelan has expressed the same idea recently by saying that 'innovation is the lifeblood of an organization' and that 'without it, not only is there no growth, but, inevitably, a slow death' (Sheelan, 2007, p. 3). There is, however, a snag that if the innovations are not well conceived, or if they are misused, they may create problems rather than solve them.

The accelerated development that the world has witnessed after the Second World War would not have been possible without an unending stream of innovations. The financial system has decidedly played an active role in this development, also as a result of innovations, including the revolution in information and communications technology. The financial system is, however, now plagued by persistent crises. According to one estimate, there have been more than 100 crises over the last four decades (Stiglitz, 2003, p. 54). Not a single geographical area or major country has been spared the effect of these crises. Even some of the countries that have generally followed sound fiscal and monetary policies have become engulfed in these crises.

This has created an uneasy feeling that there is something basically wrong somewhere. There is hence, a call for a new architecture (Camdessus, 2000, pp. 1 and 7–10; Stiglitz, 2007). The new architecture demands an innovation that could help prevent the outbreak and spread of crises or, at least, minimize their frequency and severity. Since most of the crises that the world has faced are generally of a serious nature and have been recurring persistently, cosmetic changes in the existing system may not be sufficient. It is necessary to have an innovation that would be really effective. It may not be possible to figure out such an innovation without first determining the primary cause of the crises. This is how science makes progress. It tries to determine the cause or causes of different phenomena so as to enable us to find an effective remedy for their solution.

6.2 PRIMARY CAUSE OF THE CRISES

This makes us look for the primary cause or causes of the crises. There is no doubt that there are a number of causes. However, one of the generally recognized most important causes is excessive and imprudent lending by banks[1] One cannot blame banks for this because, like everyone else, they also wish to maximize their profits. The more credit they extend, the higher will be their profit. Excessive lending, however, leads to a rise in asset prices, giving boost thereby to an artificial rise in consumption and speculative investment. Excessive lending becomes possible because of high leverage. The higher the leverage, the more difficult it is to unwind it in a downturn. Unwinding gives rise to a vicious cycle of selling that feeds on itself and leads to a serious financial crisis. It is market discipline which is expected to exercise a restraint on leverage and excessive lending. Since this has not happened, there arises the question of what is the reason for it? Is it possible that market discipline is not adequate in the financial system? If this is the case, then why is it so?

The market is able to impose a discipline through incentives and deterrents. These come through the prospect of making profit or loss. The major source of profit in the conventional system is the interest that the banks earn through their lending operations. The loss comes through the inability to recover these loans with interest. One would, therefore, expect that banks would carefully analyze their lending operations so as *not* to undertake those that would lead to a loss. There would be a check over excessive lending if the banks were afraid of suffering losses that would reduce their net profit. This does not happen in a system where profit and loss sharing (PLS) does not exist and the repayment of loans with interest is generally guaranteed.

There are two factors that save the banks from losses. The first of these is the collateral, which is necessary to manage the risk of default. The collateral can, however, do this only if it is of good quality. The banks are sometimes not very careful and rely heavily on the crutches of the collateral to extend financing for practically any purpose, including speculation. Collateral is, however, exposed to a valuation risk. Its value can be impaired by the same factors that diminish the borrower's ability to repay. The collateral, cannot, therefore, be a substitute for a more careful evaluation of the project financed. Nevertheless, the banks do not always undertake a careful evaluation because of the second factor that provides them protection. This is the 'too big to fail' concept which gives them an assurance that the central bank will bail them out (Miskhin, 1997, p. 61). Banks that are provided with such a safety net have incentives to take greater risks than they otherwise would (ibid., p. 62).

Given that banks lend excessively to maximize their profit, why is it that the depositors do not impose a discipline on the banks? They can do so in several different ways: by demanding better management, greater transparency, and more efficient risk management. If this does not work, they can always punish the banks by withdrawing their deposits. They do not, however, do so because they are assured of the repayment of their deposits with interest (ibid.). This makes them complacent and they do not take as much interest in the affairs of their financial institution as they would if they expected to suffer losses.

Instead of making the bankers as well as depositors share in the risks of business, the conventional financial system almost relieves them of the risks. The ability of the market to impose the required discipline thus gets impaired and leads to an unhealthy expansion in the overall volume of credit, to excessive leverage, to even subprime debt, and to living beyond means. This tendency of the system gets further reinforced by the bias of the tax system in favour of debt financing – dividends are subject to taxation while interest payments are allowed to be treated as a tax-deductible expense.

This shows that the absence of risk–reward sharing reduces market discipline and, thereby, introduces a fault line in the financial system. It is this fault line that makes it possible for the financier to lend excessively and also to move funds rapidly from place to place at the slightest change in the economic environment. A high degree of volatility thus gets injected into interest rates and asset prices. This generates uncertainty in the investment market, which in turn discourages capital formation and leads to the misallocation of resources (BIS, 1982, p. 3). It also drives the borrowers and lenders alike from the long end of the debt market to the shorter end. Consequently, there is a steep rise in highly leveraged short-term debt, which has accentuated economic and financial instability. The International Monetary Fund (IMF) acknowledged this fact in its May 1998 *World Economic Outlook* by stating that countries with high levels of short-term debt are 'likely to be particularly vulnerable to internal and external shocks and thus susceptible to financial crises' (International Monetary Fund, 1998, p. 83).

One may wish to pause here to ask why a rise in debt, and particularly short-term debt, should accentuate instability? One of the major reasons for this is the close link between the easy availability of credit, macroeconomic imbalances, and financial instability. The easy availability of credit makes it possible for the public sector to have a high debt profile and for the private sector to live beyond its means and to have high leverage. If the debt is not used productively, the ability to service the debt does not rise in proportion to the debt and leads to financial fragility and debt crises. The greater the reliance on short-term debt and the higher the leverage, the more severe the crises may be. This is because short-term debt is easily reversible as far as the lender is concerned, but repayment is difficult for the borrower if the amount is locked up in loss-making speculative assets or medium- and long-term investments with a long gestation period.

While there may be nothing basically wrong in a reasonable amount of short-term debt that is used for financing the purchase and sale of real goods and services by households, firms, and governments, an excess of it tends to get diverted to unproductive uses as well as speculation in the foreign exchange, stock, and property markets. Jean Claude Trichet, President of the European Central Bank, has rightly pointed out that 'a bubble is more likely to develop when investors can leverage their positions by investing borrowed funds' (Trichet, 2005, p. 4).

If we examine some of the major crises in the international financial system like the one in East Asia, the instability in the foreign exchange markets, collapse of the Long-term Capital Management (LTCM) hedge fund, and the prevailing crisis in the US financial system, we find that the easy availability of credit and the resultant steep rise in debt, particularly short-term debt, are the result of inadequate market discipline in the financial markets due to the absence of risk sharing (Chapra, 2007). In this chapter I will refer only to the collapse of the LTCM and the prevailing crisis in the US financial system.

6.2.1 The Collapse of LTCM

The collapse of the US hedge fund, LTCM, in 1998 was due to highly leveraged short-term lending. Even though the name hedge fund brings to mind the idea of risk reduction, 'hedge funds typically do just the opposite of what their name implies: they speculate' (Edwards, 1999, p. 189). They are 'nothing more than rapacious speculators, borrowing heavily to beef up their bets' (*The Economist*, 1998, p. 21). These hedge funds are mostly unregulated and are not encumbered by restrictions on leverage or short sales and are free to take concentrated positions in a single firm, industry, or sector-positions that might be considered 'imprudent' if taken by other institutional fund managers (Edwards, 2007; Sulz, 2007). They are, therefore, able to pursue the investment or trading strategies they choose in their own interest without due regard to the impact that this may have on others. They now account for close to half the trading on the New York and London stock exchanges (Sulz, 2007, p. 175).

There is a strong suspicion that these hedge funds do not operate in isolation. If they did, they would probably not be able to make large gains, and the risks to which they are exposed would also be much greater. They therefore normally tend to operate in unison. This becomes possible because their chief executives often go to the same clubs, dine together, and know each other very intimately (Plender, 1998). On the strength of their own wealth and the enormous amounts that they can borrow, they are able to destabilize the financial market of any country around the world whenever they find it to their advantage. Hence they are generally blamed for manipulating markets from Hong Kong to London and New York (*The Economist*, 1998). Mahathir Muhammad, Malaysia's ex-prime minister, charged that short-term currency speculators, and particularly large hedge funds, were the primary cause of the collapse of the Malaysian Ringgit in the summer of 1997, resulting in the collapse of the Malaysian economy (Muhammad, 1997; Stiglitz, 2007). It is difficult to know whether this charge is right or wrong because of the skill and secrecy with which these funds collude and operate. However, if the charge is right, then it is not unlikely that these funds may also have been instrumental in the collapse of the Thai Bhat and some other South Asian currencies.

The LTCM had a leverage of 25:1 in mid-1998 (Sulz, 2007, p. 179), but the losses that it suffered reduced its equity (net asset value) from the initial \$4.8 billion to \$2.3 billion in August 1998. Its leverage, therefore, rose to 50:1 on its balance-sheet positions alone. However, its equity continued to be eroded further by losses, reaching just \$600 million, or one-eighth its original value, on 23 September 1998. Since its balance-sheet positions were in excess of $100 billion on that date, its leverage rose to 167 times capital (International Monetary Fund, 1998). There was thus tier upon tier of debt, which became difficult to manage. The Federal Reserve had to come to its rescue because its default would have posed risks of systemic proportions. Many of the top commercial banks, which are supervised by the Federal Reserve and considered to be healthy and sound, had lent huge amounts to these funds. If the Federal Reserve had not come to their rescue, there may have been a serious crisis in the US financial system, with spillover and contagion effects around the world.[2] If the misadventure of a single hedge fund with an initial equity of only $4.8 billion could take the US and the world economy to the precipice of a financial disaster, then it would be perfectly legitimate to raise the question of what would happen if a number of the 9,000 hedge funds managing more than $2.8 trillion of assets got into trouble.[3]

A hedge fund is able to pursue its operations in secrecy because, as explained by former Chairman of the Board of Governors of the Federal Reserve System, Alan Greenspan, it is 'structured to avoid regulation by limiting its clientele to a small number of highly sophisticated, very wealthy individuals' (Greenspan, 1998, p. 1046). He did not, however, explain how the banks found it possible in a supposedly very well-regulated and supervised banking system to provide excessively lever-aged lending to such 'highly sophisticated, very wealthy individuals' for risky speculation when it is well known that the higher the leverage, the greater the risk of default. The unwinding of leveraged positions can cause major disruption in financial markets by exaggerating market movements and generating knock-on effects (International Monetary Fund, 1998).

This shows that a crisis can come not merely because of improper regulation of banks, as it did in East Asia, but also in a properly regulated and supervised system, as it did in the United States. Even though the hedge funds were not regulated, the banks were. Then why did the banks lend huge amounts to the LTCM and other funds? What were the supervisors doing, and why were they unable to detect and correct this problem before the crisis? Is there any assurance that the regulation of hedge funds would, without any risk sharing by banks, stop excessive flow of funds to other speculators?

6.2.2 The Prevailing Imbalances in the US Economy[4]

The lack of discipline in the financial system has also created for the United States two serious problems both of which ring a worrisome note not only for the United States but also for the world economy. These problems are the public sector budgetary deficits and the private sector saving deficiency. The federal government has been running budgetary deficits ever since 1970, except for a brief respite between 1998 and 2001. The budget moved from a surplus of $255 billion in fiscal year 2000 to a deficit of $400 billion in 2004 (Kohn, 2005; International Monetary Fund, 2007). The deficit declined thereafter to $360 and $262 and $275 billion in 2005, 2006 and 2007 but rose to $455 billion in fiscal 2008 (International Monetary Fund, 2008).

Instead of declining, the deficits are expected to rise further in the near future as a result of the efforts to bail out financial institutions, revive the economy, fulfil the generous campaign promises, and meet the retirement benefits of baby boomers. The continuing deficits had already raised the gross public debt of US Treasury to more than $10.6 trillion by 26 January 2009, $34,775 on average for every citizen (Federal Reserve, 2008). Of this, the external debt is around 27.5 per cent, more than double the 1988 figure of 13 per cent (Amadeo, 2009). The rise in external debt resulting from continuous current account deficits has had an adverse impact on the strength of the US dollar in the international foreign exchange markets.

These deficits may not have created a serious problem if the US private sector saving had not declined precipitously. Net private saving (saving by households and businesses minus investment) has been declining as a result of the borrowing and spending spree by both households and firms. This may not have been possible without loose lending by the financial system. Over the last three years (2005–2007), the net saving by households has been less than 1 per cent of the after-tax income, compared with an average of 8 per cent from 1950 to 2000 (Kohn, 2005; OECD, 2008). Government deficits combined with low private sector saving should have pushed up interest rates. This did not happen because of the inflow of funds from abroad. This inflow has, however, been only a mixed blessing because it did not only raise the US net foreign indebtedness to a record high in both absolute terms as well as a percentage of GDP but also lowered interest rates which has promoted a steep rise in consumer spending along with a boom in residential real estate prices.

This brings into focus the crucial issue of how long will the foreigners be willing to continue lending. Confidence in the strength and stability of the dollar is necessary to enable it to serve as a reserve currency. This is, in turn, not possible without the willingness of foreigners to hold dollars. What will happen if the deficits continue, create loss of confidence in the dollar, and lead to an outflow of funds from the United States? This is not just a theoretical question. In the last 40 years, the dollar has experienced four bouts of marked depreciation. Since nearly two-thirds of the world's foreign exchange holdings are still in dollars,[5] a movement out of the dollar into other currencies and commodities, as happened in the late 1960s, could lead to a sharp fall in the exchange rate of the dollar, a rise in interest rates and commodity prices, and a recession in the US economy. This might lead the whole world into a prolonged recession. The correction would then come with a vengeance when market discipline could have led to it much earlier with significantly less suffering. Accordingly, the President's Working Group on Financial Markets (PWG) has rightly concluded in its report on 'Principles and Guidelines Regarding Private Pool of Capital' issued in February 2007 that the most effective means of limiting systemic risk is to reinvigorate market discipline.

6.2.3   The Subprime Mortgage Crisis

The subprime mortgage crisis in the grip of which the US finds itself at present is also a reflection of excessive lending. Securitization or the 'originate-to-distribute' model of financing has played a crucial role in this. There is no doubt that securitization is a useful innovation. It has provided lenders greater access to capital markets, lowered transactions costs, and allowed risks to be shared more widely. The resulting increase in the supply of mortgage credit contributed to a rise in the homeowner-ship rate from 64 per cent in 1994 to 68 per cent in 2007 (Bernanke, 2007). However, even a useful innovation can have a negative impact if it is used in a way that reduces market discipline. Mortgage originators passed the entire risk of default to the ultimate purchaser of the loan security. They had, therefore, less incentive to undertake careful under-writing (Mian and Sufi, 2008; Mukkerjee et al., 2008). Consequently, loan volume gained greater priority over loan quality and the amount of lending to subprime borrowers increased. According to Mr Bernanke, Chairman of the Board of Governors of the Federal Reserve System, 'far too much of the lending in recent years was neither responsible nor prudent … . In addition, abusive, unfair, or deceptive lending practices led some borrowers into mortgages that they would not have chosen knowingly' (Bernanke, 2008). The check that market discipline could have exercised on the serving of self-interest did not, thus, come into play. This sowed the seeds of the subprime debt crisis and led to not only the financial distress of subprime borrowers but also a crisis in the US financial system which has had spillover effects on other countries.[6] Thus we can see clearly that the lack of market discipline leads first to excessive lending and then to financial crises and the suffering of a number of people.

When the system has reached a crisis point then it becomes difficult to apply the brakes. Central banks have no choice other than to lower interest rates and provide liquidity to avoid a recession. The Federal Reserve has also done the same. It has lowered interest rates and provided liquidity to the market 'to help alleviate concerns about funding' (Bernanke, 2008). While this will help reduce the intensity of the current crisis, it will also tend to aggravate the future crises by enabling the vicious cycle to continue. The liquidity made available now will enable the loose funding to continue. This will be followed by a financial crisis, which will again necessitate the pumping of further liquidity into the system to overcome the crisis. Therefore the more sensible thing to do is to simultaneously think of some effective way of introducing greater discipline into the financial system with a view to check excessive and loose lending. *The Economist* (1998) has rightly observed that 'the world needs new ways of thinking about finance and the risks it involves'. It is here where Islamic finance can make a valuable contribution to the international financial system.

6.3 THE ISLAMIC FINANCIAL SYSTEM

One of the most important objectives of Islam is to realize greater justice in human society.[7] This is not possible unless all human institutions, including the financial system, contribute positively towards this end. The financial system may be able to promote justice if, in addition to being strong and stable, it satisfies at least two conditions. One of these is that the financier must also share in the risk so as *not* to shift the entire burden of losses on the entrepreneur, and the other is that an equitable share of bank lending should become available to the poor to help eliminate poverty, expand employment and self-employment opportunities and, thus, help reduce inequalities of income and wealth.

To fulfil the first condition of justice, Islam requires both the financier and the entrepreneur to equitably share the profit as well as the loss. For this purpose, one of the basic principles of Islamic finance is: 'No risk, no gain'. If we wish to have a gain we must also be prepared to share the risk. Introduction of risk–reward sharing in the financial system should help induce the financial institutions to assess the risks more carefully and to monitor more effectively the use of funds by the borrowers. The double assessment of risks by both the financier and the entrepreneur should help inject greater discipline into the financial system, and go a long way in reducing excessive lending and making the financial system healthier. However, making just the banks share in the risk may not be enough because the desire to maximize profits may still induce the banks to indulge in excessive lending. It is, therefore, necessary to also motivate the depositors to play a more active role in the enforcement of this discipline. This will be possible if the depositors also share in the profit or loss.

However, since demand depositors do not get any return, it would not be fair to make them participate in the risks of financing. Their deposits must, therefore, be guaranteed. In contrast with this, investment depositors share in the profit and should, therefore, participate in the risks. What this will do is to turn investment depositors into temporary shareholders. Placing investment deposits in financial institutions will be like purchasing their shares, and withdrawing them will be like redeeming them. This will motivate depositors to monitor their banks, and demand greater transparency, better governance, and more effective risk management, auditing, regulation and supervision. Making the depositors participate in the risk would also help motivate them to take greater care in choosing their banks.

Instead of introducing greater discipline in this manner, the primary focus of the international financial system at present is on regulation and supervision. There is no doubt that prudent regulation and supervision are both necessary and unavoidable, and it is a matter of great relief to know that there has been substantial progress in this direction under the aegis of the Basel Committee on Banking Supervision (BCBS). Regulation and supervision cannot, however, be relied upon totally because regulation may not be applied uniformly in all countries and to all institutional money managers as a result of off-balance-sheet accounts, bank secrecy standards, and the difficulty faced by bank examiners in accurately evaluating the quality of banks' assets. The LTCM collapse as well as the prevailing financial crisis in the United States clearly show how banks can get into difficulties as a result of over-lending, even in an apparently well-regulated system. Regulation and supervision would, therefore, be more effective if they were complemented by a paradigm shift in favour of greater discipline in the financial system by making the banks, as well as investment depositors, share in the risks of financial intermediation. Just the bailing-in of banks, as is being suggested by some analysts (Calomiris, 1998; Meltzer, 1998), may not be able to take us far enough because the capital of banks may be only around 8 per cent of their risk-weighted assets. What is also necessary is to strongly motivate not only the banks to undertake careful underwriting of all loan proposals but also the depositors to be cautious in choosing their bank and to monitor their bank's affairs more carefully. The establishment of depositors' associations may make it easier for them to do so.

Islamic finance should, in its ideal form, help raise substantially the share of equity in businesses and of profit-and-loss sharing (PLS) in projects and ventures through the *mudarabah* and *musharakah* modes of financing. Greater reliance on equity financing has supporters even in mainstream economics. Professor Rogoff of Harvard University states, 'In an ideal world equity lending and direct investment would play a much bigger role' (Rogoff, 1999). He further asserts that, 'with a better balance between debt and equity, risk-sharing would be greatly enhanced and financial crises sharply muted' (ibid.). The IMF has also thrown its weight in favour of equity financing by arguing that 'foreign direct investment, in contrast to debt-creating inflows, is often regarded as providing a safer and more stable way to finance development because it refers to ownership and control of plant, equipment, and infrastructure and therefore funds the growth-creating capacity of an economy, whereas short-term foreign borrowing is more likely to be used to finance consumption. Furthermore, in the event of a crisis, while investors can divest themselves of domestic securities and banks can refuse to roll over loans, owners of physical capital cannot find buyers so easily' (International Monetary Fund, 1998).

Greater reliance on equity does not necessarily mean that debt financing is ruled out. This is because all financial needs of individuals, firms, or governments cannot be made amenable to equity and PLS. Debt is, therefore, indispensable. Debt does not, however, get created in a truly Islamic financial system through direct lending and borrowing but rather through the sale or lease of real assets via the sales- and lease-based modes of financing (*murabahah, ijarah, salam, istisna* and *sukuk*). The purpose is to enable an individual or firm to buy now the urgently needed real goods and services in conformity with his ability to make the payment later. The conditions, however, are that the asset which is being sold or leased must be real and not imaginary and that the transaction must be a genuine trade transaction with the full intention of giving and taking delivery. In the case of such sales or leases, the rate of return gets stipulated in advance and becomes a part of the deferred payment price. Since the debt is associated with real goods or services and the rate of return is fixed in advance, it will be less risky and, therefore, more attractive for banks, as compared with equity and PLS financing.

The predetermined rate of return on sales- and lease-based modes of financing may make it appear like interest-based instruments. It is, however, not so because of significant differences between the two for a number of reasons. First, as already indicated, the sales- and lease-based modes do not involve direct lending and borrowing. They are rather purchase and sale or lease transactions involving real assets. The *Shari'ah* has, in addition, imposed a number of conditions for the validity of these transactions. One of these is that the seller (or lessor) must also share a part of the risk to be able to get a share in the return. He cannot avoid doing this because of the second condition that requires the seller (financier) or lessor to own and possess the goods being sold or leased. The *Shari'ah* does not allow a person to sell or lease what he does not own and possess except in the case of *salam* and *istisna'* where the goods are not already available in the market but need rather to be produced before delivery. Once the seller (financier) acquires ownership and possession of the goods for sale or lease, he/she bears the risk. All speculative short sales, therefore, get ruled out automatically. Financing extended through the Islamic modes can thus expand only in step with the rise of the real economy and thereby help curb excessive credit expansion, which is one of the major causes of instability in the international financial markets.

Second, it is the price of the good or service sold, and not the rate of interest, that is stipulated in the case of sales- or lease-based modes of finance. Once the price has been set, it cannot be altered, even if there is a delay in payment due to unforeseen circumstances. This helps protect the interest of the buyer in strained circumstances. However, it may also lead to a liquidity problem for the banks if the buyer willfully delays payment. This is a major unresolved problem in Islamic finance. Discussions are, however, in progress among the jurists to find a *Shari'ah*-compatible solution.

6.3.1 Reducing Government Budgetary Deficits

The discipline that Islam wishes to introduce in the financial system may not materialize unless the governments reduce their borrowing from the central bank to a level that is in harmony with the goal of price and financial stability. If the governments borrow heavily from the central banks, they will provide more high-powered money to banks than is necessary and, thereby, promote excessive monetary expansion. It is essentially excessive liquidity, which, along with high leverage, enables banks to resort to lax lending. It is, therefore, necessary to have independent central banks along with legal curbs on the government's ability to borrow so that they do not run deficits in their budgets in excess of what is permissible within the framework of growth with stability.

6.4 AUTHENTICITY

This brings us to the question of authenticity in Islamic finance. In ordinary language, authentic, 'genuine' and 'bona fide' mean that there is conformity between word and deed or, in other words, the practice is exactly in keeping with what is claimed. In existentialist philosophy, it draws a distinction between the self and the non-self and refers generally to the degree to which a person is true to his own personality, spirit or character. In religious parlance it reflects the degree to which a person is true to his beliefs in spite of difficulties faced in doing so.

The way the Islamic financial system has progressed so far is only partly, but not fully, in harmony with the Islamic vision. It has not been able to come out of the straitjacket of conventional finance. The use of equity and PLS modes has been scant, while that of the debt-creating sales- and lease-based modes has been predominant. This may be condoned because of the near absence of the shared infrastructure institutions that are indispensable for reducing the difficulties faced in equity and PLS financing as a result of the principal–agent conflict of interest and the moral hazard. However, even in the case of debt-creating modes, all Islamic banks and branches or windows of conventional banks do not necessarily fulfil the conditions laid down by the *Shari'ah*. They try to adopt different legal stratagems (*hiyal*) to transfer the entire risk to the purchasers or the lessees. The result is that the Islamic financial system, as it is being practiced, does not appear to a number of its critics to be a genuine reflection of Islamic finance. If the system does not make significant progress in terms of authenticity, it will lose credibility in the eyes of the Muslim masses and the rapid progress that it has been making may not be sustainable.

6.4.1 Why the Lack of Authenticity

This raises the question of why the system has been unable to make significant headway in the direction of attaining greater authenticity. One of the primary reasons is that the institutions that are necessary to minimize the risks associated with anonymity, moral hazard, principal–agent conflict of interest, and late settlement of financial obligations have not yet been created. These institutions would enable the banks to obtain reliable information about their clients and to ensure that the funds lent by them to their clients are employed efficiently according to agreement and that the profit declared by them reflects the true picture of the business. They would also help them receive repayments on schedule, and get justice promptly in case of dispute with, or willful procrastination of payment by, their clients. They would also enable banks to gain liquidity when they need it in situations of liquidity crunch resulting from unforeseen circumstances. The establishment of such institutions would go a long way in providing a favourable environment. The longer it takes to establish such institutions, the longer it will take to move in the direction of greater authenticity. Some of the institutions that need to be created are briefly indicated below.

Centralized Shari'ah board
One of the indispensable needs of Islamic finance for realizing greater authenticity is to get verdicts that are in harmony with not just the form but also the spirit of the *Shari'ah* so as to help realize its cherished objectives (*maqasid*). This demands that the members of the *Shari'ah* board should not only be men of exemplary integrity and well-versed in the *Shari'ah*, but should also be insulated from moral hazard. This is because the *Shari'ah* board members, in spite of being individuals of high integrity, are human beings and are liable to be exposed to moral hazard. The hazard arises because every bank itself hires its own *Shari'ah* board members and pays their remuneration. In addition to being costly, particularly for small banks, this practice leads to conflicting opinions which create inconsistency and uncertainty. It also carries the potential of creating a conflict of interest. It may tempt the board members to give verdicts that are more profitable for the banks but not in keeping with the spirit of the *Shari'ah*. To overcome this problem, it is necessary to adopt some effective measures. One of these is to make full transparency mandatory with respect to the products allowed by their *Shari'ah* boards. The risk of getting a bad reputation should help induce the *Shari'ah* boards as well as the banks to be on their guard.

Another unavoidable measure is to establish a centralized *Shari'ah* board in the nature of a supreme court with members who are well-respected for their knowledge and integrity and who are also independent of banks. This will enable market participants to challenge any product which they feel is not in conformity with the spirit of the *Shari'ah*. It will also help standardize the products to the extent to which it is possible. Some differences of opinion are bound to remain. This may, however, be healthy for the financial system because it will promote innovation and also provide different alternatives for doing business instead of imposing a rigid conformity. Transparency should, however, be made mandatory so that the bank's clients and depositors know which alternative the bank has adopted. This will also help raise market discipline by enabling the bank's customers to choose for themselves a bank whose operations are in their opinion more *Shari'ah* compliant. Since standardization is necessary for the creation of an international Islamic financial market, it is imperative to have standardization at the level of not only individual countries but also all Muslim countries.

Shari'ah clearance and audit

Among the most crucial challenges before an Islamic bank is to create confidence in its depositors as well as all the other operators in the market about the harmony of its operations with the *Shari'ah*. For this purpose two important steps need to be taken. The first step is to get clearance from a *Shari'ah* board about the *Shari'ah* compatibility of all its products not only in form but also in spirit. The second step is to provide an assurance that all its transactions are actually in conformity with the verdicts of the *Shari'ah* board. The first step is like going to a legal expert to ascertain whether a specific mode of the banks operations is in conformity with the country's laws and, if not, what changes need to be introduced in it to make it so. The second is what auditors and banking supervisors do: ensuring that none of the bank's transactions violates the country's laws.

The *Shari'ah* boards are like legal experts. They can only perform the first task. It is difficult for them to perform the second task, which demands a review of all, or at least a random sample of, the different transactions that have taken place in different branches of the bank to ensure that they are in conformity with the verdict of the *Shari'ah* board. This demands a visit to the bank's premises to examine its operations in the same way as auditors and supervisors do. It is generally assumed that the *Shari'ah* boards do perform this task. However, members of the *Shari'ah* board do not have either the time or the staff to perform such a task effectively. The question that therefore arises is how to ensure the implementation of *Shari'ah* board decisions by the bank management. If this is not ensured, the existence of the *Shari'ah* board loses its meaning. There are three alternatives, which may be considered for this purpose.

One of these is for the Supervisory Authority in the country concerned to itself undertake the *Shari'ah* audit of banks in the course of its normal supervisory visits. This may not be considered desirable by Islamic banks in countries where the government and the Supervisory Authority are not favourably inclined towards Islamic banking. However it has the advantage that, if the Supervisory Authority performs the *Shari'ah* audit, they will also try to standardize the *fiqhi* decisions.

The second, more preferable, alternative is to establish independent *Shari'ah* audit firms in the private sector. These firms would have to hire and train sufficient staff to examine the transactions of banks with a view to determining whether they are in conformity with the *Shari'ah*. This alternative has the disadvantage that it would involve a proliferation of institutions. Inspectors from three different institutions would knock at the doors of banks at different times. The first of these would be from the Supervisory Authority to determine the conformity of the bank's operations with the country's laws and the principles of safe and sound banking. The second would be the *Shari'ah* auditors who would go to the bank to determine the conformity of its operations with the *Shari'ah*. The third would be the chartered auditors who would go to the banks to ensure that their financial statements have been prepared in conformity with the generally accepted accounting standards. Inspection by all these three institutions might not be convenient for banks because it would keep a number of their staff engaged in assisting these inspectors at different times, and thus add to their costs.

A third, and even more preferable, alternative is for the existing chartered audit firms to acquire the necessary expertise in the *Shari'ah* to enable them to undertake the *Shari'ah* audit. This will help avoid the proliferation of institutions with which Islamic banks have to deal. The banks would probably prefer this alternative because it will be more convenient for them to have the *Shari'ah* audit at the same time as the accounts audit.

Credit-rating agencies, chambers of commerce and trade associations

Among the shared institutions are credit-rating agencies which rate banks themselves as well as their counterparties. While such institutions exist in industrial countries, they do not at present exist in all Muslim countries. Credit-rating agencies may not be very helpful if they paint a rosy picture of the firms trying to raise equity or loans in the market. The experience of the US in the case of structured subprime loans clearly indicates the shortcomings of credit-rating agencies. Even though the concern for safeguarding their own reputation may serve as a check on rating agencies, a more effective regulatory framework needs to be developed to serve as a check on the moral hazard.

Legal reform

Even though Islamic financial institutions have been established in nearly all Muslim countries, the basic legal framework under which they operate has not evolved in the light of the *Shari'ah*. Cosmetic changes have been made in the existing conventional legal framework. It is necessary to prepare a comprehensive legal framework to bring the financial system in harmony with the *Shari'ah*. Preparing such a framework may not be an easy task because it requires expertise in *maqasid al-Shari'ah*, the *Shari'ah* compatible modes of Islamic finance, and complexities of the international financial system. Such expertise is rare. However, it is in the process of development and, hopefully, it should be possible to develop a comprehensive legal framework for financial institutions and financial markets operating on the basis of the *Shari'ah*.

External audit

The growing complexity of the banking business as well as the crises that the international financial system has witnessed have raised the function of external audit to a position of critical importance in all financial systems. It is, however, even more demanding and challenging in the Islamic financial system. It would be necessary for the external auditor to ensure not only that the bank's financial statements are prepared in all material respects in conformity with the professionally accepted financial reporting standards but also that the profit or loss declared by the bank truly reflects the bank's condition and that its profit has been derived without violating the teachings of the *Shari'ah*.

It is conventionally not considered to be the task of auditors to perform *Shari'ah* audit. They are not even equipped at present to do so. However, if this task is assigned to them in the light of what has been discussed above under the subject of *Shari'ah* audit, then the external auditors will have to create the necessary expertise to perform this task. This would demand that the training of auditors also includes necessary training in the financial aspects of the *Shari'ah*, just as it includes training in auditing and law. If such training proves to be too cumbersome for the auditors, it may also be possible for the auditing firm to hire *Shari'ah* scholars and provide them with some necessary background in auditing to be able to perform the *Shari'ah* audit.

The experience of the auditing firm Arthur Andersen has clearly revealed that the auditor should be independent and objective and there should not be anything that indicates the auditor's vested interest in protecting the bank's management. It is only such impartial audit that would create trust in the auditor's report and promote confidence in the bank. Even though it is the job of the internal controls system to prevent, or detect and correct, material misstatements arising from fraud and error, the external auditor cannot be exonerated from the responsibility of ensuring that this has been done conscientiously. He will have to design and carry out audit procedures in a way that would help reduce to an acceptably low level the risk of giving an inappropriate audit opinion.

Shari'ah courts or banking tribunals

Another indispensable requirement of the Islamic financial system is availability of some judicial facility that would help the banks recover their loans promptly from clients who unjustifiably procrastinate repayment and also help bank clients get prompt justice at a low cost when the bank is itself acting unjustly. The existence of *Shari'ah* courts or banking tribunals would be very helpful in getting prompt verdicts on the disputes of banks with their clients and vice versa. Normal civil court verdicts usually take several years in most Muslim countries.

The *Shari'ah* courts or banking tribunals would have a greater deterrent effect if the names of banks or their clients whom these courts have found to be guilty were also published in newspapers. The fear of getting bad publicity would help minimize contractual violations. Furthermore, the names of parties who violate habitually may also be sent to the chambers of commerce and trade associations for blacklisting them in order to create the same effect that social ostracism had in the Classical period when the Islamic financial system operated effectively (Chapra and Ahmed, 2002).

Audit organization

It may also be desirable to have an audit organization jointly owned by banks to evaluate the profit-and-loss accounts of those of their clients who the banks feel have tried to cheat them in a PLS arrangement. The fear of being exposed to a thorough check of their accounts by such an organization would complement the market forces in helping minimize the effort made by users of funds on a PLS basis to short-change the banks.

The creation of such an audit organization would save the individual financial institution the need to hire a large staff of auditors. It would thus create a substantial economy in expenses for all financial institutions. It would also give assurance to investors who provide their funds directly to businesses that, in case of need, they will be able to have the accounts properly examined by a qualified, impartial institution.

The whole concept of 'audit' may have to undergo a transformation in the case of primary modes of Islamic finance. Conventional auditing is 'not expressly designed to uncover management frauds'. (Elliot and Willingham, 1980). If the auditor performs a diligent audit and evaluates the financial statements according to 'the generally accepted accounting principles', the professional obligations of the auditor have been fulfilled.

The auditor has no responsibility to detect management malpractices or to determine the 'real' profit. He does not have the responsibility to check and to question (Lechner, 1980). Accounting firms generally tend to accommodate their clients, particularly the big clients who hire them. The auditor would fail in discharging his responsibility in a PLS system if he did not try to detect and disclose dishonest and questionable acts of the management and to determine the real amount of profit so as to ensure a 'fair' return to the shareholders and *mudarabah* depositors.

Depositors' associations
It is of crucial importance to establish mechanisms that would enable depositors to protect their own interest in a PLS financial system. Even demand depositors, and not just investment depositors, need such mechanisms because, even though demand deposits are guaranteed, the deposit insurance system does not generally insure demand deposits beyond a certain limit.

One of the mechanisms that could enable the depositors to protect their interest would be to have a representative on the bank's board of directors and also a voice in the shareholders' meetings The ease with which shareholders as well as depositors can participate in meetings and use their votes to influence important bank decisions or to remove directors and senior management from office, can play an important role in improving corporate governance in banks. This may, however, be difficult for depositors to do effectively because they are far more in number than shareholders when even in non-bank corporations shareholders do not necessarily attend such meetings. Moreover voting rights can be expensive for shareholders and depositors to exercise if they can do so only by attending the meetings. This would virtually guarantee non-voting. It is, therefore, necessary for depositors to appoint their representative on the board of directors. This would be easier if the formation of depositors' associations is encouraged. Such associations could also enlighten the depositors on the condition of the bank in addition to having a representative on the board and shareholder's meetings. However, until such time as such associations start functioning effectively, the external auditors may be assigned the task of acting as guardians of the depositors' interest in the same way as they are expected to guard the shareholders' interest.

Qualified pool of talent
To enable the Islamic system to fulfil the requirements of the *Shari'ah* as well as the BCBS and the IFSB and also ensure greater authenticity, it is necessary to train the management, staff and clients of banks, as well as

the general public, in the principles of Islamic finance. This will, however, not be enough. It is also necessary to create a large pool of experts and highly qualified professionals with in-depth knowledge of not only the *Shari'ah* and its objectives, but also Islamic and conventional finance and financial engineering. This would be possible if first-rate institutions were created for this purpose with the collaboration of financial institutions, central banks, universities and the governments. Directors and senior management of Islamic banks as well as *Shari'ah* advisers should also be required to take such courses. If the central banks as well as universities could make arrangements for this purpose, as is done in the case of conventional banking, the task of Islamic banks would become relatively easier.

Islamic financial market

The absence of a secondary market for Islamic financial instruments makes it extremely difficult for Islamic banks to manage their liquidity. Consequently, they end up maintaining a relatively higher ratio of liquidity than that which is generally maintained by conventional banks. This affects their profitability and competitiveness. It is, therefore, necessary to create an Islamic financial market. The establishment of the Islamic Financial Services Board (IFSB), International Islamic Financial Market (IIFM) and the Liquidity Management Centre (LMC) is a step in the right direction and will help provide the institutional infrastructure needed for an Islamic financial market.

The IFSB will help promote uniform regulatory and supervisory practices and prudential standards for Islamic *financial* institutions in the same way as is done by the BCBS. The IIFM will enhance cooperation in the field of finance among Muslim countries and financial institutions by promoting product development and harmonizing trading practices. This will serve as a catalyst for the development and promotion of a larger supply of *Shari'ah*-compatible financial instruments. The LMC will serve as an operating arm of the IIFM in the effort to facilitate the creation of an inter-bank money market that will enable Islamic financial institutions to manage their assets and liabilities effectively. It will create short-term *Shari'ah*-compatible investment opportunities by providing liquid, tradable, asset-backed treasury instruments (*sukuks*) in which these institutions can invest their surplus liquidity. It will also facilitate the sourcing and securitization of assets and trade actively in *sukuks* by offering buy/sell quotations. The three institutions will together help establish an Islamic financial market by removing the drawback experienced by Islamic banks as a result of the lack of standardization of terms and instruments and the non-availability of quality *Shari'ah*-compatible assets for trading in the secondary markets. This should help the Islamic financial system to expand at a faster rate in the future and create for itself a larger niche in the financial markets of Muslim countries.

Lender of last resort

Islamic banks also need some facility akin to the lender-of-last resort which is available to conventional banks to overcome liquidity crises when they occur suddenly as a result of unforeseen circumstances. Such a facility is available to Islamic banks at present on the basis of interest and is, therefore, unacceptable because of its incompatibility with the *Shari'ah*. Its use exposes them to charges of lack of authenticity. It may be worth considering the creation of a common pool at the central banks to provide mutual accommodation to banks in case of need. All banks may be required to contribute a certain mutually agreed percentage of their deposits to this common pool, just as they do in the case of statutory reserve requirements. They would then have the right to borrow interest-free from this pool with the condition that the net use of this facility is zero (that is, drawings do not exceed contributions) over a given period of time. In a crisis, the central banks may allow a bank to exceed the limit, with appropriate penalties, warning and a suitable corrective program. This will, in a way, be a more organized means of replacing the framework for mutual cooperation that prevailed among the *sarrafs* during the Classical period.

Reform of the stock market

Reform of the stock market is also necessary in the light of Islamic teachings to ensure that share prices reflect underlying business conditions and do not fluctuate erratically as a result of speculative forces. The discipline that the *Shari'ah* helps introduce, through the prohibition of short sales or the sale of what one does not own and possess, should greatly help in realizing this goal. In addition, rules and procedures need to be streamlined and enforced to protect investors and ensure stability and sanity in the stock market. This will help raise the confidence of savers and investors in the system and enable them to buy or sell shares in response to their circumstances or their perceptions of future market developments. Such a reform would constitute one of the most important pillars for supporting the edifice of an interest-free and equity-based economy.

6.5　ADDING ANOTHER DIMENSION OF JUSTICE

While the introduction of risk–reward sharing will help promote justice between the financier and the entrepreneur, it is also necessary to ensure that the benefit of the nation's savings that financial institutions mobilize is also shared equitably by all sectors of the economy. This is because the financial system plays a dominant role in the determination of the power base, social status and economic condition of individuals in the economy (Claessens and Perotti, 2007).

Hence no reform of the financial system may be meaningful unless it is also restructured in conformity with the socio-economic goals of Islam. The system has, however, tended to promote inequalities of income and wealth in almost all countries around the world and particularly so in countries which lack proper bank auditing and supervision and where the political system promotes cronyism. Arne Bigsten has rightly observed, that 'the distribution of capital is even more unequal than that of land' and that 'the banking system tends to reinforce the unequal distribution of capital' (Bigsten, 1987). Khwaja and Mian have shown in a recent paper that banks tend to favour politically connected firms (Khwaja and Mian, 2005). This bodes ominously for society because it leads to the recruitment of entrepreneurs from only one social class and to the failure to utilize the society's entire resource of entrepreneurial talent (Leadbearer, 1986).

For example, in Pakistan, for which data are available on the distribution of commercial bank deposits and advances by size in the State Bank of Pakistan *Bulletin*, small depositors having deposits of less than one million rupees ($16,129) were 28.2 million in number and constituted 99.6 per cent of all depositors in 2002. They contributed a total of Rs. 919.9 billion or 61.3 per cent of the banks' total deposits. Small borrowers borrowing less that Rs. 1 million and constituting 96.4 per cent of all borrowers were, however, able to get only Rs. 84.9 billion or 10.5 per cent of the banks' total advances. In sharp contrast with this, depositors of more than 10 million rupees, who constituted only 0.03 per cent of all depositors and provided only 24.8 per cent of all deposits, were able to get Rs. 628.8 billion or 77.6 per cent of total advances (see Table 6.1). What this implies is that less than 1 per cent of the borrowers were able to get more than three-quarters of the total advances. Small borrowers, thus, received far less than what they had contributed to the banks. It is even worse in nationalized banks where a number of politically well-connected big borrowers are even able to get their loans written off (Khwaja and Mian, 2005). Given such an inequitable allocation of advances, along with corruption, one cannot but expect inequalities of income and wealth to continue to rise, rather than decline, in the future – an outcome which is contrary to the socio-economic objectives of Islam.

Table 6.1   Distribution of commercial bank deposits and advances by size in Pakistan (amount in million rupees)

	2002			
	No. of Accounts	% of total	Amount	% of total
Distribution of Deposits				
Less than Rs. 100,000	26,525,861	93.70	510,998	34.06
From Rs. 100,000–1,000,000	1,677,031	5.92	408,935	27.25
From Rs. 1,000,000–10,000,000	97,785	0.35	208,204	13.88
Above Rs. 10,000,000	7,204	0.03	372.334	24.81
Total	**28,307,881**	**100.00**	**1,500,471**	**100.00**
Distribution of Advances				
Less than Rs. 100,000	906,198	78.04	22,659	2.79
From Rs. 100,000–1,000,000	213,402	18.38	62.284	7.68
From Rs. 1,000,000–10,000,000	31,293	2.70	96.620	11.91
Above Rs. 10,000,000	10,305	0.88	628.836	77.62
Total	**1,161,198**	**100.00**	**810,399**	**100.00**

Source: Derived from data given in State Bank of Pakistan, *Statistical Bulletin*.

The problem, however, is that the effort to reduce excessive lending may worsen the inequalities further by depriving primarily the small borrowers from being able to get credit because of their lack of political connection and their being considered, rightly or wrongly, as subprime. Therefore, what needs to be done is to introduce some suitable innovation in the financial system to ensure that even small borrowers are able to get adequate credit to enable them to realize their dream of establishing their own microenterprises. Any society where the poor are not able to get out of wage slavery by establishing their own enterprises and satisfying their basic needs satisfactorily from the higher income earned thereby, cannot be considered a just society. Dr Muhammad Yunus, founder of the Grameen Bank, has aptly emphasized that financing for self-employment should be recognized as a right that plays a critical role in attaining all other rights (Yunus, 1987). The Select Committee on Hunger established by the US House of Representatives concluded in its Report that 'the provision of small amounts of credit to microenterprises in the informal sector of developing countries can significantly raise the living standards of the poor, increase food security and bring about sustainable improvements in local economies' (Yunus, 1984). The Islamic financial system has hardly made any progress in accordance with this vision.

Experience has shown that microenterprises have generally proved to be viable institutions with respectable rates of return and low default rates. They have also proved to be a successful tool in the fight against poverty and unemployment. The experience of the International Fund for Agricultural Development (IFAD) is that credit provided to the most enterprising of the poor is quickly repaid by them from their higher earnings (*The Economist*, 1985). Testimony from the Grameen Bank in Bangladesh indicates a constant repayment rate of 99 per cent since the Bank's inception (Yunus, 1984).

No wonder a number of countries have established special institutions to grant credit to the poor and lower middle class entrepreneurs.[8] Even though these have been extremely useful, there are two major problems that need to be resolved. One of these is the high cost of finance in the interest-oriented microfinance system. A timely study by Qazi Kholiquz-zaman Ahmed, President of the Bangladesh Economic Association, has revealed that the effective rate of interest charged by microfinance institutions, including the Grameen Bank, turns out to be as high as 30 to 45 per cent.[9] This causes serious hardship to the borrowers in servicing their debt. They are often constrained to not only sacrifice essential consumption but also borrow from money lenders. This engulfs them unwittingly into an unending debt cycle which will not only perpetuate poverty but also ultimately lead to a rise in unrest and social tensions.[10] No wonder, the Minister of Finance for Bangladesh described micro-credit interest rates in that country as extortionate in an address he delivered at a microcredit summit in Dhaka in 2004 (Fernando, 2006). It is, therefore, important that, while the group lending method adopted by the Grameen bank and other microfinance institutions for ensuring repayment is retained, microcredit is provided to the very poor on a humane interest-free basis. This may be possible if the microfinance system is integrated with *zakah* and *awqaf* institutions. For those who can afford to bear the cost of microfinance, it would be better to popularize the Islamic modes of profit-and-loss sharing and sales- and lease-based modes of finance in Muslim countries not only to avoid interest but also to prevent the misuse of credit for personal consumption.[11]

Another problem faced by microfinance is that the resources at the disposal of microfinance institutions are inadequate. This problem may be difficult to solve unless the microfinance sector is scaled up by integrating it with the commercial banks to enable the use of a significant proportion of their vast financial resources for actualizing a crucial socio-economic goal. Commercial banks do not at present fulfil this need and the Select Committee on Hunger is right in observing that 'formal financial institutions in these countries do not recognize the viability of income generating enterprises owned by the poor' (Select Committee on Hunger, US House of Representatives, 1996. This may be because it is too cumbersome for commercial banks to get directly involved in the business of financing microenterprises. They do not, however, have to do this. They can operate through their own subsidiaries or through the institutions that already exist for this purpose, like the agricultural banks, cooperative banks, development banks and leasing and finance com-panies. Nevertheless, it is important to reduce the risk and expense of such financing for not only commercial banks but also the microfinance institutions.

The risk arises from the inability of microenterprises to provide acceptable collateral. One way of reducing the risk is to use the group lending method which has already proved its effectiveness. Another way is to establish the now-familiar loan guarantee scheme which has been introduced in a number of countries. To reduce the burden on the loan guarantee scheme it may be possible to cover the losses arising from the default of very small microenterprises from the *zakah* fund provided that the loan has been granted on the basis of Islamic modes of finance and does not involve interest. A third way is to minimize the use of credit for personal consumption by providing credit in the form of tools and equipment through the *ijara* (lease) mode of Islamic finance rather than in the form of cash. The raw materials and merchandise needed by them may be provided on the basis of *murabahah*, *salam* and *istisna'* modes. If they also need some working capital, it may be provided as *quard hassan* (interest-free loan) from the *zakah* fund.[12]

The additional expense incurred by commercial banks in evaluating and financing microenterprises also needs to be reduced. In the case of financing provided to the very poor on the basis of Islamic modes of finance, a part of the expense may also be covered from the *zakah* fund, one of the primary purposes of which is to enable the poor to stand on their own feet. For those who are not eligible for *zakah* but still deserve some help, it would be worthwhile for the governments to consider subsidizing a part of the cost, at least in the initial phase, in the interest of helping realize the cherished goals of increasing self-employment opportunities and reducing inequalities of income and wealth. As the system matures, the dependence on *zakah* as well as the government subsidy may tend to decline.

Microenterprises may not, however, be able to make a significant headway unless a substantial improvement is made in the environment for microenterprises through better access to markets and provision of the needed physical and social infrastructure. Such an infrastructure, including vocational training institutions, roads, electricity and water supply, will help increase the efficiency of microenterprises and reduce their costs, thereby enabling them to compete successfully in the market.

NOTES

1. This has been clearly recognized by the Bank for International Settlement (BIS) on p. 3 of its 78th Annual Report released on 30 June 2008 by stating that the fundamental cause of today's problems in the global economy is excessive and imprudent credit growth over a long period.
2. This was clearly acknowledged by Greenspan in the following words: 'Had the failure of the LTCM triggered the seizing up of markets, substantial damage could have been inflicted on many market participants, including some not directly involved with the firm, and could have potentially impaired the economies of many nations, including our own' (Greenspan, 1998, p. 1046).
3. The number of hedge funds is from Financial Stability Forum (www.fsforum org). The amount of assets they manage is for the third quarter of 2007 from Institutional Investor News and Hedge Asset Flows and Trends Report, 2008.
4. See Donald Kohn, member of the Board of Governors of the US Federal Reserve System, 'Imbalances in the US Economy' address at the 15th Annual Hyman Minsky Conference, the Levy Economics Institute of Bard College, Annandale-on-Hudson, New York, 22 April 2005.
5. At the end of the third quarter of 2007, 63.8 per cent of the identified official foreign exchange reserves in the world were held in United States dollars, www.imf.org/external/np/sta/cofer/eng/cofer.pdf.
6. Roughly 4.2 million mortgages were overdue or in foreclosure at the end of 2007, according to the Mortgage Bankers Association. An additional three million borrowers may default in the near future. See Herszenhorn, and Bajaj (2008).
7. See, for example, al-Qur'an, 57:25; 5:8; 4:135; 6:152; 4:58; 16:90. For references from the *Hadith*, *Fiqh* and other Islamic literature, see Chapra (1992) and Chapra (2000).
8. For the experience of microfinance institutions in some Muslim countries, see Mohammed (2008).
9. This is highly plausible because some other studies indicate even higher effective rates of interest. According to Nimal Fernando, Principal Microfinance Specialist in

the East Asia Department of the Asian Development Bank, the nominal interest rates charged by most microfinance institutions in the region range from 30 to 70 per cent a year. The effective interest rates are even higher because of commissions and fees charged by them (Nimal, 2006). According to Mannan, the effective rates range from 54 to 84 per cent (Mannan, 2007).

10. See Ahmed (2007). See also Sharma (2002). According to Sharma, 'while the Grameen Bank model of micro-credit has landed poor communities in a perpetual debt trap, the rising number of loan defaulters has given a serious setback to the Bolivian experiment'.
11. For some details see Islamic Research and Training Institute (IRTI) of the Islamic Development Bank (IDB) (2007); see also Feroz (2007).
12. For some details on the risks associated with these forms of financing, see IRTI/IDB (2007), p. 30.

REFERENCES

Ahmed, Qazi Kholiquzzaman (ed.) (2007), *Socio-Economic and Indebtedness-Related Impact of Micro-Credit in Bangladesh* (Dhaka: Bangladesh Unnayan Parishad).
Amadeo, Kimberly (2009, January), The US national debt and how it got so big? http://useconomy.about.com/od/fiscalpolicy/p/US_debt.html.
Bank for International Settlements (BIS). (1982), *Annual Report* (Basel, Switzerland: BIS).
Bank for International Settlements (BIS). (1998), *Annual Report* (Basel, Switzerland: BIS).
Bank for International Settlements (BIS). (2008), *Annual Report* (Basel, Switzerland: BIS).
Bernanke, Ben (2007, 31 August), Housing, housing finance, and monetary policy, www.federalreserve.gov/newsevents/speech/bernanke/20070831a.htm.
Bernanke, Ben (2007, 20 September), Subprime mortgage lending and mitigating foreclosures, *BIS Review*, 104.
Bernanke, Ben (2008), Fostering sustainable homeownership, Speech at the National Community Reinvestment Coalition Annual Meeting, Washington, DC, 14 March.
Bigsten, Arne (1987), Poverty, inequality and development, in Norman Gemmell, *Surveys in Development Economics* (Oxford: Blackwell).
Calomiris, C. (1998), The IMF's imprudent role as lender of last resort, *Cato Journal*, 17:3, 275–95.
Camdessus, Michael (2000, 10 January), Main principles of the future international monetary, financial system, *IMF Survey*, pp. 1 and 7–10.
Chapra. M. Umer (1992), *Islam and the Economic Challenge* (Leicester, UK: The Islamic Foundation).
Chapra, M. Umer (2000), *The Future of Economics: An Islamic Perspective* (Leicester UK: The Islamic Foundation).
Chapra, M. Umer and Ahmed, Habib (2002), *Corporate Governance in Islamic Financial Institutions* (Jeddah: IRTI/IDB, Occasional Paper No. 6).

Chapra M. Umer (2007a), The case against interest: Is it compelling?, *Thunder-bird International Business Review*, 49:2, March/April, 161–86.

Chapra, M. Umer (2007b), Challenges facing the islamic financial industry, in Kabir Hassan and Merwyn Lewis (eds), *Handbook of Islamic Banking* (Cheltenham, UK, and Northampton, MA, USA: Edward Elgar Publishing), pp. 325–53.

Claessens, Stijn and Perotti, Enricho (2007), Finance and inequality: Channels and evidence, *Journal of Comparative Economics*, 35, July, pp. 748–73.

Edwards, F.R. (1999), Hedge funds and the collapse of long-term capital management, *Journal of Economic Perspectives*, pp. 189–210.

Elliot K. and Willingham, J.J. (1980), *Management Fraud: Detection and Deterrence* (New York: Princeton, University Press).

Federal Reserve (2008, January), *Federal Reserve Bulletin*, www.federal= reserve.gov/pubs/supplement/2008/table2_41.htm.

Fernando Nimal A. (2006, May), *Understanding and Dealing with High Interest Rates on Micro-credit* (Manila: Asian Development Bank).

Feroz, Ehsan Habib (2007), The halal way to social change, *Islamic Horizons*, January/February, p. 42.

Greenspan, A. (1998), Statement before the Committee on Banking and Financial Services, US House of Representatives, *Federal Reserve Bulletin*, 1 October, pp. 1046–50.

Herszenhorn, David and Bajaj, Vikas (2008), A bipartisan bid on mortgage aid is gaining speed, *The New York Times*, 2 April, p. 2, www.nytimes.com/2008/04/02/washington/02housing.html?-th&emc=th.

International Monetary Fund (1998, May), *World Economic Outlook* (Washington, DC: IMF).

International Monetary Fund (1998, September), *World Economic Outlook* (Washington, DC: IMF).

International Monetary Fund (1998, December), *World Economic Outlook*, and *International Capital Markets* (Washington, DC: IMF).

International Monetary Fund (2007), *Yearbook* (Washington, DC: IMF).

International Monetary Fund (2008, December), *International Financial Statistics* (Washington, DC: IMF).

Iqbal, Muhammad (1954), *Payam-e-Mashriq* (Lahore: Shaykh Mubarak Ali).

Islamic Research and Training Institute (IRTI) of the Islamic Development Bank (IDB) (2007), Framework and strategies for development of islamic micro-finance services. Working Paper for IFSD Forum 2007 on Islamic Micro-finance Development: Challenges and Initiatives held Dakar, Senegal on 27 May 2007.

Keys, Benjamin, Mukkerjee, Tanmoy, Seru, Amit and Vig, Vikrant (2008, January), Did securitization lead to lax screening? Evidence from subprime loans 2001–2006, http://papers.ssrn.com/sol3/papers.cfm?abstract_id=1093137#.

Khwaja, Asim and Mian, Atif (2005), Do lenders favour politically connected firms?: Rent provision in an emerging financial market, *Quarterly Journal of Economics*, April. 120:4, 1371–1411.

Kohn, D.I. (2005), Imbalances in the US economy, *BIS Review*, Vol. 28.

Leadbearer, Charles (1996), Rags to riches: Facts or fiction, *Financial Times*, 30 December, p. 5.

Lechner Alan (1980), *Street Games: Inside Stories of the Wall Street Hustle* (New York: Harper & Row), p. 143.

Mannan, M.A. (2007), Alternative microcredit models in Bangladesh: A comparative analysis of Grameen Bank and Social Investment Bank Ltd. – myths and realities. Paper presented at the First International Conference on Enhancing Islamic Financial Services for Micro and Medium-sized Enterprises, held on 17–19 April 2007 in Negara Darussalam, Brunei.

Meltzer, A. (1998), Asian problems and the IMF, *Cato Journal*. 17:3, 267–74.

Mian, Atif and Sufi, Amir (2008, January), The consequences of mortgage credit expansion: evidence from the 2007 mortgage default crisis, http://ssrn. com/ abstract=1072304.

Miskhin, Frederic (1997), The causes and propagation of financial instability: Lessons for policymakers, in Federal Reserve Bank of Kansas City (1937), *Maintaining Financial Stability in a Global Economy*, Proceedings of a Symposium Sponsored by the FRB Kansas City, Jackson Hole, Wyoming, 28–30 August, pp. 55–96.

Muhammad, M. Mahathir (1997), Highwaymen of the global economy, *Wall Street Journal*, 3 September, p. CI.

Nadvi, Ali Ahmad al- (2000), *Jamharah al-Qawaʻid al-Fiqhiyyah fi al-Muʻamlat al-Maliyyah* (Riyadh: Sharikah al-Rajhi al-Masrafiyyah li al-Istithmar).

Obaidullah, Mohammed (2008), *Role of Microfinance in Poverty Alleviation: Lessons from Experiences in Selected IDB Member Countries* (Jeddah: IRTI/ IDB).

Organisation for Economic Co-operation and Development (OECD) (2008), *Economic Outlook 82*, Annex Tables.

Plender, J. (1998), Western crony capitalism, *Financial Times*, 3–4 October.

President's Working Group on Financial Markets (PWG) (2007, February), Principles and guidelines regarding private pool of capital, http://www. ustreas.gov/press/releases/hp272.htm.

Rogoff, K. (1999), International institutions for reducing global financial instability, *Journal of Economic Perspectives*, 4:13, 21–46.

Select Committee on Hunger, US House of Representatives (1986), *Banking for the Poor: Alleviating Poverty Through Credit Assistance in Developing Countries* (Washington, DC).

Sharma, Sudhirendhar (2002), Is micro-credit a macro trap? *The Hindu*, 25 September www.hinduonnet.com/businessline/2002/09/25/stories/2002092500 810900.htm.

Shatibi, Abu Ishaq al- (n.d.), *Al-Muwafaqat fi Usul al-Shariʻah* (Cairo: al-Maktabah al-Tijairiyyah al-Kubra).

Sheelan, Don (2007), Innovation, Wikipedia, 1 October.

State Bank of Pakistan (2002), *Statistical Bulletin* (Karachi: State Bank of Pakistan).

Stiglitz, Joseph (2003), Dealing with debt: How to reform the global financial system, *Harvard International Review*, Spring, pp. 54–9.

Stiglitz, Joseph (2007), Financial hypocrisy, *The Economist's Voice*, www. bepress. com/ev, December, pp. 1–3.

Sulz, Rene M. (2007), Hedge funds: Past, present and future, *Journal of Economic Perspectives*, 21:2, Spring, pp. 175–94.

The Economist (1998, 17 October), The risk business, p. 21.

The Economist (2004, 12 June), Funds of hedge fiends: Borrowing and betting, pp. 72–3.

The Economist (2008, 22 March), Wall Street's crisis, p. 25.

The Federal Reserve Board (2008, January), *Federal Reserve Bulletin, Statistical Supplement*, www.federalreserve.gov/pubs/supplement/2008/01/table1-4htm.

Trichet, J.C. (2005), Asset price bubbles and monetary policy, MAS Lecture, Monetary Authority of Singapore.

United States Government (2008), Treasury summary for FY 2008, http://www.fms.treas.gov/mts0908.pdf.

Wikipedia (2008), United States public debt, 25 February.

Wikipedia (2008), Grameen Bank, 2 March.

World Bank (1995), *Policy and Research Bulletin*, April–June.

Yeager, I.B. (1998), How to avoid international financial crises, *Cato Journal*, 17:3, 257–65.

Yunus, Muhammad (1984), *Group-Based Savings and Credit for the Rural Poor* (Dhaka: Grameen Bank, January).

Yunus, Muhammad (1987), The poor as the engine of development, reproduced from *The Washington Quarterly*, Autumn 1987, in *Economic Impact* (1988), 2, 31.

Zarqa, Mustafa Ahmad al- (1967), *al-Fiqh al-Islami fi Thawbihi al-Jadid* (Damascus: Matabi' Alif Ba al-Adib).

7. Challenges facing the Islamic financial industry[*]

7.1 INTRODUCTION

The prohibition of interest in Islam, as in some other major religions, and the aspiration of Muslims to make this prohibition a practical reality in their economies, has led to the establishment of the Islamic financial services industry (IFSI). The industry has made substantial progress over the last three decades after the establishment of the first Islamic bank (Dubai Islamic Bank) in 1975. The number of institutions offering *Shari'ah*-compliant services has risen, as has the number of conventional banks that have opened Islamic windows and branches. The total volume of assets that all these institutions manage has risen rapidly and so has the international acceptance of Islamic finance. Nevertheless, the industry is still in its formative stage and faces a number of challenges that need to be addressed to enable it to continue its rapid expansion without facing any crisis and, thereby, acquire greater respectability and a much greater share of the international financial market. This raises the question of what these challenges are and how they can be faced.

7.1.1 The Challenges

Challenges arise essentially from the disparity that exists between the vision of a system (where it wishes to go) and its present position (the progress that it has made so far). The greater the disparity, the more serious may be the challenges faced. The most crucial challenge that all financial systems, including the Islamic, face at present is to be sound and efficient and free from crises and instability. All the guidelines laid down by the Basle Committee for Banking Supervision (BCBS) need to be carefully considered and implemented to meet this challenge satisfactorily. However, even if the Islamic financial system meets this challenge successfully, it may still not be able to be a genuine reflection of Islamic teachings if it fails to realize the vision of Islam by actualizing justice, which is one of the primary objectives of Islam (*maqasid al-Shari'ah*) (al-Qur'an, 57:25). It may not be possible to realize this

193

vision unless all human institutions, including the financial system, contribute positively towards this end. The financial system may be able to promote justice if, in addition to being strong and stable, it satisfies at least two conditions. One of these is risk sharing by the financier so as not to shift the entire burden of losses on the entrepreneur, and the other is equitable distribution of the benefit of deposits provided by a wide spectrum of depositors to a similarly wide spectrum of the population by helping eliminate poverty, expand employment and self-employment opportunities, and reduce inequalities of income and wealth.

7.1.2   The First Condition of Justice

The first condition would be satisfied if the profit as well as loss is shared equitably by both the financier and the entrepreneur. It is against the principles of justice that, in the event of a loss, the entrepreneur bears the entire loss in spite of his hard work and entrepreneurship, while the financier gets a positive rate of return without doing anything. The sharing of risks will lead to an increase in the reliance on equity and profit-and-loss-sharing (PLS) modes of financing (*mudaraba* and *musharaka*)[1] and reduce that on debt. This will help introduce greater discipline into the financial system. If investment depositors share in the risk to get a return, they will be motivated to take more interest in the affairs of their banks and demand greater transparency and more effective management. Similarly, if the bankers also participate in the risk, they will also be motivated to evaluate loan applications more rigorously. The introduction of such a discipline in the financial system should help reduce funds available for speculation and unproductive spending and, thereby, control excessive expansion of credit and living beyond means by both the public and the private sectors. Moreover, since the rate of profit is only known ex post, it cannot change daily like the rate of interest. This along with the check on excessive credit expansion should help reduce volatility in the movement of funds and, thereby, inject greater stability into the financial markets (see Chapra, 2002, for details). No wonder Mills and Presley have stated: 'There are sufficient grounds to wish that, in hindsight, the prohibition of usury had not been undermined in Europe in the sixteenth century. More practical wisdom was embodied in the moral stand against usury than was then realized' (Mills and Presley, 1999, p. 120).

However, since it is not possible for the *mudaraba* and *musharaka* modes to accommodate all different types of financial needs. Islam has also allowed some other modes of financing (*murabaha*, *ijara* (leasing), *salam* and *istisnaa*)[2] which create debt rather than equity and in which the rate of return gets fixed in advance. *Sukuk* (asset-based Islamic bonds) have also now gained prominence as instruments for raising large amounts of finance by governments and corporations. These are based primarily on the *ijara* mode and have the advantage of converting leasing assets into *Shari'ah*-compatible financial assets which are tradable in the market (for details see Ali, 2005). There is hardly any significant need for financing that all the different modes of Islamic finance cannot together help satisfy. Nevertheless, it should be possible to create more *Shari'ah*-compatible modes in the future in response to need.

It may be argued that the above-specified debt-creating modes with a predetermined rate of return are not different from the interest-based modes. This is not so because the debt that arises in the case of these modes does not arise as a result of lending and borrowing on interest. It rather arises as a result of the sale or lease of goods and services on a deferred payment basis. The rate of return becomes a part of the price of the goods or services sold or leased. The debt, therefore, gets linked with the growth of the economy. There is, however, a danger that these modes may degenerate into purely financing devices. The *Shari'ah* has therefore laid down certain conditions for their validity. The most important of these conditions is the requirement that the seller or the lessor cannot sell or lease what he/she does not own and possess. When the financer purchases an asset for the purpose of sale or lease, he converts cash into real assets and, thereby, takes risk. The return he gets is a reward for the risk that he has taken.

7.1.3 The Second Condition of Justice

Fulfilment of the second condition of justice about the equitable distribution of credit is imperative because it would help realize the vision of Islam which is not only to improve the condition of the oppressed but also to make them leaders and heirs and to establish them firmly on earth (al-Qur'an, 28:5–6). One of the ways of actualizing this vision would be to spread the benefit of resources that become available to banks from a wide spectrum of depositors to a similarly large spectrum of the society rather than to just a few rich individuals, as the banking systems generally end up doing at present. Islamic finance will not be able to fulfil this criterion of justice if increased financing does not become available to the poor and the middle-class entrepreneurs. A number of these people have the talent, drive and innovative ability to establish a successful business enterprise, but do not have the resources they need to make use of their talents. Availability of finance would perform the function of pump priming in enabling such talented individuals not only to advance themselves economically but also to make a positive contribution to their economy.

7.1.4   The Dream and the Reality

The way the Islamic financial system has progressed so far is not in accordance with this vision. It has not been able to come out of the straitjacket of conventional finance. The use of equity and PLS modes has been scant, while that of the debt-creating sales-based modes has been predominant. Moreover, even in the case of debt-creating modes, all Islamic banks and branches or windows of conventional banks do not necessarily fulfil the conditions laid down by the *Shari‘ah*. They try to adopt different legal stratagems (*hiyal*) to transfer the entire risk to the purchasers or the lessees, in violation of the first condition of justice stated above. Significant progress does not seem to have been made even towards fulfilment of the second condition of justice, which is realization of equitable distribution of credit. The result is that the Islamic financial system, as it is being practiced, does not appear to a number of its critics to be a genuine reflection of Islamic finance.

7.2   HOW TO BE GENUINE (1): GREATER RELIANCE ON EQUITY AND PLS MODES

The most important challenge facing the Islamic financial industry is to be as genuine and authentic a reflection of Islamic teachings as is possible within the present-day environment. This would happen not only when interest was removed definitively from the economy but also when the two conditions for realizing justice specified in the introduction were genuinely fulfilled. The system would lose its raison d'être if it did not make significant progress in promoting greater reliance on equity and PLS financing in the financial system and bringing about a more equitable distribution of credit with the objective of eliminating poverty, expanding employment and self-employment opportunities and reducing inequalities of income and wealth. It is only this, which will enable the Islamic financial system to gain credibility in the eyes of the Muslim masses.

This raises the question of why the system has failed to make significant headway in using the equity and PLS modes and to bring about a relatively more equitable distribution of credit. It may not be possible to answer this question without answering some other questions, such as the following. Did the system ever operate successfully in Islamic history? What were the factors that contributed to its success? Can the system operate in a changed environment? If it can, then what are the different institutions that need to be established to enable it to operate in the modern environment when the favourable conditions that existed during the Classical period do not exist any more?

7.2.1 Financial Intermediation in Islamic History

From a very early stage in Islamic history, Muslims were able to establish a financial system without interest for mobilizing resources to finance productive activities and consumer needs. The system to finance productive activities was based largely on the profit-and-loss-sharing (PLS) modes of *mudaraba* and *musharaka*. Other modes, including interest-free loans (*qard hasan*), were also used to help finance purchases on credit by consumers as well as businesses and to help the needy.

There are no empirical data available about the operation of the Islamic system in the past. However, whatever historical evidence is available seems to indicate that the system worked quite effectively during the heyday of Muslim civilization and for centuries thereafter. According to Udovitch, the Islamic modes of financing (*mudaraba* and *musharaka*) were able to mobilize the 'entire reservoir of monetary resources of the medieval Islamic world' for financing agriculture, crafts, manufacturing and long-distance trade. They were used not only by Muslims but also by Jews and Christians (Udovitch, 1970, pp. 180, 261) to the extent that interest-bearing loans and other overly usurious practices were not in common use (Udovitch, 1981, p. 257: see also p. 268). According to Goitein, breach of the Jewish, Christian and Islamic law against interest was found in the Geniza documents 'only once in the record of a judgment even though an unusually large amount of Geniza documents deal with credit' (Goitein, 1967, pp. 255 and 250. See also Goitein, 1966, pp. 271–74). Schatzmiller has also concluded that financial capital was developed during the early period by a 'considerable number of owners of monetary funds and precious metals, without the supposed interdiction of *riba*, usury, hampering it in any way' (Schatzmiller, 1994, p. 102).

Financiers were known in the early Muslim history as *sarrafs*.[3] By the time of the Abbasid Caliph al-Muqtadir (908–932), they had started performing most of the basic functions of modern banks (Fischel, 1992). They had their own markets, something akin to Wall Street in New York and Lombard Street in London, and fulfilled all the banking needs of commerce, industry and agriculture (Duri, 1986, p. 898) within the constraints of the then-prevailing technological environment. However, since the *sarrafs* were not banks in the strictly technical modern sense, Udovitch has preferred to call them 'bankers without banks' (Udovitch, 1981).

The legal instruments necessary for the extensive use of financing through *mudaraba* and *musharaka* were already available in the earliest Islamic period (Udovitch, 1970, p. 77). These instruments, which constituted an important feature of both trade and industry and provided a framework for investment, are found in a developed form in some of the earliest Islamic legal works (pp. 77–8). Some of the institutions, practices and concepts already fully developed in the Islamic legal sources of the late 8th century did not appear in the West, according to Udovitch, until several centuries later (p. 261).

The ability to mobilize the financial resources, along with a combination of several economic and political factors (for a discussion of some of these, see Chapra, 2000, pp. 173–85), provided a great boost to trade which flourished from Morocco and Spain in the West, to India and China in the East, Central Asia in the North, and Africa in the South. The extension of Islamic trade influence is indicated not only by the available historical documents but also by the Muslim coins of the 7th to the 11th centuries found through excavations in countries like Russia, Finland, Sweden, Norway and the British Isles which were on the outskirts of the then-Muslim world (Kramers, 1952, p. 100; see also pp. 101–6). The expansion of trade generated prosperity, which, in turn, 'made possible a development of industrial skill which brought the artistic value of the products to an unequalled height' (Udovitch, 1970, p. 104). Since businesses were in general small, even the poor and middle-class entrepreneurs seem to have flourished. This takes us to the second question of what were the factors that led to the success of primary modes in the classical period.

7.2.2   Factors that Contributed to Past Success

All the functions that the *sarrafs* performed demanded minimization of the principal–agent conflict of interest so as to ensure the total confidence of all the stakeholders (*sarrafs*, and providers and users of funds) in each other. This leads us to the questions of what were the factors that made it possible to minimize the principal–agent conflict of interest in the Classical period and what can be done in modern times to create the same trust and confidence of the stakeholders in each other when the conditions have changed.

The answer lies in the support that the system received from an enabling environment. First, the market mechanism worked effectively and induced all participants in the market to do their jobs honestly and efficiently in their own long-term self-interest. This received further support from Islamic values which were generally observed by the market participants.

Second, the *sarrafs* operated in communities which were far smaller compared with the communities in which modern banks operate. Accordingly, the providers and users of funds as well as the *sarrafs* were all well-known to each other. This was further reinforced by membership of nearly all participants in tribes, guilds, fraternities or sufi orders. This established a 'moral community' with social solidarity and mutual trust and cooperation. This acted as an informal contract enforcement mechanism and served as a deterrent against cheating and fraud. Anyone who tried to cheat or procrastinate unduly became ostracized. The entire community would refrain from doing business with the guilty party. This, along with the effective operation of market forces, was further reinforced by the then-prevailing religious environment which helped create self-enforcement of religious values. This climate of mutual trust and cooperation, according to Udovitch, was not based on a casual or occasional favour, but rather 'a recognized commercial practice looming large in the discussion of partnership (*mudaraba* and *musharaka*) on the same level as deposit, pledge and similar contracts' (Udovitch, 1970, p. 102; see also Grief, 1997; Rauch, 2001).

Third, the economic environment was also less complex and, in general, there seems to have been less volatility in economic variables, particularly prices and exchange rates, than what prevails in modern times.

Fourth, the *sarrafs* were individual proprietors or partnership firms and the separation of ownership and control was not a problem. The self-interest of the *sarrafs* themselves as well as the users of funds reinforced mutual trust and confidence in a system in which *mudaraba* and *musharaka* were the primary methods available for mobilizing financial resources. They brought to the disposal of commerce and industry the entire reservoir of monetary resources of the medieval Islamic world and served as a 'means of financing, and to some extent, insuring commercial ventures, as well as providing the combination of skills and services for their satisfactory execution' (Udovitch, 1970, pp. 180, 261). The absence of a predetermined positive rate of return made everyone (rich and poor) a prospective candidate for financing by the *sarrafs*, provided that he had the necessary skill and experience for doing business successfully along with a reputation for honesty. The poor were not, therefore, necessarily at a disadvantage.

Fifth, the legal instruments necessary for the extensive use of financing through *mudaraba* and *musharaka* were also already available in the earliest Islamic period (Udovitch, 1970, p. 77). These instruments, which are found in a developed form in some of the earliest Islamic legal works (1970, pp. 77–78), were inspired by the Qur'anic requirement that all loan transactions must be consummated in writing with witnesses (al-Qur'an, 2:282). Written instruments thus became an important feature of financial inter-mediation.

Last but not least, what helped further was the strength and independence of the judicial system (*mahkamah al-qada*). The courts helped ensure the honest fulfilment of contractual obligations. It was also possible to get justice promptly at a low cost in terms of time, trouble and money. The office of the *qazi* (judge) proved to be according to Schacht one of the most rigorous institutions evolved by Islamic society. The *qudis*, along with the *ulama* (religious scholars), 'played an important part in maintaining Islamic civilization, and in times of disorder they constituted an element of stability' (Schacht, 1970, p. 558).

Consequently, a climate of trust prevailed, conflict of interest was minimized and the transactions costs of enforcing contracts were reduced. The system worked effectively. This led to an expansion of trade and helped boost commerce, industry and agriculture to an optimum level, as indicated earlier.

7.2.3   Institutions Needed to Enable the System to Work

This takes us to the next question of whether the revival of the *mudaraba* and *musharaka* modes of Islamic finance can operate successfully in the modern world when the enabling environment prevailing in the Classical period does not exist. Banks operate in relatively larger communities where all the different stakeholders (shareholders, depositors, directors, management and users of funds) do not necessarily know each other very well. In a situation of anonymity that now prevails, depositors may hesitate to entrust their savings to banks, and the banks may also be reluctant to provide financing to users on a PLS basis unless the moral hazard is reduced and a climate of trust is created between the principals and agents.

The question that, therefore, needs to be addressed is how to recreate the climate of trust that prevailed in the past. Without effectively addressing this question the primary modes of *mudaraba* and *musharaka* financing may not be able to gain ground and the banks may even try to avoid the risks associated with the secondary modes by adopting different stratagems (*hiyal*). Consequently, the claimed benefits of the Islamic system resulting from the greater reliance on equity and PLS modes may also fail to be realized. It is therefore necessary to create a new environment compatible with modern conditions to help minimize the risks and to create a climate of trust and confidence among all the participants in the Islamic financial market.

Risks are not a peculiarity of only the Islamic financial system. They are present in all financial systems: risks associated with fiduciary money, interest rate and exchange rate fluctuations, loan default, operational failures, natural calamities and a range of other human, managerial and environmental weaknesses. The Islamic financial system is equally exposed to all these risks. The only risk that gets added to the Islamic financial system is that which arises from the greater reliance on equity and PLS modes. Here also the Islamic financial system is not unique. Corporations as well as universal banks have long been exposed to similar risks and their experience in handling them can provide valuable insights to Islamic banks.

Of course it is not possible to replicate the environment that prevailed during the Classical period. It is possible, however, to create institutions that may help minimize the risks associated with anonymity, moral hazard, principal agent conflict of interest, and late settlement of financial obligations. These institutions should be able to help the banks in different ways. They should enable them to obtain reliable information about their clients and to ensure that the funds lent by them to their clients are employed efficiently according to agreement and that the profit declared by them reflects the true picture of the business. They should also help them receive repayments on schedule, and get justice promptly in case of dispute with, or willful procrastination by, their clients. They should also enable banks to gain liquidity when it is needed by them owing to unforeseen circumstances. The establishment of such institutions should go a long way to providing the favourable environment that was available to the *sarrafs* in the Classical period. If such institutions are not available, then even banks with the best corporate governance may face difficulties and the movement of the Islamic financial system in the desired direction may not be able to gain momentum. Some of the institutions that need to be created are briefly indicated below.

Credit-rating agencies, chambers of commerce and trade associations

One of these shared institutions is credit-rating agencies which rate banks themselves as well as their counterparties. In the relatively smaller communities of the Classical period, such rating was available informally without the help of any formal credit-rating agency through the operation of market discipline and the intimate personal contacts of the parties concerned. This was further reinforced by the built-in discipline of the socio-economic structure of tribes, guilds, fraternities and sufi circles. Now it is the credit-rating agencies and chambers of commerce and trade associations which can perform this task. Most Muslim countries do not at present have private credit-rating agencies. Moreover the chambers of commerce and trade associations are perhaps not concerned with enforcement of the necessary discipline.

The International Islamic Rating Agency (IIRA), which has been established in Bahrain, is a step in the right direction. It will perform a number of functions including the rating of all public and private issuers of credit instruments with respect to their financial strength, fiduciary risk and creditworthiness. It will also assess the compliance with the *Shari'ah* of financial instruments as well as their issuers. It will have a *Shari'ah* board of its own to advise it on *Shari'ah* issues. It will, thus, complement the work of the Islamic Financial Services Board (IFSB) and the Accounting and Auditing Organization for Islamic Financial Institutions (AAOIFI) in setting standards for adequate disclosure. This will help promote an international capital market for Islamic financial instruments.

Even though the IIRA will rate private non-bank organizations, it will not be possible for it to rate the thousands of counterparties with whom banks deal. It would therefore be desirable to have private credit-rating agencies in all Muslim countries to facilitate the task of Islamic banks in choosing their counterparties. In fact the establishment of such institutions would also facilitate the task of the IIRA itself in getting the information that is necessary to know the financial strength, fiduciary risk and creditworthiness of even those private issuers of financial instruments whose rating the IIRA wishes to provide.

Centralized Shari'ah board

It is also necessary to standardize the *Shari'ah* modes of financing to the extent to which this is possible. Some differences of opinion are bound to remain and this may be healthy for the financial system because it will provide different alternatives for doing business instead of imposing a rigid conformity. The establishment of a centralized *Shari'ah* board should help create the needed harmony. In the absence of such a centralized board every bank is under an obligation to have its own *Shari'ah* board. This is very costly, particularly for smaller banks. Moreover, the existence of a large number of *Shari'ah* boards leads to conflicting opinions, which creates inconsistency and uncertainty. It may be expected that, with the passage of time and the free discussion of all controversial issues, the conflicts may tend to be gradually resolved. However, in the initial phase of evolution, such a centralized board seems to be necessary to minimize the differences and to standardize the instruments of Islamic finance. Such standardization will also help pave the way for the creation of an Islamic financial market. While some Muslim countries have already standardized their instruments, it may be desirable for other countries to do the same. It is also necessary that the standardization should take place, even at the level of all Muslim countries. The *Shari'ah* Board of the Islamic Development Bank should be able to complement and accelerate the work of the OIC (Organization of the Islamic Conference) *Fiqh* Committee in the pursuit of this goal.

Shari'ah clearance and audit

Among the most crucial challenges before an Islamic bank is to create confidence in its depositors as well as all the other operators in the market about the harmony of its operations with the *Shari'ah*. For this purpose two important steps need to be taken. The first step is to get clearance from a *Shari'ah* board about the *Shari'ah* compatibility of all its products. The second step is to provide an assurance that all its transactions are actually in conformity with the verdicts of the *Shari'ah* board. The first step is like going to a legal expert to ascertain whether a specific action of the bank is in conformity with the country's laws and, if not, what changes need to be introduced in it to make it so. The second is what auditors and banking supervisors do: ensuring that none of the bank's transactions violates the country's laws.

The *Shari'ah* boards are like legal experts. They can only perform the first task. It is difficult for them to perform the second task, which demands a review of all, or at least a random sample of, the different transactions that have taken place in different branches of the bank to ensure that they are in conformity with the verdict of the *Shari'ah* board. This demands a visit to the bank's premises to examine its operations in the same way as auditors and supervisors do. It is generally assumed that the *Shari'ah* boards do perform this task. However, members of the *Shari'ah* board do not have either the time or the staff to perform such a task effectively. The question that therefore arises is how to ensure the implementation of *Shari'ah* board decisions by the bank management. If this is not ensured the existence of the *Shari'ah* board loses its meaning. There are three alternatives, which may be considered for this purpose.

One of these is for the supervisory authority itself to undertake the *Shari'ah* audit in the course of its normal supervisory visits. This may not be considered desirable by Islamic banks in countries where the government and supervisory authorities are not favourably inclined towards Islamic banking. However it has the advantage that, if the supervisory authorities perform the *Shari'ah* audit, they will also try to standardize the *fiqhi* decisions.

The second, more preferable, alternative is to establish independent *Shari'ah* audit firms in the private sector. These firms would have to hire and train sufficient staff to examine the transactions of banks with a view to determining whether they are in conformity with the *Shari'ah*. This alternative has the disadvantage that it would involve a proliferation of institutions. Inspectors from three different institutions would knock at the doors of banks at different times. The first of these inspectors would be from the supervisory authority which sends examiners to banks to determine the conformity of their operations with the country's laws and the principles of safe and sound banking. Others would be the *Shari'ah* auditors who go to the bank to determine the conformity of its operations with the *Shari'ah*. The third group would be the chartered auditors who would go to ensure that the bank's financial statements had been prepared in conformity with the generally accepted accounting standards. This might not be convenient for banks because it would keep a number of their staff engaged in assisting three inspectors at different times, and thus add to their costs.

A third, and even more preferable, alternative is for the existing chartered audit firms to acquire the necessary expertise in the *Shari'ah* to enable them to undertake the *Shari'ah* audit. This will help avoid the proliferation of institutions with which Islamic banks have to deal. The banks would probably prefer this alternative because it will be more convenient for them to have the *Shari'ah* audit at the same time as the accounts audit.

External audit
The growing complexity of the banking business as well as the crises that the international financial system has witnessed have raised the function of external audit to a position of critical importance in all financial systems. It is, however, even more demanding and challenging in the Islamic financial system. It would be necessary for the external auditor to ensure not only that the bank's financial statements are prepared in all material respects in conformity with the professionally accepted financial reporting standards but also that the profit or loss declared by the bank truly reflects the bank's condition and that its profit has been derived without violating the teachings of the *Shari'ah*.

It is conventionally not considered to be the task of auditors to perform *Shari'ah* audit. They are not even equipped at present to do so. However, if this task is assigned to them in the light of what has been discussed above under the subject of *Shari'ah* audit, then the external auditors will have to create the necessary expertise to perform this task. This would demand that the training of auditors also include necessary training in the financial aspects of the *Shari'ah*, just as it includes training in auditing and law. If such training proves to be too cumbersome for the auditors, it may also be possible for the auditing firm to hire *Shari'ah* scholars and provide them with some necessary background in auditing.

For the external auditor to be able to do an effective job of auditing, he must have independence and objectivity. The experience of the auditing firm Arthur Andersen has clearly revealed that there should not be anything that indicates the auditor's vested interest in protecting the bank's management. It is only such impartial auditing that would create trust in the auditor's report and promote confidence in the bank. Even though it is the job of the internal controls system to prevent, or detect and correct, material misstatements arising from fraud and error, the external auditor cannot be exonerated from the responsibility of ensuring that this has been done conscientiously. He will have to design and carry out audit procedures in a way that would help reduce to an acceptably low level the risk of giving an inappropriate audit opinion. The share-holders, the Board of Directors, the management and the depositors all depend on his report and it would be a pity if he failed them. The auditor's success in his job would, however, depend greatly on the work of internal auditing. If internal auditing is weak, the external auditor may find it very *difficult* to do his job effectively. The strength of the internal auditor is greatly influenced by the competence, conscientiousness and integrity of the Board of Directors and management.

Shari'ah courts or banking tribunals
Another indispensable requirement of the Islamic financial system is availability of some judicial facility that would help the banks recover their loans promptly from clients who are unjustifiably procrastinating about repayment and also help bank clients get prompt justice at a low cost when the bank is itself acting unjustly. The establishment of *Shari'ah* courts or banking tribunals would be very helpful in getting prompt verdicts on the disputes of banks with their clients and vice versa. Normal civil court verdicts usually take several years in most Muslim countries.

The *Shari'ah* courts or banking tribunals would have a greater deter-rent effect if the names of banks or their clients whom these courts have found to be guilty were also published in newspapers. The fear of getting bad publicity would help minimize contractual violations. Furthermore, the names of parties who violate habitually may also be sent to the chambers of commerce and trade associations for blacklisting to create the same effect that social ostracism had in the Classical period.

Audit organization
It may also be desirable to have an audit organization jointly owned by banks to evaluate the profit-and-loss accounts of those of their clients who the banks feel have tried to cheat them in a PLS arrangement. The fear of being exposed to a thorough check of their accounts by such an organization would complement the market forces in helping minimize the effort made by users *of* funds on a PLS basis to short-change the banks.

The creation of such an audit organization would save the individual financial institution the need to hire a large staff of auditors. It would thus create a substantial economy in expenses for all financial institutions. It would also give assurance to investors who provide their funds directly to businesses that, in case of need, they will be able to have the accounts properly examined by a qualified, impartial institution.

The whole concept of 'audit' may have to undergo a transformation in the case of primary modes of Islamic finance.[4] Conventional auditing is 'not expressly designed to uncover management frauds' (Elliot and Willingham, 1980, p. viii). If the auditor performs a diligent audit and evaluates the financial statements according to 'the generally accepted accounting principles', the professional obligations of the auditor have been fulfilled. The auditor has no responsibility to detect management malpractices or to determine the 'real' profit. He does not have the responsibility to check and to question (Lechner, 1998, p. 143). Accounting firms generally tend to accommodate their clients, particularly the big clients who hire them. The auditor would fail in discharging his responsibility in a PLS system if he did not try to detect and disclose dishonest and questionable acts of the management and to determine the real amount of profit so as to ensure a 'fair' return to the shareholders and *mudaraba* depositors.

Qualified pool of talent
To enable the Islamic system to fulfil the requirements of the *Shari'ah* as well as the BCBS, it is necessary to train both the staff and clients of banks, as well as the general public, in the principles of Islamic banking. This will not be enough, however. It is also necessary to create a large pool of experts and highly qualified professionals with in-depth knowledge of not only the *Shari'ah* and its objectives, but also Islamic and conventional finance and financial engineering. This would be possible if

first-rate institutions were created for this purpose with the collaboration of financial institutions, central banks, universities and the governments. Directors and senior management of Islamic banks as well as *Shari'ah* advisers should also be required to take such courses. If the central banks as well as universities could make arrangements for this purpose, as is done in the case of conventional banking, the task of Islamic banks would become relatively easier.

Islamic financial market

It is also necessary to create an Islamic financial market. The absence of a secondary market for Islamic financial instruments makes it extremely difficult for Islamic banks to manage their liquidity. Consequently, they end up maintaining a relatively higher ratio of liquidity than that which is generally maintained by conventional banks. This affects their profitability and competitiveness. The establishment of the Islamic Financial Services Board (IFSB), International Islamic Financial Market (IIFM) and the Liquidity Management Centre (LMC) will help provide the institutional infrastructure needed for an Islamic financial market.

The IFSB will help promote uniform regulatory and supervisory practices and prudential standards for Islamic *financial* institutions in the same way as is done by the BCBS. The IIFM will enhance cooperation in the field of finance among Muslim countries and financial institutions by promoting product development and harmonizing trading practices. This will serve as a catalyst for the development and promotion of a larger supply of *Shari'ah*-compatible financial instruments. The LMC will serve as an operating arm of the IIFM in the effort to facilitate the creation of an inter-bank money market that will enable Islamic financial institutions to manage their assets and liabilities effectively. It will create short-term *Shari'ah*-compatible investment opportunities by providing liquid, tradable, asset-backed treasury instruments (*sukuks*) in which these institutions can invest their surplus liquidity. It will also facilitate the sourcing and securitization of assets and trade actively in *sukuks* by offering buy/sell quotations. The three institutions will together help establish an Islamic financial market by removing the drawback experienced by Islamic banks of the lack of standardization of terms and instruments and the non-availability of quality *Shari'ah*-compatible assets for trading in the secondary markets. This should help the Islamic financial system to expand at a faster rate in the future and create for itself a larger niche in the financial markets of Muslim countries.

Lender of last resort

Islamic banks also need some facility akin to the lender-of-last resort which is available to conventional banks to overcome liquidity crises when they occur suddenly as the result of unforeseen circumstances. Such a facility is available to Islamic banks at present on the basis of interest and is, therefore, unacceptable because of its incompatibility with the *Shari'ah*. Its use exposes Islamic banks to a great deal of criticism. It may be worth considering the creation of a common pool at the central banks to provide mutual accommodation to banks in case of need. All banks may be required to contribute a certain mutually agreed percentage of their deposits to this common pool, just as they do in the case of statutory reserve requirements. They would then have the right to borrow interest-free from this pool with the condition that the net use of this facility is zero (that is, drawings do not exceed contributions) over a given period of time.[5] In a crisis, the central banks may allow a bank to exceed the limit, with appropriate penalties, warning and a suitable corrective programme. This will in a way be a more organized means of replacing the framework for mutual cooperation that prevailed among the *sarrafs* during the Classical period.

Reform of the stock market

Reform of the stock market is also necessary in the light of Islamic teachings to ensure that share prices reflect underlying business conditions and do not fluctuate erratically as a result of speculative forces. The discipline that the *Shari'ah* helps introduce through the prohibition of short sales or the sale of what one does not own and possess, should greatly help in realizing this goal (see Chapra, 2002). In addition, rules and procedures need to be streamlined and enforced to protect investors and ensure stability and sanity in the stock market. This will help raise the confidence of savers and investors in the system and enable them to buy or sell shares in response to their circumstances or their perceptions of future market developments. Such a reform would constitute one of the most important pillars for supporting the edifice of an interest-free and equity-based economy.[6]

7.3   HOW TO BE GENUINE (2): EQUITABLE DISTRIBUTION OF CREDIT

Finance has always been a powerful political, social and economic weapon in the world. It plays a prominent role, not only in the allocation and distribution of scarce resources, but also in the stability and growth of an economy. It also determines the power base, social status and economic condition of an individual in the economy. Hence no socio-economic reform in Muslim societies can be meaningful unless the financial system is also restructured in conformity with the socio-economic goals of Islam in which justice occupies a prominent place. Since the resources of financial institutions come from deposits placed by a wide cross-section of the population, it is only rational to regard them as a national resource in the same way as water supply coming out of a public reservoir. They must be utilized for the well-being of all sectors of the population and not for the further enrichment of the wealthy and the powerful. However, as Arne Bigsten has rightly observed, 'the distribution of capital is even more unequal than that of land' and 'the banking system tends to reinforce the unequal distribution of capital' (Bigsten, 1987, p. 156). This bodes ominously for society because it leads to the recruitment of entrepreneurs from only one social class and to the failure to utilize its entire resource of entrepreneurial talent (Leadbearer, 1986, p. 5).

Hence it is necessary to correct the tendency of the financial system to contribute to concentration of wealth by promoting an equitable distribution of credit in the economy. Micro enterprises have generally proved to be not only viable institutions with respectable rates of return and low default rates but also a successful tool in the fight against poverty and unemployment. The experience of the International Fund for Agricultural Development (IFAD) is that credit provided to the most enterprising of the poor is quickly repaid by them from their higher earnings (*The Economist*, 16 February 1985, p. 15). Testimony from the Grameen Bank in Bangladesh indicates a constant repayment rate of 99 per cent since the Bank's inception (Yunus, 1984, p. 12). The Select Committee on Hunger established by the US House of Representatives concluded in its Report that 'the provision of small amounts of credit to micro enterprises in the informal sector of developing countries can significantly raise the living standards of the poor, increase food security and bring about sustainable improvements in local economies' (US House of Representatives, 1986, p. v). Dr Muhammad Yunus, founder of the Grameen Bank. has aptly emphasized that financing for self-employment should be recognized as a right that plays a critical role in attaining all other rights (Yunus, 1987, p. 31).

No wonder a number of countries have established special institutions to grant credit to the poor and lower-middle-class entrepreneurs. Even though these have been extremely useful, they have proved not to be adequate and, therefore, unable to make significant headway in realizing the goal of equitable distribution of credit. This goal may be difficult to realize unless the microfinance sector is scaled up by integrating it with the commercial banks to enable the use of a significant proportion of their vast financial resources on a commercial basis for actualizing a crucial socio-economic goal. Commercial banks do not at present fulfil this need and the Select Committee on Hunger is right in observing that 'formal financial institutions in these countries do not recognize the viability of income generating enterprises owned by the poor' (US House of Representatives, 1986, p. v).

Commercial banks need not get directly involved in the business of financing micro enterprises if they find this to be too cumbersome. They can operate through their own subsidiaries or through the institutions that already exist for this purpose, like the agricultural banks, cooperative banks, development banks and leasing and finance companies. To enable the commercial banks to be integrated into the microfinance business, it is necessary to make it profitable for them to do so. This requires significant improvement in the environment for micro business through better access to markets and the provision of the needed physical and social infrastructure. Such an infrastructure, including vocational training institutions, roads, electricity and water supply, will help increase the efficiency of micro enterprises and reduce their costs, thereby enabling them to compete successfully in the market.

The reason normally given by commercial banks for diverting a very small proportion of their funds to micro enterprises is the greater risk and expense involved in financing a large number of small firms instead of a few large ones. Hence small enterprises are generally unable to get financing from banks and have to go to the informal sector where they are able to borrow only at prohibitive rates of interest. Thus the growth and survival of these firms is jeopardized even though they carry a great potential for increased employment and output and improved income distribution.

It is therefore necessary to reduce the risk and expense of such financing for commercial banks. The risk is great because micro enterprises are unable to provide acceptable collateral to the banks. The risk would be reduced to a substantial extent if the group solidarity method used by the Grameen Bank was employed and the financing was not provided in the form of cash loans but rather in the form of tools and equipment through the *ijara* mode of Islamic finance. The raw materials and merchandise as well as the working capital they need may be provided on the basis of *murabaha*, *salam* and *istisnaa*. These would involve greater risk than the *ijara* mode. To handle the risks involved in all such financing, it is imperative to establish the now-familiar loan guarantee scheme which has been introduced in a number of countries. It may also be possible to cover from the *zakat* fund the losses arising from the default of very small micro enterprises.

The additional expense incurred by commercial banks in evaluating and financing micro enterprises also needs to be reduced. In the case of financing provided to the very poor, the expense may also be covered from the *zakat* fund, one of the primary purposes of which is to enable the poor to stand on their own feet. For those who are not eligible for *zakat* but still deserve some help, it would be worthwhile for the governments to consider subsidizing a part of the cost, at least in the initial phase, in the interest of helping realize an important socio-economic goal of Islam. As the system matures, the dependence on *zakat* as well as the government subsidy may tend to decline.

7.3.1 Effective Corporate Governance

What has been discussed so far in the sections above has been related primarily to the challenge of gradually raising the share of equity and PLS financing in the financial system and bringing about a more equitable distribution of credit by removing the obstacles that prevent this from happening. This, however, is only one of the challenges faced. An equally important challenge is to ensure the soundness, stability and accelerated development of the system, without which it will be difficult not only to meet successfully the first challenge but also to ensure the system's survival. This necessitates effective corporate governance, prudent regulation and supervision, protection of depositors and resolution of unresolved *fiqhi* disputes. This is what will be discussed in this and the following sections.

Corporate governance has gained great prominence over the last two decades even in the conventional financial system because of continued financial instability. It would be of even greater importance in the Islamic system because of the additional risk to which the depositors would become exposed when the banks really started moving into the risk-sharing modes. This poses an important challenge before Islamic banks to improve all crucial aspects of corporate governance. The challenge will become more serious as these institutions expand and their problems become more complex. This challenge could be successfully met if the Board of Directors and senior management become more effective in the performance of their responsibilities.

For this purpose, it is important to sharpen the tools of corporate governance, the most important of which are internal controls, risk management, transparency, loan accounting and disclosure, *Shari'ah* clearance and audit, external audit, and prudential regulation and supervision. Total reliance on these would, however, not be sufficient. Moral commitment on the part of all market operators is indispensable. Without such commitment, market operators will find different ways of violating the law without being detected and punished. This will create the need for more and more legal checks and controls, which will raise transactions costs to an unbearably high level. Making them truly accountable before shareholders and depositors by the adoption of measures discussed in this chapter should also be of great help. What is also needed is the establishment of a number of shared institutions, as discussed above. Without such institutions even banks with the best corporate governance may not be able to avoid crises.

However, corporate governance is generally weak in all countries and particularly so in developing countries, in which category nearly all Muslim countries fall at present. This is because all the institutions that play a crucial role in disciplining markets and ensuring efficiency and integrity are not well-developed in these countries. Information asymmetries are more severe, market participants less experienced, and regulations, even if they exist, are not always enforced effectively and impartially because of political corruption and the general weakness of judicial systems. Disclosures are also not adequate and accounting practices are not well developed (see Prowse, 1998, p. 16). The adverse effects of ineffective corporate governance can be more serious in the case of financial institutions because their leverage is much higher, the number of their stakeholders is more extensive and the systemic risks of their failure are far more serious. There is no reason to assume that, even though the Islamic financial institutions have done fairly well so far, they have necessarily been able to escape the trappings of the prevailing weak corporate governance in developing countries. It is therefore not possible to avoid the taking of all those measures that would help improve the functioning of these institutions. The role of the Board of Directors and senior management is of crucial importance in this respect. It is gratifying to note that almost all Muslim countries are currently in the process of implementing the BCBS guidelines.

The Board of Directors
The Board of Directors cannot, however, play this role effectively if its members do not have a high degree of moral integrity as well as professional competence in banking business. They must be adequately aware of the risks and complexities involved in the banking business. In an Islamic system, they must have the additional qualification of being well-versed in the *Shari'ah* and its objectives and in particular the rationale behind the prohibition of interest. They should ensure adequate

transparency in keeping with the standards laid down by the BCBS, the IFSB and the supervisory authority of their own country through a smooth flow of relevant information to directors, senior management, auditors, supervisors, shareholders, depositors and the public according to the needs of each with a view to ensure a proper check on the affairs of the bank. They must establish a strong internal control system, proper accounting procedures, effective internal and external audit, efficient risk management and all necessary checks and balances, rules, regulations and procedures (for some of these, see Iqbal, Khan and Ahmad, 1998; Chapra and Khan, 2000; Khan and Ahmed, 2001; and al-Jarhi and Iqbal, 2001).

Experience has shown that directors do not necessarily perform their roles effectively (Mace, 1996). There are a number of reasons for this. One of these is that the Board members may not necessarily have the professional competence and the moral integrity that are needed to manage the bank efficiently. Another reason is that Board members are not always genuinely elected by shareholders and are not necessarily accountable before them. Elections do not take place regularly at defined intervals and, even if they do, evidence indicates that shareholders are not actively involved in the election or removal of directors (Prentice, 1993, p. 31). This enables Board members to perpetuate themselves and it is generally difficult to dislodge them except through takeovers. These are, however, expensive and potentially disruptive and may not, therefore, be a possible remedy except in extreme cases (Morck, Schleifer and Vishny, 1990). To correct this situation, it is necessary to have a transparent procedure for elections and to adopt measures that would enable minority shareholders and investment depositors to have a say in Board decisions. It is also necessary to enable shareholders to remove Board members in the event of their performance falling far short of what they expect. It is, therefore, imperative to institute reforms in election procedures as well as proxy rules to enable shareholders to elect competent and conscientious persons to the Board of Directors and to prevent them perpetuating themselves in spite of their poor performance.

It is also necessary to develop a legal and regulatory infrastructure to protect the rights of not only minority shareholders but also depositors (both being outsiders). In a number of countries companies are allowed to ask registered shareholders, who are unable to attend general meetings, to transfer their votes to the Board of Directors. This further strengthens the hands of the Board and enables it to control decisions at shareholder meetings. Since the transfer of voting rights often leads to far-reaching consequences, which may not always be in the interest of all stakeholders, it would be desirable to transfer voting rights to shareholder associations. if they exist. If such associations do not exist, then voting rights may be transferred to supervisory authorities or to specialized chartered firms established in the private sector to protect the interest of stakeholders, against a fee, as discussed below. All three of these institutions would perhaps be better qualified to protect the interests of stakeholders.[7]

It would also be helpful if there were an adequate number of non-executive directors on the Board. Empirical evidence in the conventional system indicates that non-executive directors influence positively a Board's capabilities to evaluate and discipline managers (Alvarez et al., 1998, p. 2). This is perhaps because such directors do not have any management responsibility and may not, therefore, have a vested interest in protecting the management. They may, therefore, be expected to attach greater weight to the interests of minority shareholders and depositors and, thereby, help inject equity into the company. If they do not come up to this expectation, they would hurt their own reputation in the directors' labour market. Removal of the Chief Executive Officer (CEO) caused by poor performance is more likely in outsider-dominated Boards than in insider-dominated ones. However. here too there are problems. If the non-executive directors have not been elected by shareholders but rather handpicked by the dominant shareholder or the CEO, they would owe their careers to him and would, therefore, 'lack the information and incentives required to provide consistent effective corporate governance' (Herzel, 1994, p. 472). There will thus be conflict of interest, which will create a lack of willingness on their part to discipline senior management (Sykes, 1994, p. 118). Moreover, Board meetings may not be frequent and non-executive directors may not, therefore, be able to monitor the activities of the company effectively and ensure correction, particularly if overt criticism of management policies in Board meetings is considered to be rude (Morck, 1994, p. 476).

Since Islamic banks are generally small compared with their conventional counterparts even in Muslim countries, leave alone the rest of the world, the amount of capital held by them is also very small. This enables concentration of shares in the hands of a few executive directors.[8] The number of non-executive directors who can serve as a check on the executive directors is also accordingly small. Since the small size as well as the concentration of shareholdings carries the potential of leading to undesired consequences for protecting the interests of all stakeholders, it is desirable to enlarge the size of banks and to institute legal reforms with the objective of reducing concentration, diversifying risks and increasing the ability of these banks to absorb losses.

It would also be desirable to introduce some other reforms to make the Board of Directors more effective in its functions. One of these, which needs to be considered seriously, is to relate the remuneration of Board members to their performance in the same way as is required in *mudaraba* contracts.[9] The directors in their capacity as *mudaribs* (managing entrepreneurs) should be compensated only for their actual expenses and not be entitled to a fixed management fee or remuneration as they do in modern corporations. Their remuneration should be a certain percentage of the profit earned by the bank, if the bank makes a profit. This must be in addition to their normal share in profit like other shareholders on the basis of their shareholdings. The percentage share of profits to be allocated to the directors for their management services must be clearly specified in the Articles of Agreement so that it is well known to the shareholders. If the corporation makes a profit. the directors receive the specified percentage of profit for their services. But if the corporation makes a loss, the directors do not, like the *mudarib*, receive a 'fee' for their management services, and should share in the losses in proportion to their stockholdings. The directors would thus have a reward for their services only if they had contributed to profits: the higher the profit, the greater their reward. This should prove to be an incentive to them for better performance.

Senior management
While the Board of Directors refers to persons who are generally not only shareholders themselves but also participate in the governance of the bank, senior management refers to the CEO and other senior members of the staff who perform management functions but are not necessarily shareholders. Modern corporations are in general not managed by their owners (shareholders) (Berle and Means, 1932: Jensen and Meckling, 1976). Instead, professional managers are hired to run the business. They are 'fiduciaries'.[10] This creates the principal–agent problem and leads to a conflict of interests. It is therefore necessary to impose restrictions on self-dealing, fraud, excessive compensation in different hidden forms, and other malpractices.

One of the most important constraints on management is that key positions should not be held by one person ('four eyes principle'). Since the CEO and the Chairman of the Board perform two distinct functions in the bank, it would be preferable to have two different persons holding these positions so that there is a clear division of responsibilities at the top of the bank to ensure independence and balance of power and authority. Neither the directors nor the management should be allowed to stay in the job if they are no longer competent or qualified to run the bank. As argued by Jensen and Ruback, poor managers who resist being replaced might be the costliest manifestation of the agency problem (cited from Jensen and Ruback, 1963, by Schleifer and Vishny, 1997, p. 743). A survey conducted by IRTI has revealed that, in all the banks covered by the survey, the positions of CEO and Chairman were held by different persons (Chapra and Ahmed, 2002). This is gratifying. However, it need not necessarily be true for banks not covered by the survey, and it is necessary to ensure that this is the case.

It is the responsibility of the Board of Directors and senior management to ensure proper internal controls, and effective management of all risks, including credit risk, liquidity risk, interest-rate risk and operational risks. Even though the exposure of most Islamic banks to these risks seems to be relatively high, they have been able to manage them fairly well so far. Nevertheless, this may not necessarily continue in the future. It is, therefore, extremely important to cultivate an effective risk management culture in these banks to ensure their competitiveness and survival in a world full of uncertainties and crises. This cannot be done, however, without the active collaboration of the Board of Directors, senior management, the *Shari'ah* scholars and bank supervisors.

7.3.2   Prudential Regulation and Supervision

A survey conducted by 1RTI has revealed that, while the overall regulatory environment for conventional banks seems to be relatively good and the variation among them is also relatively less in Muslim countries, the regulatory and institutional environment for Islamic banks does not appear to be adequate and the variation is also relatively greater (see Chapra and Ahmed, 2002. Tables 1.2, 1.3 and 1.5). This indicates that there are a number of issues confronted by the authorities with respect to the regulation and supervision of Islamic financial institutions. The first of these issues relates to the removal of all the legal obstacles that hinder the rapid expansion of Islamic financial institutions. The second issue is about the clarification, harmonization, and codification of standards of Islamic finance as much as is possible and about ensuring the compliance of these institutions with these standards: and the third issue relates to implementation of the guidelines provided by the BCBS.

The removal of legal obstacles does not seem to have received due attention so far from regulatory authorities in most Muslim countries. The laws with respect to financial institutions were formulated in these countries in the image of conventional banking before the initiation of Islamic finance. These have in general remained unchanged, with some cosmetic changes introduced here and there. For example, while interest payments continue to be tax-deductible, dividend payments do not get the same treatment in most jurisdictions. This puts firms using the Islamic modes of finance as well as Islamic banks at a disadvantage. What is needed is a thorough review of the whole legal structure so as to bring it into harmony with the needs of Islamic finance.

The harmonization of standards is a difficult task because of the differences of opinion among the jurists. While the existence of some differences is natural and healthy, an effort needs to be made to bring about as much harmony as possible. This is happening as a result of the continuing dialogue among the jurists and the role that the IDB and the IFSB are playing. Where there are differences of opinion, the differences should appear as alternative ways of conducting Islamic finance. In this case, the law should require transparency in contacts about the alternative that is being used so as to avoid misunderstanding. It also needs to be clearly stated that the liability of the financers in a *mudaraba* contract is limited to the extent of finance provided by him/her. This is generally understood to be the case. It would nevertheless be desirable to have a clear *fiqhi* verdict on this issue and the reflection of this in the laws so that no ambiguity remains. All this would help introduce greater clarity and harmony in Islamic finance and make the job of *Shari'ah* courts or banking tribunals relatively easier in the resolution of disputes.

While the successful resolution of the first two issues will enable the Islamic financial industry to grow rapidly and gain credibility in Muslim countries, the third, which is in the process of being fulfilled, will help it gain respectability in the international financial markets. All these will together help in not only promoting accelerated development of an Islamically compliant safe and sound financial system but also protecting the payments system from instability and ensuring efficient operation of the capital market and its institutions.

The regulatory authorities should not, however, make the regulations so tight and comprehensive that they may raise compliance costs unbearably and also strangulate innovation and creativity. They should, nevertheless, ensure the following:

- That the banks are preferably joint stock companies and that all the members of their Board of Directors and senior management do not belong to a single family or business group;
- That the major shareholders, and members of the Board of Directors and senior management not only enjoy a reputation for integrity and fairness as well as financial strength but also possess adequate knowledge of the *Shari'ah* and the skills and experience necessary to operate an Islamic bank in a safe and sound manner;

- That the banks have adequate risk-weighted capital in conformity with the requirements of the BCBS;
- That the banks have appropriate checks and balances, and their internal controls and risk management systems are effective to ensure not only efficient operation but also freedom from fraud, overlending, credit concentration, exploitation and mismanagement; and their non-executive directors and external auditors are independent and do not have a vested interest in supporting the banks' board or management;
- That the banks disclose adequate qualitative and quantitative information about their operations, particularly their capital, reserves, liquidity and risk profile to enable all market participants and particularly the shareholders and depositors to monitor the banks effectively.

Regulation cannot, however, be effective if it is not enforced. It should therefore be accompanied by effective supervision. The objective of supervision must be to ensure that, first, the financial system is safe and sound in accordance with the guidelines laid down by the BCBS, and, second, that it is also in conformity with the teachings of *Shari'ah*. This is what will help it gain credibility in the domestic as well as international financial markets and enable it to compete successfully and achieve an accelerated rate of growth. For this purpose the supervisory authorities will have to develop effective mechanisms to monitor and limit (and if possible, also measure) all the different types of risks to which banks are exposed. They will also have to assess the quality of the banks' loans and investments, and in particular the risk of default of a debtor, which is crucial in the case of Islamic banks. It is this assessment which may turn out to be the most critical determinant of an Islamic bank's financial condition and ability to survive. It is also important for the supervisor to ensure that the bank has in place an effective internal controls system in conformity with the nature and scale of its business and that its management has the necessary training and experience to manage the risks and to handle the challenges that it faces.

It is also important for the supervisors to develop and institute a set of indicators of financial soundness to help assess and monitor the strengths and vulnerabilities of the financial system at both micro and macro levels. At the micro level, the indicators should show the condition of individual institutions while at the macro level they should help assess and monitor the soundness and vulnerabilities of the financial system as well as the economy. The International Monetary Fund (IMF) has suggested a set of these indicators, called 'macro-prudential indicators', which include a core set as well as an enlarged set of financial soundness indicators (see Sundararajan et al., 2002, for details of these indicators, especially pp. 3 and 8).

Asymmetric information from which banks suffer makes supervision a difficult task. This difficulty is accentuated if accounting, auditing and information systems are less developed, as they are in most developing (including Muslim) countries. These difficulties make the role of share-holders and depositors absolutely crucial in monitoring the banks and strengthening the safety and soundness of the banking system. It may be hoped that the risks to which investment depositors are exposed would motivate them to monitor the banks more carefully and thereby help strengthen them. Risk-based adequacy of capital also has an important role to play. However, it cannot be relied upon fully because the problem with capital is that, while supervision can ensure its quantity, it cannot ensure its quality. Excessive reliance on capital may not, therefore, be prudent.

This call for regulation and supervision of Islamic banks is not something new, it has always been considered to be a challenge for the Islamic financial system, as is evident from the attention drawn towards it more than two decades ago by the governors of central banks and monetary authorities of the member countries of the OIC in their detailed report on 'Promotion, Regulation and Supervision of Islamic Banks', approved by them in their Fourth Meeting held in Khartoum on 7–8 March 1981. This was done at a time when Islamic banking was still in its infancy. The first fully-fledged Islamic bank had been established in Dubai in March 1975, just six years before this report. Now that Islamic banking has spread and is expected to continue to spread, regulation and supervision are even more crucial. The more conscientiously this chal-lenge is met, the better it will be for the development of a sound and healthy Islamic financial system.

However it is not just the soundness of the financial system at both the micro and the macro levels that the supervision of an Islamic financial system should be concerned about. It is also necessary to ensure that the Islamic goal of justice is also being realized. This cannot be done by means of regulation. What needs to be done is to remove the obstacles that prevent banks from being integrated with the microfinance network to be able to provide credit to a larger spectrum of society. This will necessitate the establishment of institutions that help banks overcome their difficulties in the realization of this goal, as discussed earlier.

7.3.3   Protecting the Depositors

The financial crises faced by almost three-quarters of the member countries of the IMF over the last two decades have brought into focus the question of protecting the depositors. Although effective corporate governance along with prudential regulation and supervision can greatly help protect the depositors, they cannot be considered to be sufficient and there is a need to find other ways.

Deposit insurance
Deposit insurance has received maximum attention as a way of protecting the depositors from losses, and many countries have adopted this (Laeven, 2002). Even countries which do not have deposit insurance have rescued the depositors in the case of bank failures because of the fear that refusal to do so may lead to the collapse of the financial system. If this is the case in countries where the conventional financial system prevails and the depositors do not participate in the risks of banking business, then the imperative of PLS brings into even sharper focus the challenge of protecting the depositors. While this has the hazard of making depositors complacent and, thereby, less motivated towards the monitoring of their banks' affairs, it has the advantage of making the insurance provider complement the regulatory and supervisory authorities in their task of ensuring the health of financial institutions. This raises the question of whether all deposits should be insured, as in the conventional financial system, or only the demand deposits.

Since demand depositors do not participate in the risks of banking business and do not, therefore, get a return, their deposits need to be fully protected. However, deposit insurance systems do not normally insure demand deposits beyond a certain limit. This raises the question of whether demand deposits should, or should not, be fully insured in the Islamic system. The knowledge that their deposits are protected will inspire the depositors' confidence in the Islamic financial system as a whole and prevent panics. It is of particular importance to fully protect small depositors. Large depositors may or may not be fully protected because they have the resources to monitor the condition of their banks, and giving them full protection may tend to reduce market discipline by lowering the motivation to assess the soundness of their banks.

Protecting investment depositors may, however, be in conflict with the spirit of Islamic finance. Nevertheless a case has been made by some *Shari'ah* scholars in favour of protecting small investment depositors from losses (see al-Misri, 1995). This proposal is worth considering seriously because it would remove the criticism levelled against Islamic finance that it does not protect small depositors who need income but are not able to risk the loss of their principal. Even if it is not possible to do this because of a lack of consensus on this issue, it should always be possible for banks to invest such deposits in relatively safe ventures so as to minimize the risk of loss. There also arises the question of whether large investment deposits can be insured against fraud, mismanagement and violation of the *mudaraba* contract. The answer would depend on the willingness of insurance providers to provide such insurance. However, if it is possible to have medical malpractice insurance, it should also be possible to provide insurance against fraud and mismanagement in the case of investment deposits. This would help introduce greater discipline in the financial system by also making the insurance provider assess more carefully the quality and practices of bank management and requiring greater transparency.

Keeping in view the nature of Islamic finance, it would be desirable to have an explicit insurance scheme specifying the kind and extent of coverage available to different categories of depositors. This would be better for building the depositors' confidence in the Islamic financial system. They would be aware of the extent of protection they have. In the absence of such an explicit coverage, the depositors may tend to assume a full implicit coverage, particularly in the case of large banks, because of the 'too big to fail' doctrine. This will be more costly for the financial authorities because they will have to bail out all depositors, irrespective of the size and nature of their deposits. It will also introduce a moral hazard and reduce depositor watchfulness of large banks which is necessary for greater market discipline and systemic stability.

Other ways of protecting depositors
Another way of protecting the depositors would be to allow them to have a representative on the bank's Board of Directors and also a voice in the shareholders' meetings. The ease with which shareholders as well as depositors can participate in meetings and use their votes to influence important bank decisions or to remove directors and senior management from office, can play an important role in improving corporate govern-ance in Islamic banks. However, when even shareholders do not neces-sarily attend shareholders' meetings, it may not be possible for depositors, being far greater in number than shareholders, to do so, particularly if the banks are large and have several branches, not only within the country but also abroad. Moreover, if shareholders and depositors can exercise voting rights only by attending the meetings, this will virtually guarantee non-voting and the voting rights will be almost meaningless. One way of solving the problem of non-voting would be to

transfer voting rights to the regulatory authorities who may appoint a representative on behalf of depositors on the banks' Board of Directors. The banks may perhaps resent this. It is, however, important not only for safeguarding the interests of depositors but also for systemic stability.

If such representation is ruled out, it may be desirable to encourage the formation of depositors' associations to protect the depositor's interests. If this also happens to be practically difficult, it would be worth considering the establishment of specialized chartered firms in the private sector to protect the interests of depositors, just as it is the job of external auditors to protect the interests of shareholders. Their fee could be paid by the banks out of the dividends distributed to the investment depositors. An important objection to this suggestion may be that it would lead to an unnecessary proliferation of institutions. To avoid such proliferation, external auditors may be assigned the task. It will be cheaper and more convenient if the external auditors are required to act as guardians not only of the rights of shareholders but also those of the depositors. It is also necessary to ensure that adequate transparency prevails so that the depositors know what is going on in the bank and are thus able to play a greater role in safeguarding their own interests.

There is also another aspect of safeguarding the interest of depositors in Islamic banks. The depositors would like to ensure that what they are getting is not wine with the label of honey. Compliance of Islamic banks with the *Shari'ah* in the acquisition as well as the use of funds is, therefore, an important challenge. This has already been discussed.

7.3.4　Some Unresolved Fiqhi Issues[11]

Fiqhi verdicts related to the financial system have remained dormant for a long period and, in particular, over the last two centuries, during which time the conventional financial system has made tremendous advances. However, a great deal of progress has been made over the last three decades in facing the new challenges, although a number of crucial issues still remain unresolved. It is not possible to encompass all of these in this brief chapter. Some of these, however, are discussed below for the consideration of jurists. In case it is found that the prevalent *fiqhi* opinion cannot be changed, it will be necessary for the jurists and financial experts to join hands to find practical *Shari'ah*-compatible solutions for the problems faced by Islamic financial institutions. In the absence of such solutions, the risks faced by Islamic banks may be higher and the need for capital greater. Capital standards which are significantly higher than those for conventional banks may reduce the profitability of these banks and make them less competitive.

Late settlement of financial obligations

One of the most important of these issues relates to the failure of the purchaser of goods and services under the *murabaha* mode of financing to settle payment on time even when he/she is capable of doing so. If this failure were due to strained circumstances, then Islam recommends not just rescheduling but even remission, if necessary. However, if it is due to unscrupulousness, then the question is whether a penalty can be imposed on the defaulter and whether the financier or the bank can be compensated for the damage as well as the loss of income caused by such default. If the late payment does not lead to any penalty, there is a danger that default may tend to become a widespread phenomenon through the long-run operation of path dependence and self-reinforcing mechanisms. This may lead to a breakdown of the payments system if the amounts involved are significantly large.

Scholars have expressed a number of opinions on the subject. but so far there is no consensus.[12] The conservative view allows blacklisting of the defaulter's name and also his imprisonment if the delay is unjustified, but prohibits the imposition of any monetary penalty on the defaulter or the payment of any compensation to the aggrieved party for fear that this may become a disguise for charging interest.

The possibility of blacklisting and imprisonment of the defaulter can serve as a strong deterrent and help minimize default cases provided that this can be enacted promptly. However. if the lender and police high-handedness are to be eschewed, imprisonment should not be allowed except on the basis of a court decree issued after a due process of law. This may be difficult because, given the present-day inefficient judicial system of many Muslim countries, court decisions usually take several years and involve substantial litigation costs. It is therefore imperative that special *Shari'ah* courts or banking tribunals be established, as discussed earlier, to penalize promptly the unjustifiably defaulting party and thereby help minimize default cases. Although blacklisting and imprisonment may serve as deterrents to the unjustified delaying of payments, it does not provide any relief to the aggrieved party, which has suffered damage and loss of income.

The relatively liberal view, therefore, allows the imposition of a financial penalty on the debtor who delays payment without any justification, but allows it to be made available to the aggrieved party as compensation only if the penalty is imposed by a court. However, even in the case of a court decision, there are two different views. One view permits the court to determine compensation for the damage caused by late payment as well as the loss of income suffered by the aggrieved party. The other view allows the court to determine compensation for only the actual damage but not for the loss of income. If the penalty is not determined by a court, the proceeds must be utilized for charitable objectives only and cannot be made available as compensation to the aggrieved party.

If the concept of compensation for loss becomes accepted by the jurists, there will arise the question of how to determine the compensation in a way that reduces subjectivity as well as the possibility of injustice to either the defaulting or the aggrieved party. The answer may lie in developing an index of 'loss-given-default' (LGD). It should be possible to develop and maintain such an LGD index using internationally recognized standards. The LGD will, for example, provide a schedule of the loss incurred by a bank if $100 is defaulted in payment for a given number of days. The LGD will capture all costs related to the administration of the default until its settlement, the litigation cost and the loss of income. The ultimate decision will, of course, have to be made by a special banking tribunal in keeping with the LGD schedule with adjustments for individual circumstances.

Some issues about leasing

The jurists are unanimously agreed on the need for the lessor to bear at least a part of the risk of lease financing to make the lease contract lawful. Nevertheless there are differences of opinion among them on the permissibility of different types of lease contacts.

The kind of leasing which the jurists have generally discussed in the classical *fiqhi* literature, and about the permissibility of which there is no difference of opinion, is what is now called the operating lease. This form of lease distinguishes itself from the other forms in a number of ways. First, the lessor is himself the real owner of the leased asset and therefore, bears all the risks and costs of ownership. All defects, which prevent the use of the equipment by the lessee, are his responsibility, even though it is possible to make the lessee responsible for the day-to-day maintenance and normal repairs of the leased asset. Second, the lease is not for the entire useful life of the leased asset, but rather for a specified short-term period, and ends at the end of the agreed period unless renewed by the mutual consent of both the lessor and the lessee. The entire risk is thus borne by the lessor. This has, however, the potential of introducing a moral hazard through the misuse of the leased asset by the lessee.

The financial lease helps take care of the moral hazard problem by making the lease period long enough (usually the entire useful life of the leased asset) to enable the lessor to amortize the cost of the asset with profit. At the end of the lease period the lessee has the option to purchase the asset from the lessor at a price specified in advance or at its market value at that time. The lease is not cancellable before the expiry of the lease period without the consent of both the parties. There is, therefore, little danger of misuse of the asset.

A financial lease has other advantages too. The leased asset serves as security and, in the case of default on the part of the lessee, the lessor can take possession of the equipment without court order. It also helps reduce the lessor's tax liability owing to the high depreciation allowances generally allowed by tax laws in many countries. The lessor can also sell the equipment during the lease period so that the lease payments accrue to the new buyer. This enables the lessor to get cash when he needs liquidity. This is not possible in the case of a debt because, while the prevailing *fiqhi* position allows the sale of physical assets, it does not allow the sale of financial debt instruments except at their nominal value.

Some of the jurists have expressed doubts about the permissibility of a financial lease. The rationale they give is that the long-term and non-cancellable nature of the lease contract shifts the entire risk to the lessee, particularly if the 'residual' value of the asset is also fixed in advance. The end result for the lessee may turn out to be worse than the outright purchase of the asset through an interest-bearing loan. A financial lease thus has the potential of becoming more exploitative than outright purchase. Supposing the lease contract is for five years, the lessee would have to continue making lease payments even if he does not need the asset, say, after two years. In the case of a purchase through an interest-bearing loan, the purchaser can sell the asset in the market and repay the loan, thus reducing his loss. This he cannot do in a financial lease. If he is unable to make lease payments, he may lose his stake in the asset even though he has paid a part of the asset price beyond the rental charge he would normally pay in an operating lease.

There are, however, jurists who consider a financial lease to be permissible if certain conditions are satisfied. First, the lessor must bear the risks of leasing by being the real owner of the leased asset. He cannot lease what he does not own and possess, and should be responsible for all the risks and expenses related to ownership.[13] Therefore a lease contract where the lessor acts only as an intermediary between the supplier and the lessee and plays the role of only a financier, with ownership of the asset being nothing more than a legal device to provide security for repayment of the loan and legal protection in case of default, is not allowed. In this case the lessor leases an asset before buying it and taking possession of it, and gets a reward without bearing any risk. Second, obligation of the lessee to make lease payments does not start until he has received possession of the leased asset and can continue only as long as it remains useable by him.[14] Third, all manufacturing defects and related problems should be the lessor's responsibility. The lessee can, however, be made responsible for the proper upkeep and maintenance of the leased asset. Fourth. the lease contract should be separate from, and independent of, the contract for the purchase of the residual asset. The residual value has to be market-related and cannot be fixed in advance. The purchase contract has, therefore, to be optional and not a condition for the lease contract because the quality of the asset at the end of the lease period as well as its market-related price, two of the essential requirements for a valid contract, are unknown when the lease contract is signed.

Almost all Islamic banks use the financial lease by fulfilling, or at least making an effort to fulfil, the *Shari'ah* conditions. The residual value remains a problem, but the banks have tried to overcome it by setting a small nominal value for the residual asset or transferring it as a gift from the lessor to the lessee. This does not satisfy the jurists who are opposed to the financial lease because, according to them, it does not fulfil the *Shari'ah* requirements. The residual value is automatically predetermined and becomes built into the lease payments, and thereby leads to injustice. The lessee loses the asset as well as the extra payments made by him in the case where he dies or is unable to continue lease payments. The alternative suggested by them is that the lessor should sell the asset to the lessee on an installment basis and then get it hypothecated to ensure full payment. However, once the asset is owned by the 'lessee', it is very cumbersome for the bank to get it back from him in a number of Muslim countries even if he is unable to make payments. Moreover, the ownership of the asset enables him to sell the asset and use the money, leaving the bank with nothing to fall back upon.

The jurists are agreed that the security lease (also referred to as 'financing' lease) is not acceptable from the point of view of the *Shari'ah* because it is not a lease contract in the traditional sense. It is just a financing transaction, and nothing more than a disguised security agreement. It involves the effective transfer to the lessee of all the risks and rewards associated with ownership. The security lease has therefore been ruled out from the modes of Islamic finance.

Securitization and sale of debts

There is a general agreement among the jurists that the sale of debts is not allowed except at their face value. The rationale usually given for this position is that the sale of debts involves *riba* (interest) as well as *gharar* (excessive uncertainty),[15] both of which are prohibited by the *Shari'ah*. Such a position is undoubtedly true with respect to the sale of debts incurred by borrowing money. Since it is normally not possible to sell a debt except at a discount, such a sale would be nothing but a disguised way of receiving and paying interest. It is also argued that, as a result of what is now called 'asymmetric information', the buyer of the debt may be unaware of the true financial position of the debtor and of his willingness and ability to honour the debt. Consequently there is *gharar* in the transaction. Hence the jurists have a strong rationale in not allowing the sale of debts.

The rationale does not, however, apply to debts sold by Islamic banks in modern times, for two main reasons. First, the debt is created by the sale of goods and services through the sales-based modes of Islamic finance, particularly *murabaha*. If, say, an aeroplane or a ship is sold by a bank or a consortium of banks to a government or a corporation, the debt is not incurred by borrowing money. The debt is created by the *murabaha* mode of financing permitted by the *Shari'ah* and the price, according to the jurists themselves, includes profit on the transaction and not interest. Therefore, when the bank sells such a debt instrument at a discount, what it is selling is a part of an asset and the return that the buyer is getting is not interest but rather a share of the profit that the bank has earned in the *murabaha* transaction.

Second, in the present-day sale of debts by banks, we are not talking of a debt owed by an unknown (*majhul*) person with an unknown credit rating, such that the buyer of the debt instrument does not know whether the debt will be honoured or not. The debt instruments intended to be sold are generated by the financing provided through the sales-based modes to governments and well-known corporations and firms having a high credit rating. The buyer of the debt instrument can know about the rating as much as the bank. Moreover, the debt is not unsecured. It is rather asset-based and well-secured. Its payment is therefore almost certain and there is no question of any *gharar*. The past ruling of the jurists, given in entirely different circumstances, does not, therefore, seem to fit the changed realities of modern times.

The jurists may therefore wish to reconsider their verdict, not because the earlier verdict was wrong, but because circumstances have changed. They should definitely retain the ban on sale of debts in the form of treasury bills, bonds and other such interest-based instruments which involve pure lending and borrowing against interest. However, their ruling with regard to the sale of asset-based debt instruments, which originate in the sale of real goods and services and which transfer a part of the profit, and not interest, from the original financier to the new financier, needs to be reviewed. The development of a general agreement on this important issue would help create a secondary market for such debt instruments and thereby lead to the accelerated development of an Islamic money market.

The absence of such a secondary market for debt instruments creates two major problems for banks and thereby serves as a hindrance to the further development and expansion of Islamic banking. First, the banks are stuck with the debt instrument until its maturity. There are so many uncertainties facing banks in the modern volatile financial system that, even without being guilty of overlending, it is possible for them to get into a tight liquidity situation. This may be the result of an excessive net outflow of funds from the banks for some unexpected reason. It may also be due to the failure of a major client of the bank to settle payment on time because of some unexpected developments. There may be a number of other unforeseen reasons for the liquidity crisis of an individual bank. If the bank cannot sell some of its debts to acquire the badly needed liquidity before the maturity date of those debts, it may not be able to meet its obligations or to fund more profitable opportunities for investment.

Second, it is difficult for banks to play their role of financial intermediation effectively without being able to securitize their receivables. When banks grant a big sales-based credit for an expensive item (say, an aeroplane, a ship or a building), they would like to package it into small portions and sell these to small financiers. In this way they would be able to provide a large amount of credit without straining their own resources excessively and would simultaneously be able to provide investment opportunities to small investors. If they are unable to play this role effectively, the economy may suffer from the hesitation on the part of banks to finance the purchase of costly items. Companies will have to sign loan agreements separately with numerous investors to raise a large amount. This would undoubtedly be a cumbersome task. Syndicated loans may not be a substitute for the sale of debts because, in addition to the lead bank, there are generally only a few big lenders participating in such loans. Therefore, while a large purchase may be facilitated for a major borrower, the packaging of the amount into small portions would not be possible and small financiers would not be able to benefit from the investment opportunity.

Hedging and financial engineering
Hedging has become an important instrument for the management of risks in the present-day international economic and financial environment where there is a great deal of instability in exchange rates as well as other market prices. If individuals, businesses and financial institutions do not resort to this instrument for the management of their risks, there is

a strong likelihood that they may suffer substantial losses with knock-on effects for the whole economy.

Exchange rate risks do not seem to have been common during the days of the Prophet, peace and blessings of God be on him, and the *Khilafah al-Rashidah*. The rates of exchange between gold and silver coins in the then-prevailing bimetallic monetary system were relatively stable at around ten. Such stability did not, however, persist later on. The two metals faced different supply and demand conditions, which destabilized their relative prices. The ratios sometimes moved to as low as 20, 30 and even 50 (al-Qaradawi, 1969, Vol. 1, p. 264; Miles, 1992, p. 320). This instability enabled bad coins, according to al-Maqrizi (d. 1442) and his contemporary al-Asadi (d. 1450), to drive good coins out of circulation (al-Misri, 1990, pp. 54, 66), a phenomenon which has become known since the 16th century as Gresham's Law. Such instability created difficulties for everyone, but there was no solution at that time to protect individuals and economies from its adverse effects.

To solve this problem the world abandoned the bimetallic standard and moved to the gold standard and then to the dollar exchange standard, both of which helped stabilize exchange rates because of the fixed parities. These two standards, however, created other difficult problems and had to be abandoned in favour of floating exchange rates. The farewell to fixed parities has introduced a great deal of instability in the foreign exchange markets and the risks involved in foreign trade and finance have become unduly intensified. In such an unstable climate, hedging has proved to be a boon. It has made it possible for banks and businesspeople to manage the exchange rate and price risks by passing them on to those who are willing to bear them at a certain cost.

To understand the problem, let us assume that a Saudi businessman places an order for Japanese goods worth a million dollars (Rls 3.75 million) to be delivered three months from now. If the rate of exchange is 117 Yen per dollar, and if the exchange rate remains stable, ¥117 million will become due at the time of delivery of the goods. Since exchange rates are not stable and, consequently, if the Yen appreciates over these three months by, say, 5 per cent, the Saudi importer will have to pay Rls 3.94 million for the goods instead of Rls 3.75 million. The Saudi businessman will therefore incur an unforeseen loss of Rls 190,000.

One way of protecting himself against such loss would be to purchase now the Yen that will be payable three months later. This will freeze his financial resources unnecessarily and create a liquidity crisis for him. To avoid such liquidity tightness, the alternative solution available in the conventional financial system is to purchase ¥117 million in the forward market at the current exchange rate of ¥117 per dollar plus or minus a premium or discount. All that the importer has to do is to pay a small percentage of the total amount as deposit for this purpose. Such a transaction is called hedging.

The question that therefore arises is whether the mechanism of hedging to protect the importer from exchange rate fluctuations is permissible. The verdict of the jurists so far is that hedging is not permissible. This opinion is based on three objections: hedging involves *gharar* (excessive uncertainty), interest (*riba*) payment and receipt, and forward sale of currencies. All three of these are prohibited by the *Shari'ah*.

As far as *gharar* is concerned, the objection is not valid because hedging in fact helps eliminate *gharar* by enabling the importer to buy the needed foreign exchange at the current exchange rate. The bank, which sells forward Yen, also does not get involved in *gharar*, because it purchases the Yen spot and invests them until the time of delivery. The bank therefore earns a return on the Yen that it invests for three months but also loses the return that it would have earned on the Riyals or the dollars that were used to purchase the Yen. The differential in the two rates of return determines the premium or the discount on the forward transaction.

The second objection with regard to interest can be handled by requiring the Islamic banks to invest the Yen or other foreign currencies purchased by them in an Islamically permissible manner to the extent to which it is possible for them to do so. There would not then be any interest, but rather profit earned on the investments.

The third objection is, of course, very serious. The Prophet, peace and blessings of God be on him, has clearly prohibited forward transactions in currencies. However, we live in a world where instability in the foreign exchange markets has become an unavoidable reality. It is not possible for businessmen as well as Islamic banks to reduce their exposure to this risk. How are they going to manage it? It is very risky for them to carry unhedged foreign exchange liabilities or assets on their balance-sheets, particularly in crisis situations when exchange rates are volatile. If they do not resort to hedging, they actually get involved in *gharar* more intensively. In addition, one of the important objectives of the *Shari'ah*, which is the protection of wealth (*hifz al-mal*),[16] is compromised unnecessarily.

Institutions, which provide the needed protection through hedging, are well-qualified for this service because of their greater financial resources and better knowledge of market conditions. The fee that they charge can be 'Islamized' by resort to Islamic instruments. The question, therefore, is about whether hedging could be accepted in an unstable exchange rate environment. Here we need to look at the reason (*illah*) for the prohibition of forward transactions. If the *illah* is to prevent speculation in the foreign exchange markets, which is a source of great volatility in the flow of funds and exchange rates, this could be overcome by confining hedging to only foreign exchange receivables and payables related to real goods and services.

7.4 CONCLUDING REMARKS

The Islamic financial industry has made commendable progress over the last three decades since the establishment of the first Islamic bank in Dubai in 1975. Nevertheless, the industry has a long way to go before it can hope to realize the vision for which it was established.

The vision consists of two indispensable parts. The first part relates to the removal of interest from the financial systems of Muslim countries in such an orderly manner that all their financial needs are satisfied in conformity with Islamic teachings without creating any setback for their economies. It is hoped that, with the gradual coming of age of Islamic finance, reliance on equity and the PLS modes of financing will steadily rise in Muslim countries and that on the debt-creating modes will decline until a suitable mix of the two has been achieved in accordance with the needs of accelerated development of their economies within the framework of financial health and stability. The second part of the vision is to bring about a more equitable distribution of credit so that the financial system helps reduce poverty, unemployment and concentration of income and wealth instead of continuing its existing tendency of making the rich richer at the expense of the poor.

As far as the quantitative aspect of the vision is concerned, there has been an unexpectedly rapid progress in the expansion of the industry in terms of the number of banks and the volume of deposits and assets. What has helped greatly is the recent emergence of *sukuk*, which have made it possible for governments and corporations to have access to a relatively large volume of financing. Experience so far leads to the hope that *Shari'ah*-compatible products will continue to respond to the increasing demand for these in the future to satisfy the rising financial needs of all countries until a respectable niche has been achieved in the international financial markets.

The movement into equity and PLS financing, however, has not been significant. This is because the kind of institutional infrastructure that is needed to make progress in this direction does not exist to a satisfactory level. This indicates the urgency of establishing shared institutions that would enable banks to minimize the principle–agent conflict of interest through appropriate incentives and deterrents and the prompt settlement of disputes. It is also necessary to strengthen corporate governance through well-enforced internal controls, risk management, transparency, loan accounting and disclosure, *Shari'ah* clearance and audit, external audit and prudential regulation. Total reliance on these may not, however, be sufficient. Moral commitment on the part of all market operators is indispensable. Without such commitment, market operators will be able to find clandestine ways of violating the law without being detected and punished. This will blunt the system of incentives and deterrents and accentuate the need for more and more legal checks and controls which will raise transactions costs to an unbearably high level. It may not be an exaggeration to say that no human institution can work effectively without the injection of a moral dimension in human society.

Progress in the realization of the second part of the vision – equitable distribution of credit – has not been significant. It may be difficult to realize this part of the vision without integrating the microfinance sector with the mainstream financial system. This will make available a significantly larger volume of funds for financing micro enterprises in urban and rural areas to reduce poverty, unemployment and income inequalities. Commercial banks need not enter directly into microfinance if they find this to be cumbersome. They may do it through their subsidiaries and the institutions that already exist for this purpose. If a relatively greater share of the resources of the financial system does not become available to the poor and lower middle classes, then Islamic finance will not be able to contribute positively to the realization of the *maqasid* (objectives) of *Shari'ah* and, thereby, fail to come up to the expectations of the people.

In conclusion, one may say that, even though a substantial degree of progress has been made in quantitative terms, progress toward the realization of the Islamic vision has lagged behind. This is because the Islamic system has so far been unable to escape the trappings of conventional finance. A part of the explanation lies in the difficulties faced in the successful establishment of a new system in place of the well-entrenched interest-oriented conventional system when even the necessary shared institutions do not exist to support its operations.

However, a number of things have happened that will help reduce the difficulties in the future and enable the industry to meet successfully the challenges that it faces. The most important of these is the establishment of some needed infrastructure institutions. One of these is the Islamic Development Bank. which was established in the very initial phase of Islamic finance, and is in the nature of a World Bank for Muslim countries operating on Islamic principles. It has also played a catalytic role in the accelerated development of the Islamic financial industry. Another is the IFSB, which is in the process of setting standards and guidelines for the industry. Once these guidelines are set, their implementation by the regulatory and supervisory authorities will begin. This will bring about greater harmony in the operations of the industry and help not only remove some of its weaknesses but also strengthen and expand it significantly. The establishment of the IIRA, AAOIFI. IIFM and LMC will also bring positive results. Other infrastructure institutions, particularly academic institutions for training highly qualified expertise in Islamic finance, will add further strength to the industry. The central banks have also become more active and are trying to help remove the difficulties that lie in the path of ensuring Islamization of the industry in the real sense. On the whole the future looks bright for the industry.

NOTES

* Chapter edited by M. Kabir Hassan and Mervyn K. Lewis. This chapter draws heavily on the author's previous writings. especially Chapra (1985, 1992, 2000). Chapra and Khan (2000) and Chapra and Ahmed (2002). He is grateful to the co-authors of the latter two occasional papers for their permission to adapt some of the material here. The views expressed in this chapter do not necessarily reflect the views of IRTI or IDB. The author is also grateful to Abdel-Hameed Bashir for his valuable comments on an earlier draft and to Shaikh M. Rashid and M. Rasul Hoque for the efficient secretarial assistance provided by them.
1. *Mudaraba* (commenda) refers to an agreement between two or more persons whereby one or more of them provide finance, while the others provide management. The purpose is to undertake trade, industry or service with the objective of earning profit. The profit may be shared by the financiers and the managers in any agreed proportion. The loss must, however, be borne only by the financiers in proportion to their share in total capital. The loss of the manager lies in having no return for his/her effort.
   Musharaka (partnership) is also an agreement between two or more persons. However, unlike *mudaraba*, all of the partners contribute finance as well as entrepreneurship and management, though not necessarily equally. Their share in profits can be in accordance with the agreement but the share in losses must be in proportion to their share in capital.
2. *Murabaha* (also called *bai' muajjal*) refers to a sales agreement whereby the seller purchases the goods desired by the buyer and sells them at an agreed marked-up price, the payment being settled within a specified timeframe, either in installments or a lump sum. The seller bears the risk for the goods until they have been delivered to the buyer.
   Salam refers to a sales agreement whereby full payment is made in advance against an obligation to deliver the specified fungible goods at an agreed future date. This is not the same as speculative forward sale because full, and not margin, payment is required. Under this arrangement the seller, say a farmer, may be able to secure the needed financing by making an advance sale of only a part of his expected

234   *Morality and justice in Islamic economics and finance*

output. This may not get him into delivery problems in case of a fall in output due to unforeseen circumstances.

Istisnaa refers to a sales agreement whereby a manufacturer (contractor) agrees to produce (build) and deliver a certain good (or premise) at a given price on a given date in the future. This, like *salam*, is an exception to the general *Shari'ah* ruling which does not allow a person to sell what he does not own and possess. However, unlike *salam* the price need not be paid in advance. It may be paid in installments in step with the preferences of the parties, or partly at the front end and the balance later on as agreed.

3. These were also called *sayarifah* (sing., *sayrafi*) (see the word *sarf* in Ibn Manzur, *Lisan al-'Arab*). Another less popular word used for *sarrafs* was *jahabidhah* (sing., *jahbadh*). The *sarrafs* were more widespread because they provided banking facilities to the public sector as well as an extensive private sector. The *jahabidhah* were less prevalent because they served mainly the public sector (cf., Duri, 1986, p. 898).

4. Abdul Jabbar Khan, ex-President, Habib Bank of Pakistan, has emphasized that the 'auditing system presently in vogue suffers from a number of weaknesses. There is, therefore, an urgent need for a thorough reappraisal of the existing laws and practices governing the role of auditors and for evolving a really independent auditing system' (see his privately circulated paper, 'Commercial Banking Operations in the Interest-free Framework', p. 39). See also al-Qabbani (n.d.) and Khan (1981).

5. Some of the jurists do not find this to be acceptable because it appears to them as a form of reciprocal lending (*qurud mutabadalah*) which is like deriving benefit from a loan, and hence equivalent to interest. However, some other highly respectable jurists have allowed this, provided that it does not involve the taking and giving of interest (see Ahmad and Abu Ghuddah, 1998, p. 236). Mutual help of this kind is a form of cooperative insurance, whereby the banks provide themselves with protection in case of need. Such cooperation had prevailed in Muslim history between businesses in the form of what was then called *ibda'* or *bida'ah* (see Chapra, 1985, pp. 75, 250).

6. The detailed discussion that this subject requires is beyond the scope of this chapter. For some relevant discussion on the reform of the stock market. see Chapra (1985, pp. 95–100) and Chapra (2002).

7. In Germany it is customary for individual shareholders to transfer their voting rights to banks or to shareholder associations who send their representatives to the meeting (Balling et al., 1998, p. xxii).

8. See Tables 2.3 and 2.4 in Chapra and Ahmed (2002) for the results of a sample survey conducted by IRTI. Figures have not been given above because of the small size of this sample.

9. The *mudaraba* form of business allows only normal expenses of the *mudaraba* to be charged to the *mudaraba* account. The *mudarib* is not entitled to a fixed remuneration or an absolute amount of profit specified in advance. His only entitlement beyond the normal expenses of business is a mutually agreed share in profit as a reward for his management services.

10. A fiduciary is 'a person who is entrusted to act as a substitute for another person for the sole purpose of serving that person' (Iwai, 2001).

11. This section has been adapted from Chapra and Khan (2000, pp. 71–83).

12. For a range of opinions expressed on the subject, see M.A. Zarqa and M.A. El-Gari (1991, pp. 25–27) as well as the comments by M. Zaki 'Abd al-Barr and Habib al-Kaf on pp. 61–64 of the same issue, and by Rabi' al-Rabi on pp. 67–69 of the 1992 issue of the same journal. See also al-Misri (1997, pp. 131–54; al-Zu'ayr, 1997, pp. 50–57; Abu Ghuddah and Khoja, 1997, pp. 55 and 91).

13. The jurists, however, allow the sub-lease of a leased asset even though the sub-lessor is not the owner of the asset. The sub-lessor then bears the risk, but can pass it on to the original lessor.

14. This does not mean that the lessee cannot make lease payments in advance of the lease period. However, his liability cannot start until he has received the leased asset.
15. For a detailed meaning and explanation of gharar, see Saleh (1986, pp. 49–52).
16. According to al-Ghazali (d. 1111): 'The objective of the Shari'a is to promote the well-being of the people, which lies in protecting their faith, their life, their intellect, their posterity, and their wealth. Whatever ensures the protection of these five serves public interest and is desirable' (1937, pp. 139–40). The same objectives have been upheld in the same, or a somewhat different, order by a number of other jurists. (For a discussion of these *maqasid*, see Chapra, 2000, pp. 118–23).

BIBLIOGRAPHY

Abu Ghuddah, Abd al-Fattah and Izz al-Din Khoja (1997), *Fatawa Nadwah al-Barakah, 1981–1997* (Jeddah: Shirkah al-Barakah li al-Istithmar wa al-Tanmiyah).

Ahmad, Muhay al-Din Ahmad and Abd al-Sattar Abu Ghuddah (1998), *Fatawa al-Khidmat al-Masrafiyyah* (Jeddah: Majmu'ah Dallah al-Barakah).

Ali, Salman Syed (2005), Islamic Capital Market Products: Development and Challenges. Occasional Paper No. 9, Jeddah: IRTI/IDB.

Al-Qaradawi, Yusuf al- (1969), *Fiqh al-Zakat* (Beirut: Dar al-Irshad).

Alvarez, Ana, Anson, Silvia and Mendez, Carolos (1998), The effect of board size and composition on corporate governance, in Morten Balling, Elizabeth Hennessey and Richard O'Brien (eds), *Corporate Governance, Financial Markets and Global Convergence* (The Hague: Kluwer Academic Publishers).

Balling, Morten, Hennessey, Elizabeth and O'Brien, Richard (eds) (1998), *Corporate Governance, Financial Markets and Global Convergence* (The Hague: Kluwer Academic Publishers).

Berle A. and Means, G. (1932), *The Modern Corporation and Private Property* (New York: Macmillan).

Bigsten, Arne (1987), Poverty, inequality and development, in Norman Gemmell (ed.), *Surveys in Development Economics* (Oxford: Basil Blackwell).

Chapra, M. Umer (1985), *Towards A Just Monetary System* (Leicester, UK: The Islamic Foundation).

Chapra, M. Umer (1992), *Islam and the Economic Challenge* (Leicester, UK: The Islamic Foundation).

Chapra. M. Umer (2000), *The Future of Economics: an Islamic Perspective* (Leicester, UK: The Islamic Foundation).

Chapra, M. Umer (2002), Alternative visions of international monetary reform, in Munawar Iqbal and David Llewellyn (eds), *Islamic Banking and Finance: New Perspectives on Profit-Sharing and Risk* (Cheltenham, UK and Northampton, MA, USA: Edward Elgar Publishing).

Chapra, M.U. and Khan, Tariqullah (2000), Regulation and Supervision of Islamic Banks. Occasional Paper No. 3, Jeddah: IRTI/I DI3.

Chapra, M. Umer and Ahmed, Habib (2002), Corporate Governance in Islamic Financial Institutions. Occasional Paper No.6. Jeddah: I RT1/1 DB.

Dinsdale, Nicholas and Prevezer, Martha (1994, reprinted 2001), *Capital Markets and Corporate Governance* (Oxford: Clarendon Press).

Duri, A.A. (1986), Baghdad, *The Encyclopedia of Islam*, Vol. 1 (Leiden: Brill), pp. 894–909.

Elliot. R.K. and Willingham, J.J. (1980), *Management Fraud Detection and Deterrence* (Princeton, NJ: Petrocelli Books).

Fischel, W.J. (1992), Djahbadh, *The Encyclopedia of Islam*, Vol. 2 (Leiden: Brill), pp. 382–3.

Gemmell, Norman (ed.) (1987), *Surveys in Development Economics* (Oxford: Basil Backwell).

Ghazali, Abu Hamid al- (d. 1111) (1937), *Al-Mustasfa* (Cairo: al-Maktabah al-Tijariyyah al-Kurba).

Goitein, S.D. (1966), *Studies in Islamic History and Intuitions* (Leiden: Brill).

Goitein, S.D. (1967), *A Mediterranean Society* (Berkeley and Los Angeles: University of California Press).

Grief, Avner (1997), Informal contract enforcement: Lessons from medieval trade, *The New Palgrave Dictionary of Economics and the Law*, Vol. 1 (London: Palgrave), pp. 287–95.

Herzel, Leo (1994), Corporate governance, *The New Palgrave Dictionary of Money and Finance*, Vol. 1 (London: Palgrave), pp. 472–5.

Iqbal Munawr and Llewellyn, David (eds) (2002), *Islamic Banking and Finance: New Perspective on Profit-Sharing and Risk* (Cheltenham: UK and Northampton, MA, USA: Edward Elgar Publishing).

Iqbal, Munawar, Khan, Tariqullah and Ahmad, Ausaf (1998), Challenges Facing Islamic Banking. Occasional Paper No. 2, Jeddah: IRTI/IDB.

Iwai, Katsuhito (2001), What is corporation: The corporate personality controversy and comparative corporate governance, in E. Cafaggi, A. Nicita and V. Pagano (eds), *Legal Orderings and Economic Intuitions* (London: Routledge).

Jarhi, Ma'bid al- and Muanwar Iqbal (2001), Islamic Banking: Answers to Some Frequently Asked Questions. Occasional Paper No. 4, Jeddah: IRTI/IDB.

Jensen M. and Meckling, W. (1976), Theory of the firm: Managerial behavior, agency costs and ownership structure, *Journal of Financial Economics*, 3, 305–60.

Khan, M. Akram (1981), Auditing in an Islamic framework. Unpublished Paper.

Khan, Tariqullah and Ahmed, Habib (2001), Risk Management: An Analysis of Issues in Islamic Financial Industry. Occasional Paper No. 5, Jeddah: IRTI/IDB.

Kramers, J.H. (1952), Geography and commerce, in T. Arnold and A. Guillaume (eds), *The Legacy of Islam* (London: Oxford University Press).

Laeven, Luc (2002), Bank risk and deposit insurance, *The World Bank Economic Review*, 16:1, 109–37.

Leadbearer, Charles (1986), Rags to riches: Fact or fiction, *Financial Times*, 30 December, p. 5.

Lechner, Alan (1998), *Street Games: Inside Stories of the Wall Street Hustle* (New York: Harper & Row).

Mace, Myles (1996), *Directors: Myth and Reality* (Boston, MA: Harvard Business School Press).

Miles, G.C. (1992), 'Dinar' and 'Dirham', *The Encyclopedia of Islam*, Vol. 2 (Leiden: Brill), pp. 297–9 and 319–20.

Mills, Paul and Presley, John (1999), *Islamic Finance: Theory and Practice* (London: Macmillan).

Misri, Rafiq Yunus al- (1st edn 1990, 2nd edn 1997), *Bay' al-Taqsit: Tahlil Fiqhi wa Igtisddi* (Damascus: Dar al-Qalam).

Misri, Rafiq al (1998), Hal Yajuz Istithmar Amwal al-Yatama bi al-Riba? (Is it permissible to invest the wealth of orphans on interest?), *Majallah al-Amwal*, Jeddah, 6, 1419.

Morck, Randall (1994), Corporate ownership and management, *The New Palgrave Dictionary of Money and Finance*, Vol. 1 (London: Macmillan), pp. 475–7.

Morck, R.K., Schleifer, A. and Vishny, R.W. (1990), Do managerial objectives drive bad acquisitions?, *Journal of Finance*, 45:1, 31–48.

Organization of the Islamic Conference (1981), Promotion, regulation and supervision of Islamic banks, Report prepared by a Committee of the Governors of Central Bank and Monetary Authorities of the Organization and adopted by the Governors at their fourth meeting held in Khartoum, 7–8 March.

Prentice, D.D. (1993), Some aspects of the corporate governance debate, in D.D. Prentice and P. Holland (eds), *Contemporary Issues in Corporate Governance* (Oxford: Clarendon Press).

Prentice, D.D. and Holland, P. (eds) (1993), *Contemporary Issues in Corporate Governance* (Oxford: Clarendon Press).

Prowse, Stephen (1998), Corporate governance: Emerging issues and lessons for East Asia (World Bank, www.worldbank.org/html/extdr/pos 981).

Qabbani, Thana 'Ali al- (n.d.), *Ba'd Khasa'is Tatawwur Al-Fkr al-Muhasabi al-Mu'asir wa al-Muhasabah al-Islamiyyah* (Cairo: Matabi' al-Ittihad al-Dawii li al- Bunuk al- Islamiyyah).

Rauch, James E. (2001), Business and social networks in international trade, *Journal of Economic Literature*, December, 1177–203.

Saleh Nabil A. (1986), *Unlawful Gain and Legitimate Profit in Islamic Lair: Riba, Gharar and Islamic Banking* (Cambridge: Cambridge University Press).

Schacht, J. (1970), Law and justice, in P.M. Holt, Ann Lambton and Bernard Lewis (eds), *The Cambridge History of Islam*, Vol. 2 (Cambridge: Cambridge University Press), pp. 539–68.

Schatzmiller, Maya (1994), *Labour in the Medieval Islamic World* (Leiden: Brill).

Schleifer, A. and Vishny, R. (1997), A survey of corporate governance, *Journal of Finance*, 52, 737–83.

Sundararajan. V., Enoch, C.A., San Jose, A., Hilbers, Paul L., Kruger, Russell C., Moretti, Marina and Slack, Graham L. (2002), *Financial Soundness Indicators: Analytical Aspects and Country Practices* (Washington, DC: IMF).

Sykes, Allen (1994), Proposals for a reformed system of corporate governance to achieve internationally competitive long-term performance, in N. Dinsdale and M. Prevezer (eds), *Capital Markets and Corporate Governance* (Oxford: Clarendon Press), pp. 111–27.

Udovitch. Abraham L. (1970), *Partnership and Profit in Medieval Islam* (Princeton, NJ: Princeton University Press).

Udovitch Abraham L. (1981), *Bankers Without Banks: Commerce, Banking and Society in the Islamic World of Middle Ages*, Princeton Near East Paper No. 30, Princeton, NJ: Princeton University Press.

United States House of Representatives (1986), *Banking for the Poor: Alleviating Poverty Through Credit Assistance in Developing Courtiers*, Report of the Select Committee on Hunger.

Yunus, Muhammad (1984), *Group-Based Savings Anti Credit for the Rural Poor* (Dhaka: Grameen Batik).

Yunus, Muhammad (1987), The poor as the engine of growth, *The Washington Quarterly*, 10:4, 05309.

Zarqa. M. Anas and M. Ali EI-Gari (1991), Al-Ta'wid 'an Darar al Mumatalah fi al-Dayn bayn al-Fiqh wa al-Iqtisad, *Journal of King Abdul University: Islamic Economics*, 25–37.

Zu'ayr. M. Ahd al-Hakim (1997), Fatwa and Shari'a supervision at Islamic banks, *The American Journal of Islamic Finance*, Rancho Polos Verdes, CA, 3, 4–6.

8. The global financial crisis: some suggestions for reform of the global financial system in the light of Islamic finance*

The whole world is now in the grip of a financial crisis which is far more serious than any experienced since the Great Depression. It has taken more than three trillion dollars of bail out and liquidity injections by a number of industrial countries to abate somewhat the intensity of the crisis. Nevertheless, there are fears that this crisis may have exposed the world economy to a long period of economic slowdown. There is, hence, a call for a new architecture that could help minimize the frequency and severity of such a crisis in the future (Camdessus, 2000, pp. 1 and 7–10; Stiglitz, 2007, p. 3; Baily et al., 2008, p. 44).

8.1 PRIMARY CAUSE OF THE CRISES

It is not possible to design a new architecture without first determining the primary cause of the crises. The generally recognized most important cause of almost all crises has been excessive and imprudent lending by banks.[1] This raises the question of what makes it possible for banks to resort to such an unhealthy practice that not only hurts their own long-run interest but also destabilizes the international financial system. There are a number of factors that make this possible. One of the most important of these is inadequate market discipline in the financial system.

What is it that makes it possible for the financial system to have inadequate discipline when this is considered to be a crucial and indispensable mechanism of a market economy for correcting unhealthy practices? The market is able to impose discipline only when it is able to reward efficiency and prudence and punish inefficiency and reckless-ness.[2] There would be a check on excessive lending only if the banks were afraid that this would lead to losses, souring of their reputation, and bankruptcy. This does not happen in a system where profit-and-loss-sharing (PLS) does not exist, the repayment of loans with interest is generally assured, and 'the too big to fail' concept ensures survival. The false sense of immunity from losses introduces a fault line into the system. Banks do not, therefore, undertake a careful evaluation of loan applications. This leads to an unhealthy expansion in the overall volume of credit, to excessive leverage, and to an unsustainable rise in asset prices, living beyond means, and speculative investment. Unwinding later on gives rise to a steep decline in asset prices, and to financial fragility and debt crises, particularly if this is also accompanied by over-indulgence in short sales. John Galbraith (1990) has documented the role of debt and leverage in the speculative booms of the last three centuries. Even according to the G-20 Summit held on 15 November 2008, excessive leverage was one of the root causes of 'vulnerabilities in the system' (G-20, 2008). Inadequate discipline, thus, promotes excessive lending and high leverage, and leads first to a bubble and then to a debt crisis. This injects built-in instability into the financial system (see Fisher, 1992, pp. 24–44; and Minsky, 1975).

8.2   THE SUBPRIME MORTGAGE CRISIS

The subprime mortgage crisis in the grip of which the US finds itself at present, did not come out of the blue. In has been preceded by a number of other crises which had sent ripples through the financial markets. Some of these crises are the stock market crash of 1987, the Long-Term Capital Management (LTCM) collapse in 1998, and the 'dot.com' bubble burst in 2000. All of these are classic examples of excessive and imprudent lending resulting from the absence of PLS and a false sense of assurance against losses.

There are a number of factors that lead to this false assurance. One of these is the collateral. Collateral is, of course, indispensable for managing the risk of default. The collateral can, however, perform this function only if it is of good quality. But collateral is exposed to a valuation risk. Its value can be impaired by the same factors that diminish the borrower's ability to repay. If there is no risk-sharing, the bank will have little incentive to undertake a careful evaluation of the collateral and will extend financing for any purpose including speculation and gambling. The collateral cannot, therefore, by itself be a substitute for a more careful evaluation of the project financed. Moreover, the sale of collateral, and particularly of mortgaged houses does not only cause a great deal of hardship to their owners but is also extremely costly for the banks themselves. Transactions costs of foreclosures can easily dissipate close to or more than one-third of the total value of the home being re-possessed (Summers, 2008, p. 11).

A second factor that provides protection against losses is securitization which switched the 'originate-to-hold' model to the 'originate-to-distribute' model of financing. This enables the banks to sell the debt, transfer the risk of default to the purchasers, and use the proceeds to make more loans and increase their profit. However, the problem they encountered in this was that, while rational purchasers would be willing to buy the prime debt they would be reluctant to buy the subprime debt. This problem was solved by the creation of collateralized debt obligations (CDOs). Prime and subprime debts were mixed and securitized by trenching them into different groups with varying degrees of risk and maturity. Since complex models were used for this purpose, the CDOs became difficult to understand, and made their purchasers rely on rating agencies. The rating agencies also used, in turn, complex computer models to predict the likelihood of default. Independent judgment of the risk involved, therefore, became difficult (see Baily et al., 2008, pp. 34–45). There would have been no problem in this if the rating agencies had not suffered from conflict of interests and provided accurate ratings. However, since they were paid by banks and hedge funds which organized and sold these structured securities, they did not have adequate incentive to perform proper risk analysis of the underlying assets. They issued their ratings on the basis of information that was provided to them without certifying its accuracy. The high ratings plus the relatively higher yields on these CDOs, made it easier for mortgage originators to pass the risk of default to the ultimate purchasers. Unscrupulous lenders also used deceptive tactics to sell adjustable rate mortgages (ARMs) with low introductory 'teaser' rates to promote the sale of debt to unsophisticated borrowers. Loan volume accordingly gained greater priority over loan quality and the amount of lending to subprime borrowers and speculators increased steeply (Mian and Sufi, 2008, p. 4; and Keys et al., 2008).

A great deal of fraud was, thus, involved in the sale of CDOs. The number of *reported* cases of mortgage fraud increased by more than 15 times from roughly 3,500 in 2000 to 53,000 in 2007 (Barth and Yago, 2008). This has been acknowledged by Mr Bernanke, Chairman of the Board of Governors of the Federal Reserve System, who stated in one of his speeches that 'far too much of the lending in recent years was neither responsible nor prudent. ... In addition, abusive, unfair, or deceptive lending practices led some borrowers into mortgages that they would not have chosen knowingly' (Bernanke, 2008, p. 1). Even Christopher Cox, Chairman of the Securities and Exchange Commission, acknowledged that 'there's no question that somewhere in this terrible mess many laws were broken' (Blough, 2008). The check that market discipline could have exercised on the serving of self-interest did not, therefore, come into play.

Even the supervisors, who are expected to ensure orderly operation of the market and to punish the culprits failed to perform their task effectively by following the policy of minimal regulation and supervision of private markets that has been pursued over the last three decades. They did not take serious notice of the 'abusive, unfair, or deceptive lending practices' and did not take any effective measures to nip them in the bud. The newly promoted complex and opaque financial innovations, therefore, thrived in an environment of easy and loose monetary policy.

A third factor that further reduced underwriting standards is the spread of derivatives like credit default swaps (CDSs) which made it possible for lenders to insure themselves against the risk of default. The buyer of the swap (creditor) paid a premium to the seller (a hedge fund) for the compensation he will receive in case the debtor defaults. Even though this innovation would have resulted in further reducing underwriting standards, it may not have caused much harm if the hedge funds had also performed some scrutiny and sold the swaps to just the actual lending banks. They, however, sold them also to a large number of other institutions and individuals who were willing to bet on the default of the debtor. These swap holders, in turn, resold the swaps to others. The whole process continued several times. While a genuine insurance contract indemnifies only the insured party against losses *actually* suffered, in the case of CDSs the hedge funds and insurers had to compensate several other swap holders who had not suffered any loss from default. In addition to this betting on debt default, there was also betting in the case of interest rates and exchange rates far in excess of the genuine need for hedging. As a result of all this, risk became excessively accentuated and made it well nigh impossible for the hedge funds and banks to honour their commitments. The notional amount of all outstanding derivatives is estimated by the Bank for International Settlements (BIS) to have risen to $683.7 trillion in June 2008[3] (BIS, November 2008, p. 20), more than 12 times the world GDP of $54.3 trillion in 2007 (World Bank, 2008). Of even greater risk was the fact that a large proportion of derivatives contracts became concentrated in the hands of relatively few dealers who were interlinked to one another through different credit instruments. The default of even one could quickly destabilize all the others and lead to a financial crisis. No wonder George Soros described derivatives as 'hydrogen bombs', and Warren Buffett called them 'financial weapons of mass destruction'.

A fourth factor that has tended to provide a false sense of security is the 'too big to fail' concept which provides an assurance to 'big' banks that the central bank will come to their assistance and bail them out. Banks which are provided with such a safety net have incentives to take greater risk than they otherwise would (Miskhin, 1997, p. 62).

Given that banks lend excessively to maximize their profit, why is it that the depositors do not impose a discipline on the banks? They can do this in several different ways: by demanding better management, greater transparency, and more efficient risk management. If this does not work, they can always punish the banks by withdrawing their deposits. They do not, however, do so in the conventional financial system because they are assured of the repayment of their deposits with interest. (Mishkin, 1997, p. 62). This makes them complacent and they do not take as much interest in the affairs of their financial institution as they would if they expected to suffer losses.

The false sense of immunity from losses provided to bankers as well as depositors impairs the ability of the market to impose the required discipline. This, along with the easy monetary policy pursued by the Federal Reserve, led to an unhealthy expansion in the overall volume of credit, to excessive leverage, to subprime debt, and to living beyond means. This tendency of the system got further reinforced by two other factors. One of these was the excessive use of complex computer models which few people understood. These models took the place of human judgment and left little incentive for bank management to use their own knowledge and skills to assess the actual risk of the underlying assets. The second factor was the bias of the tax system in favour of debt financing – dividends are subject to taxation while interest payments are allowed to be treated as a tax-deductible expense.

The result is that a number of banks have either failed or have had to be bailed out or nationalized by the governments in the US, the UK, Europe and a number of other countries. This generated fear and uncertainty in the market and led to a credit crunch, which has made it hard for even healthy banks and firms to find financing. There is a lurking fear that this might be only the tip of the iceberg and a lot more may follow if the crisis causes a prolonged recession and leads to defaults on the part of credit card institutions, corporations, and derivatives dealers.

8.3   MAKING A HUMANE ARRANGEMENT FOR SUBPRIME BORROWERS

Introduction of greater discipline into the financial system will most probably result in depriving subprime borrowers of access to credit. This will certainly not be a healthy and acceptable development in any society which stands for socio-economic justice. The financial system is like a reservoir of financial resources mobilized by banks from a wide spectrum of depositors. There is, therefore, no reason why only a small proportion of the public should benefit from this pool of financial resources. The ground reality, however, is that primarily the rich benefit from it. In the US, a substantial part of the total credit extended by banks goes to the largest non-financial corporations which exercise significant political power at both state and federal levels (Kotz, 1978, p. 143). The Patman Report as well as the Securities and Exchange Commission Report drew similar conclusions (United States Securities and Exchange Commission, 1971, pp. 124–25. See also, United States Congress, House Banking and Currency Committee, Subcommittee on Domestic Finance, 1968, p. 5). Although financial institutions deny that they exercise significant influence over non-financial corporations to which they supply capital, one would tend to agree with Kotz's observation that 'historical experience indicates that such assurances cannot be taken at face value' (Kotz, 1978, p. 119).

Justice demands that the essential needs of all sectors of society should be equitably fulfilled. Without this the underprivileged would be exposed to a life full of difficulties. This would ultimately accentuate social unrest, conflict, crime and lower rates of economic growth. It is, therefore, in the interest of social health to enable even subprime borrowers to have access to a reasonable amount of credit at affordable rates, within the constraints of their ability to repay, to enable them to purchase a home, pursue higher education or vocational training, and establish micro enterprises. They are also human beings just like the rich and privileged, and their needs also need to be fulfilled in every society that stands for human brotherhood.

While social responsibility demands that financial institutions also make a contribution towards the fulfilment of this need, it is too much to expect them to satisfy this need fully. It is, therefore necessary to make some alternative arrangement for this purpose. There could be several ways of doing this. One of these is to enable subprime borrowers to fulfil their own needs on a self-help basis. Cooperatives have proved to be very effective and have been established in a number of countries around the world (Buckley, 1994; Jones and Millin, 1999; Cizakca, 2000; Bremer, 2004). One such venture is the 'housing finance cooperative' whereby a group of people form a society to raise funds among themselves to enable them to buy and maintain a home.

Such a cooperative, however, needs a sufficient amount of seed money to get started. Members' contributions would not be adequate for this purpose and would need to be reinforced by contributions from the government and society. Instead of spending trillions of dollars to resuscitate the financial system after a serious crisis has been triggered by the default of subprime borrowers, why not make a reasonable provision in the budget and also invite contributions from banks, corporations and rich individuals to provide a part of the seed money for the establishment of non-profit cooperative housing societies. Once established, the cooperatives should be self-sustaining. Every effort should be made to ensure that the loans are repaid. However, if a borrower faces difficulty as a result of job loss, back-breaking medical bills, or some other serious problem, the members should give him respite and, in extreme circumstances, even write off the balance of the loan or a part of it. For providing such relief, the cooperative would also have to act as an insurance provider. It could do this by purchasing CDSs from hedge funds for genuine hedging and not gambling. This would not only ensure justice and harmony in society but also save the financial system from serious crises. The US already has experience in the area of co-ops through the National Cooperative Business Association (NCBA) which helped in the establishment of the National Cooperative Bank in 1978 and remains the premier cross-sectional link among co-ops in the US.

8.4 THE PREVAILING IMBALANCES IN THE US ECONOMY

Introduction of greater discipline into the financial system may not succeed unless a discipline is also injected into the government finances. The US federal government has been running budgetary deficits ever since 1970, except for a brief respite between 1998 and 2001. The budget moved from a surplus of $255 billion in fiscal year 2000 to a deficit of $412 billion in 2004 (Kohn, 2005, pp. 1–2; and IMF, August 2008, p. 602). The deficit declined thereafter to $360, $262 and $275 billion in 2005, 2006 and 2007 respectively (IMF, December 2008, p. 1204), but increased to $455 billion in 2008.[4] Instead of declining, the deficits are expected to rise further in the near future as a result of the efforts to bail out financial institutions, revive the economy, fulfil the generous campaign promises, and meet the retirement benefits of baby boomers. Mr Obama has already warned Americans to be prepared for 'the unparalleled prospect of trillion dollar deficits for years to come' (Zeleny and Andrews, 2009). This prospect has immediately become reflected in the 2009 budget for which the estimated deficit has been raised by the non-partisan Congressional Budget Office to an unprecedented to $1.7 trillion in March 2009 from an already high level of $1.2 trillion in January 2009.[5]

The continuing deficits had already raised the gross public debt of US Treasury to $10.6 trillion by 26 January 2009, $34,775 on average for every citizen.[6] Of this, the external debt is around 27.5 per cent, more than double the 1988 figure of 13 per cent (Amadeo, 2009). The rise in external debt resulting from continuing current account deficits has had an adverse impact on the strength of the US dollar in the international foreign exchange markets.

These deficits may not have created a serious problem if the US private sector saving had not declined precipitously. Net private saving (saving by households and businesses minus investment) has been declining as a result of the borrowing and spending spree by both households and firms. One of the reasons for this spending spree is the culture of consumerism. A vast array of unwarranted wants, including aimless fashions and unnecessary model changes, has been systematically promoted through advertising. 'All forms of consumer persuasion affirm that', asserts Galbraith, 'the consumption of goods is the greatest source of pleasure, the highest measure of human achievement' (Galbraith, 1972, p. 153). False symbols of prestige are thus being promoted and wants are being made infinite and insatiable as compared with 'real' human needs.[7]

The culture of consumerism may not have gained strength and momentum if the financial system had not become an accomplice. The typical US household owned 13 credit cards in 2008, and the total household debt had grown from $705 billion, or 60 per cent of disposable income, in 1974 to $7.4 trillion, or 134 per cent of disposable income, in mid-2008 (Zakaria, 2008). In addition, credit has also been promoted for speculation when the purpose of credit should essentially be to finance productive investments and not speculative buying or hoarding. Paul Volker, ex-Chairman of the Federal Reserve, had in a letter to the chief executives of all member banks, warned against speculative loans, loans made to retire stocks, loans to finance takeovers, and loans involving any extraordinary finance, 'except as they clearly involve the improvement in the nation's productive capabilities' (Volker, 1979, p. 110).

However, since the Second World War, the banking system has played the crucial role of enabling both the public and the private sectors to perpetuate their insatiable claims on the economy by performing the dual function of creating as well as promoting the lust for borrowing through easy access to credit. Governments have also financed their excessive spending by borrowing substantial amounts from the Federal Reserve (printing money). This has provided high-powered money to not only the US banks but also the banks around the world, thereby enabling them to expand credit in the prevailing proportional reserve system.

As a result of rise in spending, the net saving by households has been less than 1 per cent of after-tax income over the last three years (2005–2007), compared with an average of only 8 per cent from 1950 to 2000 (Kohn, 2005, p. 1; and OECD, 2008, Annex Table 23). Government deficits combined with low private sector saving should have pushed up interest rates. This did not happen because of the inflow of funds from abroad. This inflow has, however, been only a mixed blessing because it did not only raise the US net foreign indebtedness to a record high in both absolute terms as well as a percentage of GDP but also lowered interest rates which promoted a further rise in consumer spending along with a boom in assets prices, particularly of residential real estate.

This brings into focus the crucial issue of how long will the foreigners be willing to continue lending. Confidence in the strength and stability of the dollar, and the willingness of foreigners to hold dollars, is indispensable for enabling it to serve as a reserve currency and for ensuring the inflow of foreign funds into the US. What will happen if the deficits continue, create loss of confidence in the dollar, and lead to an outflow of funds from the United States? This is not just a theoretical question. In the last 40 years, the dollar has experienced four bouts of marked depreciation. Since nearly two-thirds of the world's foreign exchange holdings are still in dollars,[8] a movement out of the dollar into other currencies and commodities, as happened in the late 1960s, could lead to a sharp fall in the exchange rate of the dollar, a rise in interest rates and commodity prices, and a recession in the US economy. This might lead the whole world into a prolonged recession. The correction would then come with a vengeance when market discipline could have led to it much earlier with significantly less suffering. Accordingly, the President's Working Group on Financial Markets (PWG) has rightly concluded in its report on 'Principles and Guidelines Regarding Private Pool of Capital', issued in February 2007, that the most effective means of limiting systemic risk is to reinvigorate market discipline.

8.5 THE ISLAMIC FINANCIAL SYSTEM

One of the most important objectives of Islam is to realize greater justice in human society. According to the Qur'an all the messengers of God were sent to promote justice (57:25) and any society where there is no justice will ultimately head towards decline and destruction (20:111). One of the essential requisites for ensuring justice is a set of rules or moral values, which everyone accepts and complies with faithfully. The financial system may be able to promote justice if, in addition to being strong and stable, it satisfies at least two conditions. One of these is that the financier should also share in the risk so as not to shift the entire burden of losses to the entrepreneur or the borrower, and the other is that an equitable share of the society's financial resources becomes available to even the poor on affordable terms in keeping with their ability to repay so as to enable them to realize their dream of owning their own homes, pursuing higher education and vocational training, and establishing their own microenterprises.

To fulfil the first condition of justice, Islam requires both the financier and the entrepreneur to equitably share the profit as well as the loss. For this purpose, one of the basic principles of Islamic finance is: 'No risk, no gain.' This should help motivate financial institutions to assess the risks more carefully and to effectively monitor the use of funds by borrowers. The double assessment of risks by both the financier and the entrepreneur should help inject greater discipline into the system, and go a long way in not only increasing efficiency in the use of resources but also reducing excessive lending.

However, making just the banks share in the risk may not be enough because the desire to maximize profits may still induce the banks to indulge in excessive lending. It is, therefore, necessary to also motivate the depositors to play a more active role in the enforcement of this discipline. This will be possible if the depositors also share in the profit or loss. Since demand depositors do not get any return, it would not be fair to make them participate in the risks of financing. Their deposits must, therefore, be *fully* guaranteed. In contrast with this, investment depositors should participate in the risks. What this will do is to turn investment depositors into temporary shareholders. Placing investment deposits in financial institutions will be like purchasing their shares, and withdrawing them will be like redeeming them. This will motivate depositors to monitor their banks, and demand greater transparency, better governance, and more effective risk management, auditing, regulation and supervision. Making the depositors participate in the risk would also help motivate them to take greater care in choosing their banks.

Instead of introducing greater discipline in this manner, the primary focus of the international financial system at present is on regulation and supervision. There is no doubt that prudent regulation and supervision are both necessary and unavoidable, and Mr Greenspan, ex-Chairman of the Federal Reserve, also acknowledged at a Congressional hearing on 23 October 2008 'that his belief in deregulation had been shaken' (Andrews, 2008).

It is, accordingly, a source of great relief that substantial progress has been made in the direction of regulation and supervision under the aegis of the Basel Committee on Banking Supervision (BCBS). Regulation and supervision cannot, however, be relied upon totally for a number of reasons. First, regulation generally tends to follow the events that create the need for regulation and it also takes a long time to reach an agreement. It took three weeks to reach an agreement in the case of the Bretton Woods system when it had been already preceded by more than two years of technical preparation (*The Economist*, 2008a, p. 13). Basel II also took a long time and, even though it is not yet fully in force, enhancements to it have been proposed in the light of weaknesses revealed by the ongoing financial crisis (BCBS, 16 January 2009). Some of its primary flaws are its reliance on rating agencies and the banks' own models of risk management, which have both proved to be unreliable during the prevailing crisis.[9] The complexity of these models would also make the job of supervisors extremely difficult unless they have training in evaluating these models and the assumptions that lie behind them.

Second, regulation may not be applied uniformly in all countries and to all institutional money managers as a result of off-balance-sheet accounts, bank secrecy standards, and the difficulty faced by bank examiners in accurately evaluating the quality of banks' assets. The LTCM collapse as well as the prevailing financial crisis in the US clearly show how banks can get into difficulties as a result of overlending even in an apparently well-regulated system.

Third, regulations will not be effective unless there is moral consciousness among individuals to create an inner urge in them to abide by the regulations. Without such a consciousness, they would tend to adopt a number of clandestine ways of doing what is wrong without being detected and punished even in a political and judicial system which is not corrupt and unfair. The creation of a foolproof social, legal and judicial environment of rules or values may lead to an endless piling of law upon law. This may not only make the legal system very complex and cumbersome but also raise transactions costs to an unbearably high level. There is, hence, need to motivate individuals to abide by values voluntarily under all circumstances even when this hurts their self-interest and it is possible for them to get away undetected.

Since such consciousness does not exist among all individuals, incentives and deterrents are indispensable for motivating individuals to fulfil their obligations. The society does this through prestige, disgrace and ostracization; the market does this through profit and loss; and the government does this through awards, fines and imprisonment. No society can succeed in ensuring justice in an environment of general moral decline and violation of moral norms. Market discipline also has an important role to play. However, if even market discipline is flawed, a greater burden has to be borne by the regulatory and supervisory authorities. They need to try harder to ensure order and safeguard the public interest. Those who violate the regulations need to be punished. Without such punishment violation may become attractive and spread as a result of path dependence and self-reinforcing mechanisms, making it very difficult thereafter to curb the violation.

The prevailing crisis has shown that the financial system suffered from weaknesses on all these counts. Not only has individual and social moral consciousness become dented as a result of greed and general moral decline, but even market discipline has been inadequate and the supervisory authorities have been lax in the effective performance of their role. It is surprising that the supervisory authorities allowed fraud to prevail for such a long time under their own eyes in the hope of market forces being able to curb it effectively even when market discipline has itself been weak.

Regulation and supervision would not, therefore, be truly effective unless they are complemented by a paradigm shift in favour of greater moral consciousness, adequate market discipline, and more effective supervisory surveillance. Just the bailing-in of banks, as suggested by some analysts (Calomiris, 1998; Meltzer, 1998; Yeager, 1998) may not be able to take us far enough. The capital that banks are required to hold is only 8 per cent of their risk-weighted assets and the prevailing crisis has shown that banks' losses may be far in excess of this. This has led Greenspan to give an indication to *The Economist* that banks will now need a much higher ratio, perhaps 15 per cent, to soothe depositors and investors (*The Economist*, 2008c, p. 52). When listed non-financial companies have capital to assets ratios of 30–40 per cent (Rajan and Zingales, 1995), there seems to be no reason why banks should not have more than 8 per cent. What is also necessary is to strongly motivate not only the banks to undertake careful underwriting of all loan proposals but also the depositors to be cautious in choosing their bank and monitoring their bank's affairs more carefully.

Islamic finance is a morally oriented system committed to the realization of justice in human society. Its first target is the reform of the human being himself. The Qur'an clearly emphasizes that 'God does not change the condition of a people until they change their own inner selves' (13:11). However, this stress on the character uplift of individuals has become weakened even in Muslim countries as a result of centuries of decline. In addition to raising the moral consciousness of individuals, Islam also lays stress on making market discipline and supervisory vigilance (*hisbah*) more effective.

There are several requisites for making market discipline more effective. One of these is the prospect of profit or loss. For this purpose Islamic finance aims at raising substantially the share of equity and profit-and-loss-sharing (PLS) in businesses. Greater reliance on equity financing has supporters even in mainstream economics. Henry Simons, writing after the Second World War under the strong influence of the Great Depression, argued that economic instability would be minimized if no resort were made to borrowing, particularly short-term borrowing, and if investments were held in the form of equity (Simons, 1948, pp. 231–39). Hyman Minsky, whose 'financial instability hypothesis' is now getting greater attention, argued that when each firm finances its own cash flow and plans to invest its own retained profits, there is no problem of effective demand, the financial system is robust and investment has great inertia. But when firms can raise outside finance by borrowing from rentiers or banks, the system is prone to instability (Minsky, 1975). Professor Rogoff of Harvard University, writing more recently, states that in an ideal world equity lending and direct investment would play a much bigger role. He further asserts that 'with a better balance between debt and equity, risk-sharing would be greatly enhanced and financial crises sharply muted' (Rogoff, 1999, p. 40).

Greater reliance on equity does not necessarily mean that debt financing is ruled out. This is because all the financial needs of individuals, firms, or governments cannot be made amenable to equity and PLS. Debt is, therefore, indispensable, but should *not* be promoted for living beyond means, speculation, and gambling. Islam does not allow all three of these. To ensure this, the Islamic financial system does not allow the creation of debt through direct lending and borrowing. It rather requires the creation of debt through the sale or lease of real goods and services by means of its sales- and lease-based modes of financing (*murabahah, ijarah, salam, istisna* and *sukuk*). The purpose is to enable an individual or firm to buy now the urgently needed real goods and services in conformity with his/her ability to make the payment later.

Islam has, however, also laid down a number of conditions to ensure that credit expands in step with the growth of the real rector. Some of these conditions are:

1. The asset which is being sold or leased must be *real*, and not imaginary or notional;
2. The seller must own and possess the goods being sold or leased;
3. The transaction must be a genuine trade transaction with the full intention of giving and taking delivery; and
4. The debt cannot be sold and thus the risk of default associated with it must be borne by the lender himself.

The first condition will help eliminate most of the speculative and gambling transactions which involve notional goods and which constituted a major part of the derivatives transactions during the current crisis. The second condition will help ensure that the seller (or lessor) also shares a part of the risk to be able to get a share in the return. Once the seller (financier) acquires ownership and possession of the goods for sale or lease, he/she bears the risk. This condition will put a constraint on short sales, and thereby remove the possibility of a steep decline in asset prices during a downturn. The *Shari'ah* has, however, made an exception to this rule in the case of *salam* and *istisna* where the goods are not already available in the market and need to be produced or manufactured before delivery. This will help ensure that financing expands in step with the rise of the real economy and thereby help curb excessive credit expansion.

The third and the fourth conditions will not only help eliminate a great deal of speculative and derivatives transactions where there is no intention of giving or taking delivery, but also motivate the creditor to be more cautious in evaluating the credit risk. This will prevent an unnecessary explosion in the volume and value of transactions and also help keep the rise in debt to be in step with the rise of the real economy. It will also release a greater volume of financial resources for the real sector and, thereby, help expand employment and self-employment opportunities and the production of need-fulfilling goods and services.

The discipline that Islam wishes to introduce in the financial system may not materialize unless the governments reduce their borrowing from the central bank to a level that is in harmony with the goal of price and financial stability. Even borrowing from the private sector should be primarily for development that will increase its ability to repay.

Borrowing for meeting current spending needs to be avoided except in extreme circumstances. This is because borrowing does not eliminate the ultimate need for sacrifice. Without this consciousness about the ultimate need for sacrifice, the need for borrowing is most likely to become path dependent.

A number of objections may be raised here against these conditions. One of these is that hedging is a genuine need of the economy and the restrictions specified above may stand against it. Genuine hedging or insurance which is undertaken by a person or firm to provide protection against losses *actually* incurred has been recognized by Muslim jurists. However, what is prohibited is 'hedging' that is not related to a real transaction and is rather of a speculative and gambling nature. A second objection may be that all these conditions will tend to shrink the size of the economy by reducing the number and volume of derivatives trans-actions. There is no doubt that the number of transactions will be reduced. However, it will be primarily those transactions which are of a speculative and gambling nature and are generally recognized to be zero-sum games. These have rarely contributed significantly to total real output. The compounded annual rate of growth of total outstanding derivatives between 2000 and 2007 was 29.9 per cent per annum while that in total real world output was only 3.1 per cent per annum.[10] Hence a decline in speculative and gambling transactions is not likely to hurt the real economy significantly. While a restriction on such transactions will cut the commissions earned by speculators during an artificially gener-ated boom, it will help them avert losses and bankruptcy that become unavoidable during the decline and lead to a financial crisis.

8.6 INJECTING ANOTHER DIMENSION OF JUSTICE

The injection of greater discipline into the financial system may tend to deprive the subprime borrowers from access to credit even in the Islamic system as it would in the conventional system. Therefore, justice demands that some suitable innovation be introduced in the financial system to ensure that even small borrowers are able to get adequate credit at affordable terms to realize their dream of owning their own homes, pursuing education and vocational training, and establishing micro-enterprises. In Pakistan, for example, while 61.3 per cent of commercial banks' deposits came from 99.6 per cent of all depositors in 2002, 78 per cent of total advances went to less than 1 per cent of the borrowers (based on data about commercial bank deposits and advances by size given in the State Bank of Pakistan, *State Bank Bulletin*, 2003). Small

Morality and justice in Islamic economics and finance

borrowers, thus, received far less than what small depositors had contributed to the banks. It is even worse in nationalized banks where a number of well-connected borrowers are even able to get their loans written off (Khwaja and Mian, 2005). Such injustice prevails not only in Pakistan but also in nearly all countries around the world, even though in varying degrees. Given such an inequitable allocation of credit, along with corruption, one cannot but expect inequalities of income and wealth to continue to rise, rather than decline, in the future – an outcome which is contrary to the socio-economic objectives of Islam. This makes it necessary to introduce some mechanism in the financial system that would help divert a reasonable proportion of the society's financial resources to the poor. It is also necessary that such borrowers be given a respite in case they are unable to service their debt due to strained circumstances (job loss, serious illness or unforeseen financial setbacks). If necessary, their debt may also be written off instead of putting them into the serious hardship that seizure of collateral causes.

It should be possible to do this in the Muslim world by adopting two measures.[11] One of these is to use the *zakah* and *awqaf* resources to make interest-free loans (*qurud hasanah*) available to the very poor who are unable to get credit from the conventional financial system and, even if they are able to get it, the cost is too burdensome. The adoption of this measure should save them from the excruciating burden of interest. Even though the interest-based microfinance system has helped a number of borrowers, it has also crushed a significant number of others. A timely study by Dr Qazi Kholiquzzaman Ahmed, President of the Bangladesh Economic Association, has revealed that the effective rate of interest charged by microfinance institutions, including the Grameen Bank, turns out to be as high as 30 to 45 per cent.[12] This causes serious hardship to the borrowers in servicing their debt. They are often constrained to not only sacrifice essential consumption but also borrow from money lenders. This engulfs them unwittingly into an unending debt cycle which will not only perpetuate poverty but also ultimately lead to a rise in unrest and social tensions (Ahmed, 2007, pp. xvii–xix; see also Sharma, 2002).[13] No wonder, the Minister of Finance for Bangladesh described microcredit interest rates in that country as extortionate in an address he delivered to the very poor on a humane interest-free basis without the requirement of collateral which they are not able to submit. Integration of the microfinance system with the *zakah* and *awqaf* institutions should make it possible to grant interest-free loans. Adoption of the group lending method used by the Grameen Bank and some other microfinance institutions should help greatly in ensuring repayment without the requirement of collateral.

This will, of course, not be sufficient because the *zakah* and *awqaf* institutions have become weakened as a result of centuries of Muslim decline. Even though their revival has started, their resources are not adequate at present to extend credit to a large number of poor entrepreneurs. Therefore, the other measure that needs to be taken is to integrate the commercial banks with their vast resources into the microfinance network. Those who can afford to bear the cost of microfinance should go to the commercial banks or other specialized institutions established for this purpose and borrow on the basis of the Islamic modes of profit-and-loss-sharing and sales- and lease-based modes of finance, not only to avoid interest but also to prevent the misuse of credit for personal consumption.[14] The two measures can together make it possible to satisfy a substantial part of the credit needs of the poor.

Integrating the commercial banks into the microfinance network does not in any way mean that they should be *forced* to provide credit to the poor. Any attempt of this nature is bound to fail. An effort should rather be made to remove the obstacles that prevent the commercial banks from lending to the poor. This leads to the question of why the commercial banks do not lend to the poor. There are two major reasons for this. One of these is the higher cost of evaluating loan applications and the other is the greater risk. To enable the banks to give greater credit to the poor, it is necessary to reduce not only the cost but also the risk associated with such financing.

As far as the cost is concerned, it is very expensive and cumbersome for banks to deal with a large number of small borrowers. It is more economical for them to lend to a few people and not worry about the others. Consequently, as indicated earlier, credit goes primarily to the rich. To reduce the cost, it may be possible to use the *zakah* and *awqaf* resources for evaluating loan proposals of those poor people who are eligible for *zakah*. Since one of the most important objectives of *zakah* is to enable the poor to stand on their own feet, the extra cost of evaluation may be met partly from the *zakah* fund, provided that the loan is extended in accordance with the Islamic modes of finance. The balance of the cost should be borne partly by the bank as a part of social responsibility and partly by the government through subsidy. The more help the poor receive in this manner, the greater will be the contribution made to the reduction of poverty and inequalities of income and wealth.

The other measure that needs to be taken is to reduce the risk of default. Even though experience around the world shows that poor people have generally been faithful in their repayments, it is necessary to reduce the risk of default even further. For those who are eligible for *zakah* and are unable to repay their loans because of some genuine problem, *zakah* may be used to offset the losses from default, provided again that the Islamic modes of finance are used for lending. This is in harmony with one of the objectives of *zakah* which is to forgive the debt of those who are unable to repay because of strained circumstances. Offsetting the entire amount may tend to lead to moral hazard. Therefore, only a part of the loss from default may be offset though the *zakah* fund. For those who are not eligible for *zakah*, the banks should resort to the purchase of CDSs to minimize their risk. The loan guarantee scheme that exists in many countries may also be introduced, provided that appropriate measures are adopted to prevent its misuse by politically connected borrowers.

Thus, we can see that the Islamic financial system has the potential of minimizing the severity and frequency of financial crises by getting rid of the major weaknesses of the conventional system. It introduces greater discipline into the financial system by requiring the financier to share in the risk. It links credit expansion to the growth of the real economy and minimizes speculation and gambling by allowing credit primarily for the purchase of real goods and services which the seller owns and possesses and the buyer wishes to take delivery. It also requires the creditor to bear the risk of default by prohibiting the sale of debt, thereby ensuring that he evaluates the risk more carefully. In addition, Islamic finance can also help reduce the problem of subprime borrowers by providing credit to them at affordable terms. This will save the billions that are spent after the crisis to bail out the rich bankers. Such billions do not, however, help the poor because their home may have already become subject to foreclosure and auctioned at a give-away price.

8.7   ISLAMIC FINANCE IN PRACTICE

The problem, however, is that Islamic finance is still in its infancy and commands a very small proportion of international finance (see *The Economist*, 2008b, p. 72). In addition, it does not genuinely reflect the ethos of Islamic teachings. The use of equity and PLS is still very small while that of debt-creating modes is preponderant. Moreover, even in the case of debt-creating modes, all the conditions laid down by the *Shari'ah* are not being faithfully observed by the use of legal stratagems (*hiyal*). This is partially due to a lack of proper understanding of the ultimate objective of Islamic finance, the non-availability of trained personnel, and the absence of a number of shared or support institutions that are needed to minimize the risks associated with anonymity, moral hazard, principal/ agent conflict of interest, and late settlement of financial obligations (see Chapra, 2009b). In addition, consumerism has also been rapidly expanding in Muslim countries and promoting living beyond means. Financial institutions exploit this tendency to expand credit to raise their income. In addition there is a great deal of corruption in government finances which, along with inefficiency and wasteful spending, has led to high levels of budgetary deficits, which are financed by domestic as well as external borrowing. The financial system in Muslim countries is, thus, not capable at present of either promoting socio-economic justice or playing a significant role in contributing to the health and stability of the international financial system. It is, however, expected that the system will gradually gain momentum as a result of the ongoing revival of Islam and complement the efforts now being made internationally to promote the health and stability of the global financial system.

8.8 IS THIS OF ANY RELEVANCE TO THE CONVENTIONAL SYSTEM?

Since the existing architecture of the conventional financial system has existed for a long time, it may perhaps be too much to expect the international community to undertake a radical structural reform of the kind that the Islamic financial system envisages. However, the adoption of some of the elements of the Islamic system, which are also a part of the Western heritage, is indispensable for ensuring the health and stability of the global financial system. These are:

1. The proportion of equity in total financing needs to be increased and that of debt reduced.
2. Leverage needs to be controlled to ensure that credit does not exceed the ability of the borrowers to repay.
3. Credit needs to be confined primarily to transactions that are related to the real sector so as to ensure that credit expansion is more or less in step with the growth of the real economy and does not promote destabilizing speculation and gambling.
4. It may be better if, in conformity with traditional banking, the banks hold the debt on their books until maturity. This would ensure careful underwriting. However, if this is not considered desirable because of the restraint it will impose on the genuine expansion of credit and profits of financial institutions, the sale of collateralized debt obligations (CDOs) may be permitted, provided that there is full transparency about their quality to enable the purchaser to know exactly what he is getting into. It would also be desirable to make the financial instruments simpler because the

more complex the instrument, the lesser the possibility of people understanding it clearly, and the greater the opportunity for fraud. It would also be desirable to have the right of recourse for the ultimate purchaser of the CDOs so as to ensure that the debt originator has adequate incentive to underwrite the debt carefully. In case this is found to be practically difficult, all securitizers should be required to retain a meaningful part of the securities they issue, as suggested by Mr Greenspan in his testimony before the House Committee of Government Oversight and Reform (2003).

5.   While there may be no harm in the use of credit default swaps to provide protection to actual lenders, it needs to be ensured that the swaps do not become instruments for wagering. Their hedging role should be confined to the actual lenders. Similarly, the derivatives market needs to be properly regulated to allow only hedging and to remove the element of gambling that has inflated the outstanding amount of derivatives to a mind-boggling height.

6.   All financial institutions, and not just the commercial banks, need to be properly regulated and supervised so that they remain healthy and do not become a source of systemic risk.

7.   Some arrangement needs to be made to make credit available to subprime borrowers at affordable terms to enable them to buy a home, pursue higher education or vocational training, and establish their own small and micro enterprises. In case they get into difficulty for no fault of theirs and are unable to pay their installments on time, they should be given sufficient respite to enable them to improve their condition and be able to repay the debt. For those who are unable to pay, the society should help them instead of throwing them out on the street through foreclosure and auction of their homes.

NOTES

*   This chapter is a revised and updated version of a lecture the author delivered at the Institute of Bankers in London on 10 November 2008. A brief version of this lecture without references and footnotes was published in the *New Horizon* (2009a), a magazine of the Institute of Islamic Banking and Insurance, London. The views expressed in this chapter are the author's own and do not necessarily reflect those of IRTI or IDB. The author is grateful to Mr Muhammad Tarq, Dr Sami Al-Suwailem, Dr Tariqullah Khan and Dr Salman Syed Ali for valuable comments on an earlier draft, and to Shaikh Muhammad Rashid for the excellent secretarial assistance provided.
1.   This is clearly recognized by the Bank for International Settlements (BIS) in its 78th Annual Report released on 30 June 2008 by stating that the fundamental cause of

today's problems in the global economy is excessive and imprudent credit growth over a long period (p. 3).

2. There is a well-known Arabic proverb which says: 'Whoever is secure from punishment may do what he pleases'.

3. These derivatives included (in trillions of US$):
   - Credit default swaps, 57.3
   - Foreign exchange contracts, 63.0
   - Interest rate contracts, 458.3
   - Equity linked contracts, 10.2
   - Commodity contracts, 13.2
   - Unallocated, 81.7.

4. Treasury Summary for FY 2008 (http:#www.fms.treas.gov/mts/ints0908.pdf).

5. Congressional Budget Office, Blogrunner, 18 January 2009 and 21 March 2009.

6. According to the US National Debt Clock, the US national debt has been increasing by $3.60 billion per day since 28 September 2007. The clock has already run out of digits when the statutory ceiling on the national debt has been raised to $11.315 trillion to accommodate the expected rise in debt.

7. A number of expressions have been used by economists to describe this phenomenon. These include the 'bandwagon' effect, the 'snob' effect, and the 'Veblen' effect. For representative definitions of these, see Leibenstein (1976), pp. 51–52.

8. At the end of the second quarter of 2008, 62.3 per cent of the identified official foreign exchange reserves in the world were held in United States dollars, down from 77.4 per cent in the first quarter of 2001 (Based on data given in www.imf.org/external/np/sta/cofer/eng/cofer.pdf).

9. For a discussion of the shortcoming of Basel II, see, Bichsel and Blum, 2005.

10. These rates of growth are based on data for total outstanding OTC derivatives given in BIS, Regular OTC Derivatives Market Statistics (assessed on 13 November 2008, www.bis.org), and on the data for nominal GDP given in World Development Indicators (WDI)/World Bank Database Online (assessed on 24 November 2008). The rate of growth in nominal GDP was 7.9 per cent per annum over this period.

11. The cooperative movement should also be promoted in Muslim countries even though it has encountered a number of difficulties in some developing countries. This is because, as a result of poverty and lack of education, it has not been able to become a grassroots movement. It has been promoted by governments and, therefore, suffers from bureaucratic red tape, corruption and inefficiency (see Deb, 2006, and Samantary, 2004).

12. This is highly plausible because some other studies indicate even higher effective rates of interest. According to Nimal Fernando (2006), Principal Microfinance Specialist in the East Asia Department of the Asian Development Bank, the nominal interest rates charged by most microfinance institutions in the region range from 30 to 70 per cent a year. The effective interest rates are even higher because of commissions and fees charged by them (p. 1). According to Mannan (2007), the effective rates range from 54 to 84 per cent (pp. 2 and 12).

13. According to Sharma (2002), 'while the Grameen Bank model of micro-credit has landed poor communities in a perpetual debt trap, the rising number of loan defaulters has given a serious setback to the Bolivian experiment' (p. 2).

14. For some details see IRTI/IDB (2007), p. 30; and Feroz (2007), p. 42.

REFERENCES

Ahmed, Qazi Kholiquzzaman (ed.) (2007), *Socio-Economic and Indebtedness-Related Impact of Micro-Credit in Bangladesh* (Dhaka: Bangladesh Unnayan Parishad).

Amadeo, Kimberly (2009, January), The US national debt and how it got so big, http://useconomy.about.com/od/fiscalpolicy/p/US_debt.html.

Andrews, Edmund (2008), Greenspan concedes error on regulation, *The New York Times*, 23 October.

Baily, Martin, Litan, Robert and Johnson, Mathew (2008), The origins of the financial crisis (The Initiative on Business and Public Policy at the Brookings Institution), November.

Bank for International Settlements (BIS) (2008, June), *78th Annual Report* (Basle: BIS).

Bank for International Settlements (BIS) (2008, November), *Monetary and Economic Department*, OTC Derivatives Market Activity in the First Half of 2008 (Basle: BIS).

Barth, James and Yago, Glenn (2008), Demystifying the mortgage meltdown: What it means for Main Street, Wall Street and the US financial system, Presentation at the Milken Institute, 2 October.

Basle Committee on Banking Supervision (BCBS) (2009, January), Enhancements to the Basel II framework.

Bernanke, Ben (2008), Fostering sustainable homeownership, Speech at the National Community Reinvestment Coalition Annual Meeting, Washington, DC, 14 March.

Bichsel, Robert and Blum, Jürg (2005), Capital regulation of banks: Where do we stand and where are we going? (Swiss National Bank Quarterly Bulletin).

Blough, Les (2008), Alan Greenspan's 18 year crime spree was a 'mistake', *Axis of Logic*, 23 December.

Bowles, Samuel et al. (1983), *Beyond the Waste Land: A Democratic Alternative to Economic Decline* (Garden City, NY: Anchor Press/Doubleday).

Bremer, J. (2004), Reviving traditional forms for building social justice. Paper presented at the CSID Fifth Annual Conference in Washington, DC, on 'Defining and Establishing Justice in Muslim Societies'.

Buckley, R.M. (1994), Housing finance in developing countries: A review of World Bank's experience, in K. Datta and G.A. Jones (eds) (1999), pp. 44–55.

Calomiris, C. (1998), The IMF's imprudent role as lender of last resort, *Cato Journal*, 17:3, 275–95.

Camdessus, Michael (2000), Main principles of the future international, monetary, financial system, *IMF Survey*, 10 January, pp. 1 and 7–10.

Chapra, M. Umer (2008), *Muslim Civilization: The Causes of Decline and the Need for Reform* (Leicester, UK: The Islamic Foundation).

Chapra, M. Umer (2009a), The global financial crisis: Can Islamic finance help?, *New Horizon*, January, pp. 20–23.

Chapra, M. Umer (2009b), Authenticity of Islamic finance, *Business Islamica* (Dubai), February, pp. 44–9.

Cizakca, Murat (2000), *A History of Philanthropic Foundations: The Islamic World from the Seventh Century to the Present* (Istanbul: Bogazici University Press).

Congressional Budget Office, Blogrunner, 18 January 2009 and 21 March 2009.

Datta, K. and G.A. Jones (eds) (1999), *Housing and Finance in Developing Countries* (London: Routledge).

Deb, Alok Kumar (2006), World cooperative movement, www.tripurainf.com/citizen-services/helping_bytes/helping10.shtm.

Fernando Nimal A. (2006), *Understanding and Dealing with High Interest Rates on Micro-credit* (Manila: Asian Development Bank).

Feroz, Ehsan Habib (2007), The halal way to social change, *Islamic Horizons*, January/February, p. 42.

Fisher, Irving (1992), The debt–deflation theory of great depressions, in Michael Bordo, *Financial Crises* (Aldershot, UK and Brookfield, VT, USA: Edward Elgar Publishing).

G-20 Summit (2008), Decelerate of the summit on financial markets and the world economy, Washington, DC: White House, 15 November.

Galbraith, John (1972), *The New Industrial State* (New York: New American Library).

Galbraith, John (1990), *A Short History of Financial Euphoria* (Penguin, USA).

Greenspan, Alan (2008), Greenspan testimony on sources of financial crisis, *The Wall Street Journal*, online, 23 October 2008, http://blogs.wsj.com/economics/2008/10/23/greenspan-testimony-on-sources-of-financial-crisis.

International Monetary Fund (2008), Currency composition of official foreign exchange reserves, www.imf.org/external/np/sta/cofer/eng/cofer/pdf.

International Monetary Fund (August and December 2008), *International Financial Statistics*.

Islamic Research and Training Institute (IRTI) of the Islamic Development Bank (IDB) (2007), Framework and strategies for development of Islamic micro-finance services. Working Paper for IFSD Forum, 2007, on *Islamic Micro-finance Development: Challenges and Initiatives*, held in Dakar, Senegal, on 27 May 2007.

Jones, G.A. and Millin, D. (1999), Housing finance and non-governmental organizations in developing countries, in K. Datta and G.A. Jones (eds) (1999), pp. 26–45.

Keys, Benjamin, Mukkerjee, Tanmoy, Seru, Amit and Vig, Vikrant (2008, January), Did securitization lead to lax screening? Evidence from subprime loans 2001–2006, http://papers.ssrn.com/sol3/papers.cfm?abstract_id=1093137# Paper Download.

Khwaja, Asim and Mian, Atif (2005), Do lenders favour politically connected firms?: Rent provision in an emerging financial market, *Quarterly Journal of Economics*, April.

Kohn Donald (2005), Imbalances in the US economy, Address delivered at the 15th Annual Hyman Minsky Conference in the Levy Economics Institute of Bard College, Awnabdable-on-Hudson, New York, 22 April (BIS Review, 28/2005).

Kotz, D.M. (1978), *Bank Control of Large Corporations in the US* (Berkeley, CA: University of California Press).

Leibenstein, Harvey (1976), *Beyond Economic Man* (Cambridge, MA: Harvard University Press).

Mannan, M.A. (2007), Alternative microcredit models in Bangladesh: A comparative analysis of Grameen Bank and Social Investment Bank Ltd – myths and realities. Paper presented at the First International Conference on Enhancing Islamic Financial Services for Micro and Medium-sized Enterprises, held on 17–19 April 2007 in Negara Brunei Darussalam.

Meltzer, A. (1998), Asian problems and the IMF, *Cato Journal*, 17:3, 267–74.

Mian, Atif and Sufi, Amir (2008, January), The consequences of mortgage credit expansion: Evidence from the 2007 mortgage default crisis, http://ssrn. com/ abstract = 1072304.

Minsky, Hyman (1975), *John Maynard Keynes* (New York: Columbia University Press).

Mishkin, Frederic (1997), The causes and propagation of financial instability: Lessons for policymakers, in Federal Reserve Bank of Kansas City, *Maintaining Financial Stability in a Global Economy*, Proceedings of a Symposium Sponsored by the FRB Kansas City, Jackson Hole, Wyoming, 28–30 August, pp. 55–96.

Organisation for Economic Co-operation and Development (OECD) (2008), *Economic Outlook 82*, Annex Table 23, www.oecd.org/document/61/ 0,3343,en2649_201185_2483901_1_1_1_1,00.html.

President's Working Group on Financial Markets (2007), Principles and guidelines regarding private pool of capital.

Rajan, Raghuram and Zingales, Luigi (1995), What do we know about capital structure? Some evidence from international data, *Journal of Finance*, 50:5.

Rogoff, K. (1999), International institutions for reducing global financial instability, *Journal of Economic Perspectives*, 4:13, 21–46.

Samantaray, P.C. (2004), Hundred years of cooperative movement: Emerging issues and challenges, *Orissa Review*, December, pp. 7–12, http:// orissagov.nic.in/e-magazine/orissareview/dec2004.

Sharma, Sudhirendhar (2002), Is micro-credit a macro trap?, *The Hindu*, 25 September, www.hinduonnet.com/businessline/2002/09/25/stories/20020925 00810900.htm.

Simons, Henry (1948), *Economic Policy for a Free Society* (Chicago, IL: University of Chicago Press).

State Bank of Pakistan (2003), *Statistical Bulletin*.

Stiglitz, Joseph (2007), Financial hypocrisy, 21 November, nakedcapitalism.com/ 2007/11/joseph-stiglitz-financial-hyprocrisy.html.

Summers, L. (2008), America needs a way to stem foreclosures, *Financial Times*, 25 February, p. 11.

The Economist (2008a), Redesigning global finance, 15 November, p. 13.

The Economist (2008b), Savings and souls, 6 September, pp. 72–4.

The Economist (2008c), The end of the affair, 22 November, pp. 51–2.

United States Congress, House Banking and Currency Committee, Subcommittee on Domestic Finance (1968), *Commercial Banks and their Trust Activities: Emerging Influence on the American Economy*, 90th Congress, Second Session, p. 5.

United States Securities and Exchange Commission (1971), *Institutional Investor Study Report*, House Document 62-4 referred to the House Committee on Inter-State and Foreign Commerce, pp. 124–5.

Volker, Paul (1979), Cited in *Fortune*, 17 December, p. 110.

World Bank (2008), World Development Indicators (WDI) World Bank Database Online, accessed on 24 November 2008.

Yeager, I.B. (1998), How to avoid international financial crises, *Cato Journal*, 17:3, pp. 257–65.

Zakaria, Fareed (2008), A more disciplined America, *Newsweek Business*, 11 October, www.newsweek.com/nd.1163449.

Zeleny, J. and Andrews, E. (2009), Obama warns trillion dollar deficits potential, *The New York Times*, 7 January, www.nytimes.com/2009/01/07/us/politics/07 obama.html? th&emc =th.

Index

call for 216–19
effectiveness of 31–2, 249–51
enforcement of 242
failure of 145–6, 242
progress on 249
reliance on 31–2, 149–50, 168
state role 49–50, 78, 84–5
religious scholars (*ulama*) 110, 200
religious worldviews 27–8, 42, 45,
    69–70, 73
    growth of 87
    see also Islamic worldview
Rheinstein, Max 112
Ricardo, David 53
Richards, Alan 124
risk assessment 171–2
risk management 165, 172, 211, 213,
    216, 218, 228–32, 243, 249
risk-aversion 150
risk-sharing 248–9
    absence of 10–11
    differentiation with interest-based
        modes 195
    and Islamic financial system 154–6
    support for 149–51
    see also profit-and-loss sharing (PLS)
        system
Robbins, Lionel 48
Roded, Ruth 108
Rogoff, K. 150–51, 173, 251
Rosenthal, Franz 33, 96–7
Ruskin, John 43, 72

Sachs, Jeffrey D. 113, 138
sacrifice 23–4, 32, 45–7, 49, 68, 72–6,
    79, 84–6, 253–4
salam financing 155, 161, 173–4, 187,
    194–5, 210–11, 251–2
sales-based finance modes 155, 173–5,
    196, 227–8, 251–2, 255
sanctions, defaulters 223–4
Sandefur, Gary 80
al-Sarakhsi, Shams al-Din 53
Sarton, George 33–4, 60, 108
Saunders, John J. 108
saving, decline in 12, 36–7, 46, 50, 68,
    101, 113, 118, 122–4, 142, 147–8,
    153–4, 169, 184, 246–7

Say's Law 49
Scarth, W. 142
Schacht, J. 200
Schadwick, Owen 88
Schatzmiller, Maya 107–8, 197
Schleifer, A. 216
schools, removal of religious and moral
    education 72
Schumpeter, Joseph 34, 51, 61, 88
Schwartz, A. 143
Schweitzer, Alfred 93
secular democracies 109
secular worldview 36, 41–3, 45, 70, 72,
    74–5, 77–81, 109
securitization 170–71, 182, 207, 226–8,
    241
security leases 226
self-employment, financing 186–8,
    195–6, 209
self-enforcement 32, 199
self-interest 21–5, 27, 31, 42, 44–8,
    70–73, 75
self-reinforcing mechanisms 26, 35, 86,
    118, 124, 223, 250
self-sufficiency 53
sellers, ownership of goods sold or
    leased 183, 195, 208, 252–3, 256
Sen, Amartya 44, 47, 59, 87
senior management 215–17
Serageldin, Ismail 99
Sezgin, F. 34
shareholders
    accountability to 212–13
    depositors as 154, 172, 248–9
    election of boards 181, 213–14, 221
    limited liability 113–15
    protection of 213–14
    risk-sharing 149
    role in enforcement of discipline
        218–19
    satisfying objectives of 8–9
    senior managers as 215
    voting rights 181, 213–14, 221–2
Shari'ah 96, 100, 103, 109, 116, 161
    compliance with 177, 182–3, 193,
        195–6, 206–8, 218, 222, 226–7,
        231, 256–7

women, position of 108–10
worldviews
   need for a proper worldview 68–9
   role in economics 41–2
   see also Enlightenment worldview;
      Islamic worldview, religious
      worldviews; secular worldview

Yago, Glenn 241
Yalcintas, N. 35

Yeager, I.B. 149, 250
youth employment 2
Yunus, Muhammad 186, 209

zakah institutions 187–8, 211, 254–6
Zakaria, Fareed 246
Zakat 49
al-Zarqa, Mustafa A. 163
Zeleny, J. 246
Zingales, Luigi 250